Teaching Social Studies in Grades K–8

Teaching Social Studies in Grades K–8

Information, Ideas, and Resources for Classroom Teachers

THOMAS P. RUFF
Washington State University

ALLYN AND BACON
Boston   London   Toronto   Sydney   Tokyo   Singapore

Copyright © 1994 by Allyn and Bacon
A Division of Simon & Schuster, Inc.
160 Gould Street
Needham Heights, Massachusetts 02194

Library of Congress Cataloging-in-Publication Data

Ruff, Thomas P.
    Teaching social studies in grades K–8 : information, ideas, and
resources for classroom teachers / Thomas P. Ruff.
        p.   cm.
    Includes bibliographical references.
    ISBN 0-205-14606-6
    1. Social sciences—Study and teaching (Elementary)—United
States. 2. Education, Elementary—United States—Activity programs.
I. Title.
LB1584.R814   1993
372.83'044—dc20   93-19503
                                                                         CIP

Printed in the United States of America
10 9 8 7 6 5 4 3 2 1   97 96 95 94 93

This book is dedicated to
the very special people in my life:
my mother Rosann, my wife Nancy,
and my daughters Tracy, Kristina, and Anne.

Thank you for your love, support, and encouragement.

Contents

CHAPTER 3   Global and Multicultural Education   68

CHAPTER 4   Our American Heritage   89

CHAPTER 7   **Basic Information: Classroom Applications**   **167**

Preface

There are a great many tradebooks available that were written expressly to train teachers on how to teach social studies. Essentially, they follow a similar format: (1) identify and define the social sciences, (2) present rationales for teaching social studies, (3) review curricular trends, and (4) illustrate some instructional options. *This is not one of those books!*

As important as it is to know about social studies education, such knowledge does not automatically prepare one to become an effective social studies teacher! Generally, most classroom teachers agree that social studies is important, but very few have the knowledge or the skills to teach history and geography effectively. Consequently, most tradebooks on social studies education are of little help in the daily planning and teaching of content information. What teachers need, I believe, are concrete ideas and examples of how to help students learn social studies content in a more dynamic way. In essence, they need direction and ideas on how to supplement the text and make it more interesting, relevant, and applicable to students' daily lives – to make social studies fun!

As the title implies, *Teaching Social Studies in Grades K–8* is an informative idea and resource guide that proposes to do just that. Not only will this book give teachers information but it will also provide many functional and creative activities designed both to motivate and educate. The text clearly illustrates that social studies, by itself or integrated with other subjects, can become an exciting and worthwhile adventure for teachers as well as their students. Thus, the process of teaching and learning about social studies will become a more rewarding and meaningful experience for all.

Acknowledgments

A very special thank you is extended to my teaching and research assistants who gave so generously of their time and energy in the completion of this project: Darcy Bruggman, Norma Downey, Tom Fletcher, Amy Hausrath, Lisa Malcolm, Christy Nielsen, David Serwat, and Paige Vandebrake. I wish also to give my gratitude to the following reviewers who read and thoughtfully commented on the manuscript: Bill Lamperes, Principal of Centennial High School, Fort Collins, Colorado, and Jenny Nelson, Gonzaga University, Spokane, Washington.

A teacher affects eternity;
He can never tell where his influence stops. —HENRY ADAMS

CHAPTER 1

Perspectives

We Americans are the best informed people on earth as to the events of the last twenty-four hours; we are not the best informed as to the events of the last sixty centuries—WILL and ARIEL DURANT

SOCIAL STUDIES EDUCATION FOR THE YEAR 2000 AND BEYOND

During the past several years, social studies education has come under intense scrutiny by friend and critic alike. Scholars working independently or on various committees and commissions have spent considerable amounts of time surveying kindergarten through grade 12 curriculum, analyzing standardized test scores, and interviewing teacher and students, and have come to many of the same conclusions: (a) Americans are functionally illiterate in history, geography, and civics; and (2) most of the surveyed remember hating social studies, finding it boring, irrelevant, and all too frequently based on the memorization of isolated facts that had nothing to do with their respective lives.

The problems, as Shakespeare once reminded us, are not in the stars but in ourselves. Simply stated, until classroom teachers view social studies as a relevant school subject and make it a meaningful learning experience for their students, nothing will ever really change. The challenge is to give teachers knowledge, appropriate and usable materials, skills to integrate the subject matter into the curriculum, and the ability to make social studies fun, interesting, and applicable for all students.

This chapter has several purposes: (1) to review the current state of social studies curriculum and anticipate future innovations; (2) to provide classroom teachers with social studies knowledge and information and appropriate classroom resources; (3) to provide field-tested, classroom-ready learning activities; and (4) to provide learning activities that integrate social studies with many other subject areas like mathematics, art, music, and science, to mention only a few.

This is not a reform package that will resolve all the problems previously stated. Rather, it is intended as an information guide and resource for those who work daily to shape the minds, hearts, and futures of children—the classroom teachers. It is on their shoulders that the burden of curriculum implementation directly rests and it is on their knowledge, skills, and commitment that we must entrust and rely on if social studies is to become a valuable academic component, especially in the first eight years of formal schooling.

WHAT IS SOCIAL STUDIES?

Traditionally, social studies is that part of the kindergarten through grade 12 school curriculum concerned particularly with history, geography, and civic education. More recently, it has also included economics, sociology, anthropology, psychology, and career education. And, most recently, it has been infused into the greater humanities areas with art, music, and literature. The fundamental objectives are to provide each student with knowledge of history, geography, and civic education and to make each person a responsible proactive citizen.

REVISION AND RESTRUCTURE

It is said that with each crisis comes opportunity and so it seems as we begin to read and reflect on the many commission and committee reports currently being circulated. While they each illustrate programmatic and curricular inadequacies, they also provide some sensible solutions and, of course, opportunities to revise and restructure kindergarten through grade 12 social studies education.

Clearly, there are too many reports to discuss within the context of this chapter, but it is important to review some of the more prominent studies and cite their respective recommendations. The reports that will be reviewed in the next several pages are the Bradley Commission, a study done under the auspices of the *National Commission on Social Studies in the Schools* entitled "Charting a Course: Social Studies for the 21st Century," and the California Social Science Framework. Another study, though not specifically reviewed in these pages but well worth mentioning, is the California-based Center for the Study of History, which also has similar recommendations for social studies curriculum.

Although each group being reviewed here did have different membership, started in different years, and probably had different agendas, it is interesting to note that all came to many of the same conclusions.

1. History and geography remain at the core of kindergarten through grade 12 social studies curriculum.
2. History should be taught chronologically.
3. The subject matter should be taught in depth.
4. Social studies should be integrated more into existing curricula (especially in literature and literacy development).
5. Global education should be introduced early in the elementary grades.
6. Multicultural education should be integrated into the kindergarten through grade 12 experience.
7. Non-Western history and geography should be given a more important role in the curriculum.
8. Civic education is an essential component for students who live in a participatory democracy such as ours.

9. Classroom teachers should be trained or retrained in history and geography education.
10. New and more appropriate teaching/learning materials should be developed for classroom use.

The Bradley Commission

The Bradley Commission on History in Schools was created in 1987 in response to the concern over the inadequacy, both in quality and in quantity, of the history taught in U.S. schools. The Commission set itself two goals: to examine what contributes to the effective teaching of history and to make recommendations on the curricular role of history as the core of the social studies.

The Commission reported that 15 percent of all U.S. students did not take any U.S. history and 50 percent did not take any courses in world history at the high school level. The Commission made the following recommendations:

1. The knowledge and habits of mind to be gained from the study of history are indispensable to the education of citizens in a democracy. The study of history should, therefore, be required of all students.
2. Such study must reach well beyond the acquisition of useful information in order to develop judgment and perspective.
3. The curricular time essential to develop the genuine understanding and engagement necessary to exercising judgment must be considerably greater than that presently common in American school programs in history.
4. The kindergarten through grade six social studies curriculum should be history-centered.
5. This Commission recommends to the states and to local school districts the implementation of a social studies curriculum requiring no fewer than four years of history among the six years spanning grades seven through twelve.
6. Every student should have an understanding of the world that encompasses the historical experiences of peoples of Africa, the Americas, Asia, and Europe.
7. History can best be understood when the roles of all constituent parts of society are included; therefore, the history of women, racial and ethnic minorities, and men and women of all classes and conditions should be integrated into historical instruction.
8. The completion of a substantial program in history (preferably a major, minimally a minor) at the college or university level should be required for the certification of teachers of social studies in the middle and high schools.
9. College and university departments of history should review the structure and content of major programs for their suitability to the needs of prospective teachers, with special attention to the quality and liveliness of those survey courses whose counterparts are most often taught in the schools: world history, Western civilization, and American history. (pp. 7–8)

Charting a Course: Social Studies for the 21st Century

In 1985, the National Council for the Social Studies, the American Historical Association, the Carnegie Foundation for the Advancement of Teaching, and the Organization of American Historians formed a coalition and established the National Commission on Social Studies in the Schools. The Commission's tasks included examining the content and effectiveness of instruction in the social studies in U.S. elementary and secondary schools, determining goals of the social studies, and establishing priorities of importance in the field. It also charged its own Curriculum Task Force to make specific recommendations for reform and to disseminate its findings as "forcefully and persuasively" as possible.

The Commission's recommendations were first published in November of 1989 in a publication entitled "Charting a Course: Social Studies for the 21st Century" and clearly outlined both the substance and structure of a kindergarten through grade 12 social studies curriculum. It listed the characteristics of a social studies program, outlined the goals, and discussed specific grade-level curriculum. They are as follows:

1. A well-developed social studies curriculum must instill a clear understanding of the roles of citizens in a democracy and provide opportunities for active, engaged participation in civic, cultural, and volunteer activities designed to enhance the quality of life in the community and in the nation.
2. A complete social studies curriculum provides for *consistent* and *cumulative* learning from *kindergarten* through *twelfth grade*. At each grade level, students should build upon knowledge and skills already learned and should receive preparation for the levels yet to come. Redundant, superficial coverage should be replaced with carefully articulated in-depth studies.
3. Because they offer the perspectives of time and place, history and geography should provide the matrix or framework for social studies; yet concepts and understandings from political science, economics, and the other social sciences must be integrated throughout all social studies courses. By the end of twelfth grade, students would then have a firm understanding of their principles and methodologies.
4. *Selective* studies of the history, geography, government, and economic systems of the major civilizations and societies should together receive attention at least equal to the study of the history, geography, government, economics, and society of the United States. A curriculum that focuses on only one or two major civilizations or geographic areas while ignoring others is neither adequate nor complete.
5. Social studies provides the obvious connection between the humanities and the natural and physical sciences. To assist students' perceptions of the interrelationships among branches of knowledge, integration of other subject matter with social studies should be encouraged whenever possible.
6. Content knowledge from the social studies should not be treated merely as received knowledge to be accepted and memorized, but as the means through which open and vital questions may be explored and confronted. Students must be made aware that just as contemporary events have been shaped by actions taken by people in the past, they themselves have the capacity to shape the future.
7. Reading, writing, observing, debating, role-play or simulations, working with statistical data, and using appropriate critical thinking skills should be an integral part of social studies instruction. Teaching strategies should help students to become both independent and cooperative learners who develop skills of problem solving, decision making, negotiation, and conflict resolution.
8. Learning materials must incorporate a rich mix of written matter, including original sources, literature, and expository writing; a variety of audiovisual materials including films, television, and interactive media; a collection of items of material culture including artifacts, photographs, census records, and historical maps; and computer programs for writing and analyzing social, economic, and geographic data. Social studies coursework should teach students to evaluate the reliability of all such sources of information and to be aware of the ways in which various media select, shape, and constrain information.
9. A complete social studies curriculum for students can only be provided through the support of school boards, school administrators, and the community. Teachers must be granted appropriate in-service opportunities for

enhancing their content knowledge and their abilities to use appropriate teaching strategies. Above all, teachers must be provided substantial blocks of time in which to prepare course outlines, teaching guides, and lesson plans.

10. The core of essential knowledge to be incorporated in the instructional program at every level must be selective enough to provide time for extended in-depth study and must be directed toward the end goals of social studies education—the development of thoughtful Americans who have the capacities for living effective personal and public lives. (pp. 3–4)

History-Social Science Framework for California Public Schools, Kindergarten Through Grade Twelve

In 1987, the California State Board of Education adopted a framework for teaching history-social studies education for grades kindergarten through 12. It was a direct and powerful response to the widespread concern and demand for renaissance of the teaching of history and geography in the kindergarten through grade 12 system. Like many of the other studies and reports, it places history and geography at the hub and establishes a sequential curriculum that allows students to understand the development of their own nation as well as other major civilizations and cultures.

The framework integrates history and geography with the humanities and social science; it is designed to enrich the content at the early grades and to teach civic values throughout the sequence. It also involves ethical concepts and values as well as religious and secular notions and how they impacted history, and it recognizes the plurality of U.S. society. Finally, it spends considerable time reviewing appropriate and responsible citizenship in a representative democracy. Specifically, the framework states the following:

1. This framework is centered in the chronological study of history. History, placed in its geographic setting, establishes human activities in time and place. History and geography are the two great integrative studies of the field. In examining the past and present, students should recognize that events and changes occur in a specific time and place; that historical change has both causes and effects; and that life is bounded by the constraints of place. Throughout this curriculum, the importance of the variables of time and place, when and where, history and geography, is stressed repeatedly.

2. This framework proposes both an integrated and correlated approach to the teaching of history-social science. The teacher is expected to integrate the teaching of history with the other humanities and the social science disciplines. The teacher is also expected to work with teachers from other fields (such as the language arts, science, and the visual and performing arts) in order to achieve correlation across subjects. Within the context of this framework, history is broadly interpreted to include not only the political, economic, and social arrangement of a given society but also its beliefs, religions, culture, arts, architecture, law, literature, sciences, and technology.

3. This framework emphasizes the importance of history as a story well told. Whenever appropriate, history should be presented as an exciting and dramatic series of events in the past that helped to shape the present. The teacher should endeavor to bring the past to life and to make vivid the struggles and triumphs of men and women who lived in other times and places. The story of the past should be lively and accurate as well as rich with controversies and forceful personalities. While assessing the social, economic, political, and cultural contest of events, teachers must never neglect the value of good storytelling as a source of motivation for the study of history.

4. This framework emphasizes the importance of enriching the study of history with the use of literature, both literature of the period and literature about the

period. Teachers of history and teachers of language arts must collaborate to select representative works. Poetry, novels, plays, essays, documents, inaugural addresses, myths, legends, tall tales, biographies, and religious literature help to shed light on the life and times of the people. Such literature helps to reveal the way people saw themselves, their ideas and values, their fears and dreams, and the way they interpreted their own times.

5. This framework introduces a new curricular approach for kindergarten through grade three. In recognition of the shrinkage of time allotted to history-social science instruction in these grades in the recent past, and the need for deeper content to hold the interest of children, this framework proposes enrichment of the curriculum for these grades. While the neighborhood and the region provide the field for exploratory activities related to geography, economics, and local history, the students will read, hear, and discuss biographies, myths, fairy tales, and historical tales to fire their imagination and to whet their appetite for understanding how the world came to be as it is.

6. This framework emphasizes the importance of studying major historical events and periods in-depth as opposed to superficial skimming of enormous amounts of material. The integrated and correlated approach proposed here requires time; students should not be made to feel that they are on a forced march across many centuries and continents. The courses in this framework identify specific eras and events that are to be studied in-depth so that students will have time to use a variety of nontextbook materials, to think about what they are studying, and to see it enrich detail and broad scope.

7. This framework proposes a sequential curriculum, one in which knowledge and understanding are built up in a carefully planned and systematic fashion from kindergarten through grade twelve. The sequential development of instruction that proceeds chronologically through the grades will minimize gaps in students' knowledge and avoid unnecessary repetition of material among grades. Teachers in each grade will know what history and social science content and which skills their students have studied in previous years. At each grade level, some time will be designated for review of previously studied chronological periods with attention to differing themes, concepts, or levels of difficulty of understanding.

8. This framework incorporates a multicultural perspective throughout the history-social science curriculum. It calls on teachers to recognize that the history of community, state, region, nation, and world must reflect the experiences of men and women and of different racial, religious, and ethnic groups. California has always been a state of many different cultural groups, just as the United States has always been a nation of many different cultural groups. The experiences of all these groups are to be integrated at every grade level in the history-social science curriculum. The framework embodies the understanding that the national identity, the national heritage, and the national creed are pluralistic and that our national history is the complex story of many peoples and one nation, of *e pluribus unum*, and of an unfinished struggle to realize the ideals of the Declaration of Independence and the Constitution.

9. This framework increases the place of world history in the curriculum to three years (at grades six, seven, and ten), organized chronologically. While emphasizing the centrality of Western civilizations as the source of American political institutions, laws, and ideology, the world history sequence stresses the concept of global interdependence. Special attention is given to the study of non-Western societies in recognition of the need for understanding the history and cultures of Asian, African, and other non-Western peoples. At each grade level, the world history course should integrate the study of history with the other humanities.

10. This framework emphasizes the importance of the application of ethical understanding and civil virtue to public affairs. At each grade level, the teacher of history and the social sciences will encourage students to reflect on the individual responsibilities and behaviors that create a good society, to consider

the individual's role in how a society governs itself, and to examine the role of law in society. The curriculum provides numerous opportunities to discuss the ethical implications of how societies are organized and governed, what the state owes to its citizens, and what citizens owe to the state. Major historical controversies and events offer an appropriate forum for discussing the ethics of political decisions and for reflecting on individual and social responsibility for civic welfare in the world today.

11. This framework encourages the development of civic and democratic values as an integral element of good citizenship. From the earliest grades, students should learn the kind of behavior that is necessary for the functioning of a democratic society (sportsmanship, fair play, sharing, and taking turns). They should receive opportunities to lead and to follow and learn how to select leaders and how to resolve disputes rationally. They should learn about the value of due process in dealing with infractions, and learn to respect the rights of the minority, even if this minority is only a single, dissenting voice. These democratic values should be taught in the classroom, in the curriculum, and in the daily life of the school. Whenever possible, opportunities should be available for participation and for reflection on the responsibilities of citizens in a free society.

12. This framework supports the frequent study and discussion of the fundamental principles embodied in the United States Constitution and the Bill of Rights. In addition to the customary three years of United States history in grades five, eight, and eleven and the course in "Principles of American Democracy" in grade twelve, the history-social science curriculum places a continuing emphasis on democratic values in the relations between citizens and the state. Whether studying United States history or world history, students should be aware of the presence or absence of the rights of the individual, the rights of minorities, the right of the citizen to participate in government, the right to speak or publish freely without governmental coercion, the right to freedom of religion, the right to trial by jury, the right to form trade unions, and other basic democratic rights.

13. This framework encourages teachers to present controversial issues honestly and accurately within their historical or contemporary context. History without controversy is not good history, nor is such history as interesting to students as an account that captures the debates of the times. Students should understand that the events in history provoked controversy as do the events reported in today's headlines. Students should try to see historical controversies through the different perspectives of participants. These controversies can best be portrayed by using original documents such as newspapers, court decisions, and speeches that represent different views. Students should also recognize that historians often disagree about the interpretation of historical events and that today's textbooks may be altered by future research. Through the study of controversial issues, both in history and in current affairs, students should learn that people in a democratic society have the right to disagree, that different perspectives have to be taken into account, and that judgments should be based on reasonable evidence and not on bias and emotion.

14. This framework acknowledges the importance of religion in human history. When studying world history, students must become familiar with the basic ideas of the major religions and the ethical traditions of each time and place. Students are expected to learn about the role of religion in the founding of this country because many of our political institutions have their antecedents in religious beliefs. Students should understand the intense religious passions that have produced fanaticism and war as well as the political arrangements developed (such as separation of church and state) that allow different religious groups to live amicably in a pluralistic society.

15. This framework proposes that critical thinking skills be included at every grade level. Students should learn: to detect bias in print and visual media; to recognize illogical thinking; to guard against propaganda; to avoid

stereotyping of group members; to reach conclusions based on solid evidence; and to think critically, creatively, and rationally. These skills are to be taught within the context of a curriculum that offers numerous opportunities to explore examples of sound reasoning and examples of the opposite.

16. This framework supports a variety of content-appropriate teaching methods that engage students actively in the learning process. Local and oral history projects, writing projects, debates, simulations, role playing, dramatizations, and cooperative learning are encouraged, as is the use of technology to supplement reading and classroom activities and to enrich the teaching of history and social science. Video resources such as video programs and laser discs, computer software, and newly emerging forms of educational technology can provide invaluable resources for the teaching of history, geography, economics, and the other disciplines.

17. This framework provides opportunities for students' participation in school and community service programs and activities. Teachers are encouraged to have students use the community to gather information regarding public issues and become familiar with individuals and organizations involved in public affairs. Campus and community beautification activities and volunteer service in community facilities such as hospitals and senior citizen or day care centers can provide students with opportunities to develop a commitment to public service and help link students in a positive way to their schools and communities. (pp. 4–8)

It is important to be aware and understand what is being proposed for kindergarten through grade 12 social studies education. These commissions and their respective reports will have a direct impact on the curriculum, the textbooks and other teaching/learning materials, and most certainly on the pre- and in-service training given to classroom teachers.

REFERENCES

Bradley Commission on History in Schools. (1988). *Building a History Curriculum: Guidelines for Teaching History in Schools.* Educational Excellence Network.

California State Board of Education. (1987, July). *History-Social Science Framework for California Public Schools Kindergarten Through Grade Twelve.*

National Commission on Social Studies in the Schools. (1989, November). *Charting a Course: Social Studies for the 21st Century.*

CHAPTER 2

Geography: Gateway to Understanding the World in Which We Live

In the end we will conserve only what we love. We will love only what we understand. We will understand only what we are taught—SENEGALESE PROVERB

GEOGRAPHY AND THE SOCIAL STUDIES

If history is the heart of the social studies curriculum, then geography is certainly the soul. Geography has historically and traditionally occupied a position of central importance in the social studies curriculum; now, with the momentous events of modern times, the study of geography has taken on a more significant role and clearly underscores the need to teach it from a global perspective at all academic levels.

Even with its central importance, geography, like history, has been neglected, especially in the K–8 system. This has happened because elementary school teachers have not been adequately prepared to teach social studies and they lack the knowledge and skills to be effective. Also, they generally place higher value on other components in the K–6 school curriculum. The teaching of geography has also suffered because of the frequently stereotyped notions that teaching it has all too frequently meant coloring maps, memorizing physical features, and memorizing irrelevant facts. In short, too much time was spent coloring maps or compiling charts, graphs, and appendices and too little time was spent in critical thinking and other inquiry-oriented learning activities.

The National Council for Geographic Education and the Association of American Geographers have prepared a document that clearly identifies the five central themes on which a K–12 program in geography should focus: (1) *location,* the position on the earth's surface; (2) *place*, the physical, human, or other characteristics that distinguish one place from another; (3) *human/environmentinteractions*, the primary use of the land, where most people live, and how people modified or were modified by the environment; (4) *movement*, the relationships among and between places through the movement of people, concepts, and material goods; and (5) *regions*, specific areas that display some commodities like language, government, customs, vegetation, and climate.

Classroom teachers should have little difficulty finding ways to infuse elements of geography in not only social studies units but throughout the entire curriculum. Virtually every subject area in the school day (science, reading, mathematics, physical education, and literacy development) can be taught in association with geography and global education.

The primary-grade teacher can initiate geography-oriented studies by consciously expanding the existing curriculum to include basic information about the world in which we live. Besides the traditional lessons of having children identify basic concepts like the shape of the globe, water and land masses, the poles, and so on, the teacher can also introduce geography and global concepts. As stories are read, songs are sung, and art is created, the teacher can—by using maps, globes, and atlases—identify who people are, where they live, and how they relate and interact with us.

The intermediate-grade teacher also has opportunities to infuse geographic and global education into the curriculum. For example, creating units of study with applications in literature for independent and/or group study. To expand the curriculum, the teacher might utilize tall tales like "Captain Stormalong," "Joe Magarac," "Mike Fink," "Paul Bunyan," "John Henry," "Windwagon Smith," or "Pecos Bill" to illustrate geographic themes. Reviewing the concepts of location, place, and human/environment interactions would be especially appropriate in the study of myths and tall tales for these grade levels.

A skillful teacher could also direct students into discussions regarding regionalism, social attitudes and values, and historical perspectives by utilizing literature, music, and art. For example, having students read and react to Native-American folktales as presented by such notable authors as Christie Harris, John Bierhorst, Paul Goble, or John Steptoe would not only expand their knowledge of Native-American cultures but also serve as a springboard to studying the history, art, music, literture, and values of the many cultures that make the United States of America the great nation that it is today. Discussions of this type would also serve as appropriate background information as students prepare to study U.S. and world history during the remainder of their formal school years.

At the middle school level, teachers can introduce students to more current global issues, thereby creating greater awareness of other people, their locations and respective cultures. Besides atlas and almanac exercises, the teacher might also introduce students to the literature of some selected groups like the Jewish culture and the writings of Isaac Bashevis Singer, Yuri Suhl, and Uri Shulevitz; Asian cultures and the works of Ed Young, Al-Ling Louis, and Yoshiko Uchida; African-American cultures as illustrated by Ashley Bryan, Verna Aardema, and Julius Lester; or Native-American cultures as presented by Christie Harris, John Bierhurst, and Jamake Highwater.

In essence, at every grade level teachers can infuse global and geographic content and concepts in accordance with the traditional daily curriculum. By using the suggested five themes, a teacher can greatly enhance children's knowledge not only about themselves and their world but also enhance their understanding of concepts like culture, race, and ethnicity.

The following are some motifs that can serve as the basis for individual, group, and/or teacher-directed studies in geography education and global awareness:

WHAT DO THEY MEAN?
- Names of continents
- Names of countries
- Names of states
- Names of regions
- Names of cities

WHERE DID THEY COME FROM?
- The foods we eat
- The clothes we wear
- The cars we drive
- The holidays we celebrate
- The appliances we use

WHAT DO THEY TELL US ABOUT OUR WORLD?
- Stories, myths, folklore, folktales, legends, motifs, and heroes and heroines
- Money and coins
- Postage stamps
- Advertising
- Newspapers, television, and radio
- Entertainers
- Art and music

The following section contains basic data about the planet on which we live. Included are facts, information, a map, and several teacher-directed activities for classroom use.

PLANET EARTH

- The earth is at least 4.5 billion years old.
- Earth's one of nine known planets in this solar system.
- Earth is the third closest planet to the sun—only Venus and Mercury are closer.
- It rotates on its axis once every 23 hours, 56 minutes, and 4.09 seconds.
- The earth revolves around the sun once every 365 days, 6 hours, 9 minutes, and 9.54 seconds.
- The surface of the planet is 196,939,000 square miles.
- It measures 24,902 miles around the equator.
- It measures 24,860 miles from pole to pole to pole.
- The earth contains seven continents and four major oceans.
- The shape of Earth is not round; rather, it is an oblate spheroid. That means it is slightly flattened at the poles and bulges at the center.
- Three-fourths of the surface is water, but less than 1 percent is drinkable.
- Some 99 percent of the atmosphere is less than 50 miles above the surface of the planet.
- The estimated population is about 5.3 billion.

Continents and Oceans

On the surface of the earth large bodies of land and vast bodies of water called *continents* and *oceans,* respectively. Water separates most of the continents—

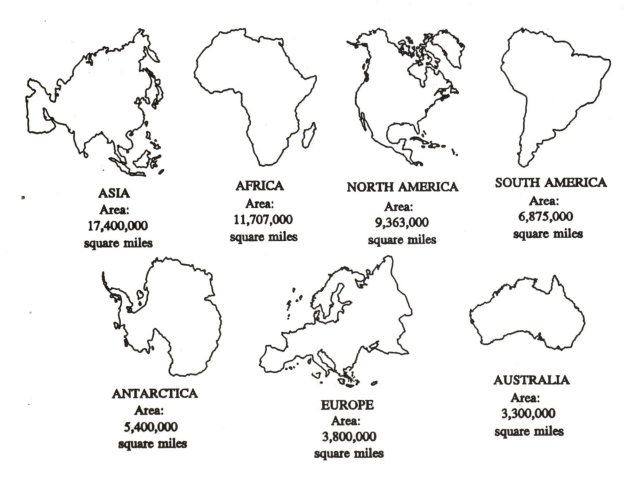

ASIA
Area:
17,400,000
square miles

AFRICA
Area:
11,707,000
square miles

NORTH AMERICA
Area:
9,363,000
square miles

SOUTH AMERICA
Area:
6,875,000
square miles

ANTARCTICA
Area:
5,400,000
square miles

EUROPE
Area:
3,800,000
square miles

AUSTRALIA
Area:
3,300,000
square miles

only Asia and Europe are not separated by a body of water. There are seven continents. They are:

1. Africa
2. Antarctica
3. Asia
4. Australia
5. Europe
6. North America
7. South America

There are four oceans. They are:

1. Arctic Ocean
2. Atlantic Ocean
3. Indian Ocean
4. Pacific Ocean

Significant Facts about Planet Earth

OCEANS AND SEAS	AREA IN SQUARE MILES
Pacific Ocean	64,186,000
Atlantic Ocean	31,862,000
Indian Ocean	28,350,000
Arctic Ocean	5,427,000
Caribbean Sea	970,000
Mediterranean Sea	969,000
South China Sea	895,000
Bering Sea	875,000
Gulf of Mexico	600,000
Sea of Okhotsk	590,000
East China Sea	482,000
Sea of Japan	389,000
Hudson Bay	317,500
North Sea	222,000
Black Sea	185,000
Red Sea	169,000
Baltic Sea	163,000

IMPORTANT ISLANDS	AREA IN SQUARE MILES
Greenland	840,000
New Guinea	305,000
Borneo	290,000
Madagascar	226,400
Baffin	195,928
Sumatra	164,000
New Zealand	103,736
Honshu	88,000
Great Britain	84,400
Celebes	72,986
Java	48,842
Newfoundland	42,031
Cuba	40,533
Luzon	40,420

Iceland	39,768
Mindanao	356,537
Ireland	31,743
Hispaniola	29,399
Hokkaido	28,983
Sri Lanka	25,332
Taiwan	13,836
Vancouver	12,079
Sicily	9,926
Bahamas	5,382
Jamaica	4,232
Hawaii	4,038
Cyprus	3,572
Puerto Rico	3,435

MAJOR MOUNTAINS	HEIGHT IN FEET
Everest, Nepal-China	29,028
Godwin Austen (K2), Pakistan	28,250
Kanchenjunga, Nepal-India	28,208
Lhotse, Nepal-China	27,923
Makalu, Nepal-China	27,824
Dhanlagari, Nepal	26,810
Nanga Parbat, India	26,610
Annapurna, Nepal	26,504
Gasherbrum, Pakistan-China	26,140
Nanda Devi, India	25,645
Rakaposhi, Pakistan	25,550
Kamet. India	25,447
Gurla Mandhada, China	25,355
Kongur Shan, China	25,325
Tirich Mir, Pakistan	25,230
Gongga Shan, China	24,790
Muztaga, China	24,757
Communism Peak, CIS	24,599
Pobeda Peak, CIS	24,406
Chomo Lhari, Bhutan-China	23,997

LAKES AND INLAND SEAS	AREA IN SQUARE MILES
Caspian Sea	143,243
Lake Superior	31,700
Lake Victoria	26,828
Lake Huron	23,010
Lake Michigan	22,300
Aral Sea	15,830
Lake Tanganyika	12,650
Lake Baykal	12,162
Great Bear Lake	12,096
Lake Nyasa	11,550
Great Slave Lake	11,269
Lake Erie	9,910
Lake Winnipeg	9,417
Lake Ontario	7,340
Lake Ladoga	7,104
Lake Balkhash	7,027
Lake Chad	5,300
Lake Onega	3,710

Lake Eyre	3,500
Lake Titicaca	3,200
Lake Nicaragua	3,100
Lake Athabaca	3,064

IMPORTANT RIVERS	LENGTH IN MILES
Nile, Africa	4,240
Amazon, South America	4,163
Yangtze, China	3,900
Mississippi, Missouri, USA	3,741
Yangtze, China	3,434
Ob-Irtysh, CIS	3,362
Congo (Zaire), Africa	2,920
Hwang (Yellow), China	2,877
Amur, Asia	2,744
Lena, CIS	2,734
Congo, Africa	2,718
Mackenzie-Peace, Canada	2,635
Mekong, Asia	2,610
Niger, Africa	2,548
Volga, CIS	2,194
Yukon, Alaska-Canada	1,979
St. Lawrence, Canada-USA	1,885
Rio Grande, Mexico-USA	1,885
Danube, Europe	1,802
Indus, Asia	1,800
Brahmaputra, Asia	1,700
Euphrates, Asia	1,700
Ganges, India	1,550
Irrawaddy, Burma	1,325

TEACHER-DIRECTED ACTIVITIES FOR STUDENTS

1. Using a globe, identify and locate the continents and oceans. Pay particular attention to the size, shape, and relative location to other continents and oceans.
2. Discuss why Greenland and the Arctic are not continents and why large bodies of water like the Mediterranean Sea are not considered oceans.
3. Review each continent in terms of population and land area. Which has the largest rivers, most mountains, greatest lakes, biggest deserts, and the most or least people living there?
4. Identify on each continent the dominant races and the ethnic and religious groups. Trace your family history and see if you can discover where your ancestors were from before they came to the United States of America.
5. Identify the most common surnames on some of the continents (e.g., Smith and Johnson in North America, Garcia and Martin in Europe, Wang in Asia, etc.).
6. Divide into groups and research one continent to share with your classmates. Report such information as the number of countries on the continent; the various ethnic and racial groups, important leaders; and the geography, history, and cultural differences (music, art, and languages) among the people on the continent. Also identify the most interesting and/or colorful national flags. Reproduce some of them and discuss their uniqueness and what they represent.

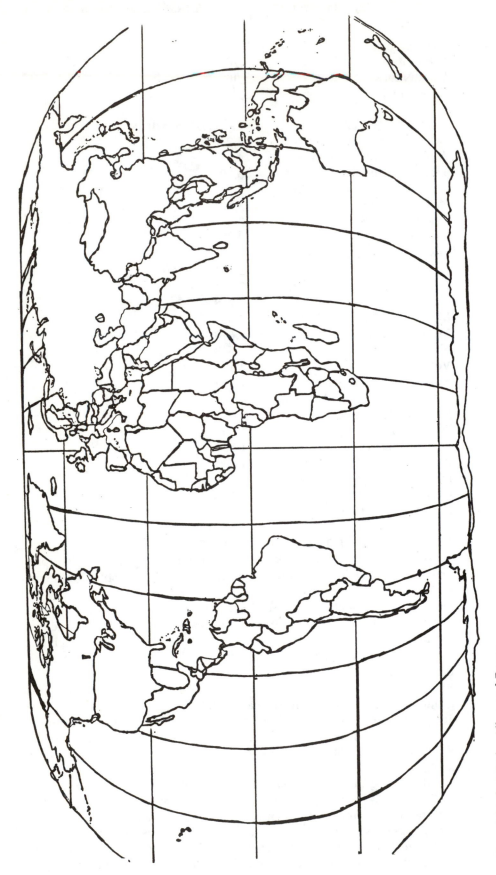

THE CONTINENTS

Africa

Area: 11,707,500 square miles; 20 percent of the world's land
Population: 795,000,000; 14.9 percent of the total world population
Political Divisions: 52 independent countries and 5 dependencies
Biggest Nation: Sudan, 967,494 square miles
Smallest Nation: Seychelles, 171 square miles
Northern-Most Nation: Tunisia
Southern-Most Nation: South Africa
Western-Most Nation: Senegal
Eastern-Most Nation: Seychelles
Coastline: 22,921 miles
Highest Elevation: Mt. Kilimanjaro, 19,340 feet
Lowest Elevation: Lake Assal, −552 feet below sea level
Principal Rivers: Nile, Congo, Niger, Zambezi, Red Volta, White Volta

Principal Lakes: Victoria, Tanganyika, Nyasa, Nasser, Kariba, Chad, Turkana

Principal Mountain Ranges: Atlas, Volta, Drakensberg, Cameroon, Mitumba

Principal Deserts: Sahara, Kalahari, Namib

Largest City: Cairo, Egypt

Distinct Languages: More than 1,700; 30 percent of all world languages

INDEPENDENT COUNTRIES OF AFRICA

Name	Sq. Miles	Population 1991 (approx.)	Capital	Date of Independence
Algeria	919,595	25,086,000	Algiers	1962
Angola	481,354	7,402,000	Luanda	1975
Benin	43,484	3,757,000	Porto-Novo	1960
Botswana	231,805	872,000	Gaborone	1966
Burkina Faso	105,568	30,438,000	Quagadougou	1960
Burundi	10,747	5,662,000	Bujumbura	1962
Cameroon	179,569	11,807,000	Yaoundé	1960
Cape Verde	1,557	339,000	Praia	1975
Central African Republic	240,535	2,879,000	Bangui	1960
Chad	495,755	4,718,000	N'Djamena	1960
Comoros	838	490,000	Moroni	1975
Congo	132,064	1,615,000	Brazzaville	1960
Djibouti	8,494	333,000	Djibouti	1977
Egypt	386,662	43,876,000	Cairo	3100 B.C.
Equatorial Guinea	10,830	382,000	Malabo	1968
Ethiopia	471,778	51,375,000	Addis Ababa	1000 B.C.
Gabon	103,347	1,206,000	Libreville	1960
Gambia	4,127	632,000	Banjul	1965
Ghana	92,100	12,394,099	Accra	1957
Guinea	94,926	5,257,000	Conakry	1958
Guinea-Bissau	13,948	861,000	Bissau	1974
Ivory Coast	124,504	8,555,000	Yamoussoukro	1960
Kenya	224,961	25,200,000	Nairobi	1963
Lesotho	11,720	1,406,000	Maseru	1966
Liberia	43,000	1,984,000	Monrovia	1847
Libya	679,362	3,227,000	Tripoli	1952
Madagascar	226,658	9,393,000	Antananarivo	1960
Malawi	45,747	6,283,000	Lilongwe	1964
Mauritania	397,954	1,718,000	Nouakchott	1960
Mauritius	790	977,000	Port Louis	1968
Morrocco	172,414	21,090,000	Rabat	1956
Mozambique	302,330	10,966,000	Maputo	1975
Namibia	317,827	1,063,000	Windhoek	1990
Niger	489,191	5,577,000	Niamey	1960
Nigeria	356,669	118,865,000	Lagos	1960
Rwanda	10,169	5,340,000	Kigali	1962
São Tomé, Principie	372	88,000	São Tomé	1975
Senegal	75,750	6,033,000	Dakar	1960
Seychelles	171	67,000	Victoria	1976
Sierra Leone	27,925	3,651,000	Freetown	1961

Name	Sq. Miles	Population 1991 (approx.)	Capital	Date of Independence
Somalia	246,241	3,830,000	Mogadishu	1960
South Africa	471,445	30,815,000	Pretoria	1931
Sudan	967,500	19,330,000	Khartoum	1956
Swaiziland	6,704	617,000	Mbabane	1968
Tanzania	363,708	19,973,000	Dar es Salaam	1963
Togo	21,622	2,670,000	Lomé	1960
Tunisia	63,170	6,677,000	Tunis	1956
Uganda	91,067	14,620,000	Kampala	1962
Zaire	905,563	30,500,000	Kinshasa	1960
Zambia	290,586	6,800,000	Lusaka	1964
Zimbabwe	150,803	7,870,000	Harare	1980

DEPENDENCIES AND OTHER POLITICAL UNITS IN AFRICA

Name	Sq. Miles	Population 1991 (approx.)	Capital	Status
Ascension	34	1,500	none	Administered through St. Helena
Canary Islands	2,808	1,407,000	Santa Cruz de Tenerife	
Madeira	307	269,000	Funchal	Portuguese Territory
Mayotte	144	77,000	Dzaoudzi	Overseas Dept. of France
Reunion	969	263,000	Saint-Denis	Overseas Dept. of France
St. Helena	47	6,657	Jamestown	Colony of the United Kingdom
Western Sahara	102,703	174,000	None	Administered through St. Helena

SOME INTERESTING FACTS ABOUT AFRICA

- Africa has more independent nations (52) than any other continent.
- It is the only continent through which the Equator and the Tropics of Cancer and Capricorn pass.
- Africa covers about a fifth of the earth's land area and has nearly an eighth of its population.
- Africa contains the world's largest desert—the Sahara—which is roughly the size of the United States.
- Africa contains the world's longest river—the Nile.
- Northern Africa is populated mostly by Arabs and Egyptians; central Africa is populated mostly by blacks; and in the southern third of the continent there are pockets of white populations—living mostly in South Africa.
- Although blacks make up the greatest majority of the African population, they are divided into more than 800 ethnic groups.
- About two-thirds of all Africans live in rural areas, but the continent does have large cities such as Cairo (Egypt), Nairobi (Kenya), and Lagos (Nigeria).
- The average life expectancy among Africans is about 49 years (compared to 75 years for Americans).

- Africa has two of the great ancient civilizations—Egypt and Ethiopia.
- There are more than 800 languages and dialects spoken in Africa.
- Mining accounts for more than half of Africa's exports. However, only five nations—South Africa, Libya, Nigeria, Algeria, and Zambia—produce about 90 percent of these minerals.
- South Africa is the world's largest producer of gold.
- The continent produces three-fourths of the world's cobalt.
- Portugal, in 1975, was the last European nation to give up its African colonies.
- Desmond Tutu of South Africa and Anwar Sadat of Egypt won Nobel Peace Prizes.

SOME HISTORICAL FIGURES IN AFRICAN HISTORY

Cleopatra	Stephen Bantu Biko
Hannibal	Paul Kruger
Vasco da Gama	Cecil John Rhodes
Bartholomeu Dias	Robert Mugabe
Johan van Riebeeck	Momar Ghadaffi
Haile Selassi I	Frederik W. de Klerk
Shaka	Jomo Kenyatta
Cetewayo	Abdel Nasser
Houari Boumedienne	David Livingstone
Mangosuthu Gatsa Buthelezi	Albert Schweitzer
Nelson Mandela	Anwar Sadat
Desmond Tutu	Sir Henry M. Stanley

TEACHER-DIRECTED ACTIVITIES FOR STUDENTS

1. Look at the following three maps of Africa.

1910

1950

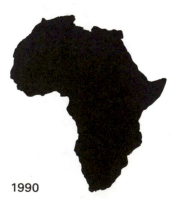

1990

   a. What does the black represent in all the maps?
   b. What are the capitals of Egypt, Ethiopia, Liberia, and South Africa? What do they have in common?
   c. Name the last country in Africa to become an independent nation.
   d. Hand draw your own map of Africa and fill in Mt. Kilimanjaro, the Sahara, the Nile River, the Drakensberg, and Lake Victoria.

2. Choose one of the personalities listed under Some Historical Figures in African History and list reasons why this person made the list.
3. Make a list of the animals that can be found in Africa. Using magazines

and newspapers, cut out pictures of these animals and make a collage in the shape of the African continent.

4. Read *Mufaro's Beautiful Daughters* by John Steptoe. After reading this African folktale, pinpoint Zimbabwe, the Limpopo River, and Bulawayo on a map of Africa.

Antarctica

Area: 5,500,000 square miles; 9.5 percent of the earth's land surface
Coastline: 19,800 miles
Highest Point: Vinson Massif, 16,864 feet
Lowest Point: Sea level
Extreme Temperatures: +58°F; −127°F
Average Annual Rainfall: 0.8 inch
Major Mountain Ranges: Antarctic Peninsula, Elsworth, Whitmore
Chief Glaciers: Beardmore, Lambert, Rennick, Recoverg

SOME INTERESTING FACTS ABOUT ANTARCTICA
- Antarctica is the fifth largest continent.
- The continent is larger than Australia and Europe.
- Some 98 percent of the continent is covered in ice or snow.
- The southern magnetic pole is located in eastern Antarctica.
- Antarctica is divided into two subcontinents: East Antarctica and West Antarctica.
- There are 45 species of birds, including 3 types of penguins—the Antarctic petral, the Emperor penguin, and the South Polar penguin.
- A few plants do grow on the continent, such as lichens, mosses, liverworts, molds, and yeasts, which grow along coastal areas.
- Only a few insects spend their entire lives on the continent, but the waters around Antarctica are teeming with life throughout the year.
- Traces of copper, chrome, gold, iron, lead, manganese, and zinc are found on Antarctica.
- The continent borders the Atlantic, Pacific, and Indian Oceans.
- The average elevation is estimated at 7,500 feet above sea level, which makes Antarctica the "highest" continent on planet Earth.

- At its densest, the ice cap is about 15,700 feet deep.
- Originally, 12 nations established more than 50 scientific stations on the continent and nearby islands. They include Argentina, Australia, Belgium, Chile, France, Great Britain, Japan, New Zealand, Norway, the Commonwealth of Independent States, the Union of South Africa, and the United States. Since the original stations were established, other nations have initiated research stations. They include Poland (1977), Germany (1981), Brazil (1983), India (1983), China (1985), Uraguay (1988), and Italy (1987).
- Roald Amundsen of Norway was the first person to reach the magnetic South Pole.
- Admiral Richard Byrd was the first to fly over the South Pole.
- In 1991, the National Science Foundation (NSF) developed and maintains three year-round facilities in Antarctica: (1) Amundsen-Scott South Pole Station, (2) McMurdo Station on Ross Island, and (3) Palmer Station on Anvers Island.
- A great deal of the current scientific research conducted in Antarctica is being focused on the depleting ozone layer.

TEACHER-DIRECTED ACTIVITIES FOR STUDENTS

1. Research the "race" to the South Pole. Role-play the characters and simulate the events of this exciting historical event.
2. Imagine that rich deposits of gold, chrome, or uranium are known to exist in Antarctica. What would be the major stumbling blocks to exploiting these minerals?
3. Draw a map of Antarctica to scale. Superimpose maps of Australia and Europe over this map and discuss the relative size and area of these three continents.
4. How do mites, ticks, and other insects survive the harsh temperatures of Antarctica?
5. Draw a compass and fill in the major points. Hold the compass over a world map and pinpoint the North Pole and South Pole.
6. Discuss what it would be like to be a scientist living in Antarctica at one of the scientific stations. How would you pass the time and what would you do for recreation?
7. Speculate on the future of the continent.

Asia

Area: 17,128,000 square miles; 30 percent of earth's land surface
Population: 3.2 billion; 59 percent of the total world population
Political Divisions: 43 independent nations and 4 dependencies
Biggest Nation: Russia, 6,592,812 square miles
Smallest Nation: Maldives, 115 square miles
Northern-Most Nation: Russia
Southern-Most Nation: Indonesia
Western-Most Nation: Turkey
Eastern-Most Nation: Russia
Coastline: 80,205 miles
Highest Elevation: Mt. Everest, Nepal, 29,028 feet
Lowest Elevation: Shore of Dead Sea, Israel/Jordan, −1,310 feet below sea level

Principal Rivers: Amur, Euphrates, Yangtze, Ob, Ganges, Indus, Salween, Mekong
Principal Lakes: Lake Baikal, Caspian Sea, Aral Sea
Principal Mountain Ranges: Himalayas, Karakoram
Principal Deserts: Gobi, Rub al Khali, Kara Kum
Largest Cities: Seoul, Korea; Moscow, Russia; Tokyo, Japan
Distinct Languages: Hundreds of languages and thousands of dialects

INDEPENDENT NATIONS OF ASIA

Name	Sq. Miles	Population 1990 (approx.)	Capital	Date of Independence
Afghanistan	251,773	17,666,000	Kabul	1747
Bahrain	265	531,000	Manama	1971
Bangladesh	55,598	118,702,000	Dhaka	1971
Bhutan	18,147	1,550,000	Thimphu	1907
Brunei	2,226	299,000	Bandar Seri Begawan	1984
Burma	261,789	38,541	Rangoon	1948
Cambodia	69,898	7,147,000	Phnom Penh	1953
China	3,696,032	1,130,883,000	Beijing	1766 B.C.
Commonwealth of Independent States (Asia)				1991
Kazakhstan	1,048,300	16,538,000	Alma-Ata	1991
Kirghizia	76,641	4,291,000	Frunze	1991
Tadzhikistan	55,251	5,112,000	Dushanbe	1991

INDEPENDENT NATIONS OF ASIA (Continued)

Name	Sq. Miles	Population 1990 (approx.)	Capital	Date of Independence
Turkmenistan	188,455	3,534,000	Ashkhabad	1991
Uzbekistan	173,591	19,906,000	Tashkent	1991
Cyprus	3,572	708,000	Nicosia	1960
India	1,269,219	871,208,000	New Delhi	1947
Indonesia	578,173	181,904,000	Jakarta	1949
Iran	636,300	55,647,000	Teheran	550 B.C.
Iraq	169,235	18,782,000	Baghdad	3500 B.C.
Israel	7,900	4,647,000	Jerusalem	1948
Japan	145,870	124,025,000	Tokyo	660 B.C.
Jordan	37,475	3,172,000	Amman	1946
Korea, North	46,540	23,432,000	P'yongyang	1948
Korea, South	38,625	44,018,000	Seoul	1948
Kuwait	6,880	2,154,000	Al Kuwait	1961
Laos	91,428	4,167,000	Vientiane	1949
Lebanon	4,015	3,026,000	Beirut	1943
Malaysia	127,317	17,689,000	Kuala Lumpur	1963
Maldives	115	227,000	Male	1965
Mongolia	604,250	2,295,000	Ulaanbaatar	1921
Myanmar	261,789	42,546,000	Vangon	1989
Nepal	56,827	19,591,000	Kathmandu	1775
Oman	120,000	1,517,000	Muscat	1740
Pakistan	307,374	122,666,000	Islamabad	1947
Philippines	116,000	66,826,000	Manila	1946
Qatar	4,416	380,000	Doha	1971
Saudi Arabia	839,000	13,366,000	Riyadh	1932
Singapore	240	2,728,000	Singapore	1965
Sri Lanka	25,333	17,639,000	Colombo	1948
Syria	71,498	12,941,000	Damascus	1946
Taiwan (China)	13,900	20,923,000	Taipei	1949
Thailand	198,115	56,454,000	Bangkok	1938
Turkey	300,946	52,144,000	Ankara	1923
United Arab Emirates	32,278	2,253,000	Abu Dhabi	1971
Vietnam	127,246	67,290,000	Hanoi	1954
Yemen	207,286	9,746,000	San'a	1991

DEPENDENT NATIONS

Name	Sq. Miles	Population 1990 (approx.)	Capital	Status
Gaza Strip	146	564,000	Gaza	Occupied by Israel
Hong Kong	1,126	5,756,000	Victoria	British Crown dependency (until 1997)
Macau	6.5	436,000	Macau	Portuguese territory (until 1999)
West Bank	2,263	1,053,000	—	Occupied by Israel

SOME INTERESTING FACTS ABOUT ASIA
- China is the largest nation (population) in the world, with over 1.3 billion people.
- Russia, which lies in both Asia and Europe, is the largest nation (land area) in the world.
- The highest point in the world (Mt. Everest in Nepal) and the lowest point in the world (Lake Baykal in the CIS) are both in Asia.
- Bangladesh, India, Hong Kong, Singapore, and Eastern China are the most densely populated areas in the world.
- All the world's great religions began in Asia.
- The continent of Asia has more people living on it than any other continent—about 3.2 billion!
- There are five landlocked nations in Asia: Afghanistan, Mongolia, Bhutan, Nepal, and Laos.
- Nepal is the world's only Hindu monarchy.
- The Great Wall of China is one of the very few human-made objects that can be seen from outer space.
- There are several Archipelagos in Asia: the islands of Japan, the Philippines, and Indonesia.

SOME INTERESTING ASIAN PERSONALITIES

Mohandas Gandhi	Jesus of Nazareth
Hammurabi	Sun Yat-Sen
Kublai Khan	Ho Chi Minh
Genghis Kahn	Indira Ghandi
Buddha	Confucius
Moses	Norodom Sihanouk
Mohammed	Golda Meier
Hirohito	Mustapha Kemal
Corazon Aquino	Yasir Arafat
King Hussein I (Jordan)	Suharto

TEACHER-DIRECTED ACTIVITIES FOR STUDENTS
1. Use a world almanac to find the latest population figures for China, Japan, India, South Korea, Vietnam, and Pakistan. Now draw a pie graph showing the population distribution in these areas as compared to the United States, Egypt, and Brazil.
2. Although it is difficult to separate the whole of the Middle East from Asia, which countries do you think make up the Middle East? Make a list of these countries and defend your choices.
3. Find and write out two verses or quotes from each of the following holy books: the Old Testament, the New Testament, the Koran, the Bagavad Gita. What do they have in common? How are they different?
4. Who was the first person to climb Mt. Everest? Who was his guide? What are the people called who live in the Mt. Everest area? What are the major problems facing mountain climbers in the Himalayas?
5. What major historical event has taken place close to the Red Sea? the Mekong River? the Euphrates and Tigris Rivers?

Australia

Area: 2,966,150 square miles (including Tasmania); 5 percent of the earth's land surface

Population: 16,930,000; 2 percent of the total world population

Coastline: 17,366 miles (including Tasmania)

Highest Elevation: Mt. Kosciusko, 7,310 feet

Lowest Elevation: Lake Eyre, −52 feet below sea level

Principal Lakes: Lake Argyle, Lake Gordon (Tasmania), Lake Eyre, Lake Torrens

Principal Rivers: Darling, Murry

Principal Mountain Ranges: Snowy Mountains, MacDonnell Range, Musgrave Range, Great Dividing Range

Principal Deserts: Great Victorian Desert, Gibson Desert, Great Sandy Deserts, Simpson Desert

Largest City: Sydney

Principal Language: English

STATES IN AUSTRALIA

Name	State Capital	Sq. Miles	Population
Australian National Capital	Canberra	930	249,207
New South Wales	Sydney	309,500	5,401,881
Northern Territory	Darwin	519,700	154,848
Queensland	Brisbane	666,900	2,587,315
South Australia	Adelaide	380,070	1,345,945
Tasmania	Hobart	26,200	436,535
Victoria	Melbourne	87,900	4,019,478
Western Australia	Perth	975,100	1,406,929

OCEANIA

Name	Sq. Miles	Population	Capital	Year of Independence
New Zealand	103,736	3,389,000	Wellington	1907
Fiji	7,055	760,000	Suva	1970
Kiribati	291	70,000	Bairiki	1979
Nauru	8	9,200	Yaren (district)	1968
Solomon Islands	10,639	335,000	Honiara	1978
Tonga	270	101,300	Nukualofa	1970
Tuvalu	10	9,100	Fongafale	1978
Vanuatu	5,700	165,000	Vila	1980
Western Samoa	1,133	186,000	Apia	1962
Papua New Guiena	178,704	3,822,000	Port Mosby	1975

OTHER POLITICAL UNITS OF THE PACIFIC

Name	Sq. Miles	Population	Capital	Status
French Polynesia	1,622	190,181	Papeete	Overseas Territory of France
New Caledonia	7,376	153,215	Noumea	Overseas Territory of France
Wallis & Futuna	106	14,910	Matautu	Overseas Dept. of France
Cook Islands	92	18,187	Avarua	Associated with New Zealand
Nive	100	2,019	Alofi	Associated with New Zealand
Tokelau	4	1,700	none	Territory of New Zealand
Pitcairn Islands	2	56	Adamstown	Colony of United Kingdom

EXTERNAL TERRITORIES

Name	Sq. Miles	Population
Ashmore and Carter Islands	2	0
Australian Antarctic Territory	2,362,875	0
Kiritamati	52	3,000
Cocos and Keeling Islands	5	600
Heard and McDonald Islands	183	0
Norfolk Island	14	2,000

SOME INTERESTING FACTS ABOUT AUSTRALIA
- Australia is the only country that is also a continent.
- Australia is the sixth largest country in the world and the smallest continent.
- It is one of only two continents located completely in the southern hemisphere.
- Australia comes from the Latin word, *australis,* which means south.
- Queen Elizabeth II of England is the official head of state. Australia is a constitutional monarchy.
- Australia began as a British penal colony.
- About one-third of the continent is desert.
- The Great Barrier Reef, the world's largest coral reef, is located off the coast of Australia.
- The native population, the Aborigines, have been in Australia for about 4,000 years.
- Australia has about 150 species of marsupials living on the continent. Some of the more famous are kangaroos, wallabies, wombats, and koalas.
- Two of the strangest animals on the continent are the platypus and the echidnas.

- The emu of Australia and the ostrich of Africa are essentially the same creature.
- The flag of Australia has a small British flag, five stars representing the southern constellation, and a larger star representing the country's state and territories.

SOME INTERESTING AUSTRALIAN PERSONALITIES

Evonne Goolagong Cawley	Helen Reddy
Lew Hoad	John Newcombe
Olivia Newton-John	Dawn Fraser
Edmund Barton	Dame Judith Anderson
Robert Hawke	Herb Elliot
Rod Laver	Errol Flynn
Ron Clarke	Randolph Stow

TEACHER-DIRECTED ACTIVITIES FOR STUDENTS

1. Why is Australia a continent when other large islands like Borneo and Greenland are not?
2. Identify and list the important sports champions from Australia (Olympic and world champions) and discuss the importance of athletics in Australia.
3. Who are the Aborigines and where did they come from? What is their situation today in Australia?
4. What is the Great Barrier Reef and why is it such a great tourist attraction?
5. Using almanacs and other resource books, chronicle the major events in the history of Australia from its beginnings as a penal colony to its present status as a constitutional monarchy.
6. Using newspapers and magazines, review the historical relationship between the United States and Australia during the past 50 years.

Europe

Area: 4,057,000 square miles, 7 percent of the earth's land surface
Population: 499,000,000; 9.3 percent of the total world population
Political Divisions: 47 independent nations, 7 dependencies
Biggest Nation: Russia
Smallest Nation: Vatican City
Northern-Most Nation: Russia
Southern-Most Nation: Greece (Crete)
Western-Most Nation: Iceland
Eastern-Most Nation: Russia
Coastline: 37,887 miles
Highest Elevation: Mt. Elbrus, 18,510 feet
Lowest Elevation: Shore of Caspian Sea, −92 feet below sea level
Principal Rivers: Volga, Rhine, Don, Danube, Oder, Elbe, Po, Seine, Thames
Principal Lakes: Caspian Sea, Ladoga, Onega
Major Bodies of Water: Mediterranean Sea, Black Sea, Baltic Sea, North Sea, Adriatic Sea, Aegean Sea
Principal Mountain Ranges: Alps, Apennines, Balkans, Carpathians, Pyrenees, Ural
Principal Deserts: None
Largest Cities: Moscow (Russia), London (England), Paris (France)
Distinct Languages: 50 languages with more than 100 dialects

INDEPENDENT NATIONS OF EUROPE

Name	Sq. Miles	Population	Capital	Date of Independence
Albania	11,100	3,275,000	Tirane	1912
Andorra	180	57,000	Andorra la Vella	1288
Austria	32,377	7,555,000	Vienna	1918
Belgium	11,783	9,897,000	Brussels	1830
Bosnia and Hercegovinia	19,741	4,116,000	Sarajevo	1992
Bulgaria	42,823	8,930,000	Sofia	1908
Croatia	21,829	4,600,000	Zagreb	1992
Czech Republic	30,464	10,500,000	Prague	1993
Denmark	16,638	5,121,000	Copenhagen	950
Estonia	17,413	1,573,000	Tallinn	1991
Finland	130,559	4,953,000	Helsinki	1917
France	211,208	56,813,000	Paris	1792
Germany	137,855	78,000,000	Berlin	1990 (reunited)
Greece	50,944	10,044,000	Athens	1827
Hungary	35,919	10,664,000	Budapest	1867
Iceland	39,800	252,000	Reykjavik	1944
Ireland	27,136	3,601,000	Dublin	1921
Italy	116,320	57,489,000	Rome	1861
Latvia	24,595	2,681,000	Riga	1991
Liechtenstein	62	29,000	Vaduz	1719
Lithuania	25,170	3,690,000	Vilnius	1991
Luxembourg	998	383,000	Luxembourg	963

INDEPENDENT NATIONS OF EUROPE (Continued)

Name	Sq. Miles	Population	Capital	Date of Independence
Macedonia	9,928	1,914,000	Skopje	1992
Malta	122	354,000	Valletta	1964
Monaco	0.73	29,000	Monaco	1911
Netherlands	14,405	14,903,000	Amsterdam	1641
Norway	149,405	4,171,000	Oslo	1905
Poland	120,728	38,269,000	Warsaw	1918
Portugal	35,553	9,915,000	Lisbon	1143
Romania	91,700	23,155,000	Bucharest	1861
San Marino	24	23,000	San Marino	1631
Slovenia	7,819	1,900,000	Ljubljana	1991
Slovakia	18,917	5,000,000	Bratslavia	1993
Spain	194,889	39,499,000	Madrid	1479
Sweden	173,732	8,371,000	Stockholm	1523
Switzerland	15,943	6,485,000	Bern	1648
European Commonwealth of Independent States (European)				
Armenia	11,506	3,283,000	Yerevam	1991
Azerbaijan	33,436	7,029,000	Baku	1991
Byelorussia	80,154	10,200,000	Minsk	1991
Georgia	26,911	5,449,000	Tbilisi	1991
Moldavia	13,012	4,341,000	Kishinev	1991
Russia	6,592,812	147,386,000	Moscow	1992
Ukraine	233,089	51,704,000	Kiev	1991
United Kingdom	94,248	57,658,000	London	1801
Vatican City	.17	1,000	Vatican City	1929
Yugoslavia (Serbia and Montenegro)	39,000	10,337,000	Belgrade	1992

DEPENDENT NATIONS OF EUROPE

Name	Sq. Miles	Population	Capital	Status
Azores	888	252,000	Ponta Delgada	Autonomous region of Portugal
Balearic Islands	1,936	755,000	Palma	Province of Spain
Channel Islands	75	145,000	St. Peter Port St. Helier	British Crown Colonies
Faeroe Islands	540	48,000	Torshavn	Self-governing community of Denmark
Gibraltar	2.3	35,000	Gibraltar	British Crown dependency
Isle of Man	22	70,000	Douglas	British Crown dependency
Svalbard	24,000	3,942	Longyearbyen	Territory of Norway

SOME INTERESTING FACTS ABOUT EUROPE
- Europe is the second smallest continent.
- Europe is bordered on the north by the Arctic Ocean, on the west by the

Atlantic Ocean, on the south by the Mediterranean Sea, and on the east by the Black Sea and the Caucasus mountains.

- Mt. Elbrus is the highest point in Europe—18,510 feet.
- The highest elevations and the most rugged relief are found in the Alps, the Pyrenees, the Sierra Nevada, and the Caucasus mountains.
- The Volga River is the continent's longest river—2,291 miles. Other major rivers are the Danube, Rhine, Vistula, Elbe, and Oder.
- Lake Ladoga in northeastern Europe is the largest lake at 6,826 square miles.
- Europe has four regional climate types: Maritime climate of the west, Transitional climate of central Europe, Continental climate of the northeast, and Mediterranean climate of southern coastal Europe.
- The most extensive forest zone in Europe is located in northern (former Soviet Union) Europe, north of the Volga River.
- Wildlife in northern Europe include elk, reindeer, brown bear, wolf, badger, beaver, and sable; in middle Europe, mink, wild cat, deer, wild boar, and bison; in southern Europe, wild goat, sheep, bear, and wildcat; in eastern plains (Steppe), rodents, fox, and rabbits; and in Caspian Sea region, sheep.
- The primary crops of Europe are wheat and barley.
- Europe has the world's leading reserve in just one metal—mercury (40 percent). Europe also has 13 percent of the world's lead, 20 percent of ilmenite, and 15 percent of zinc. Europe, along with South America, is the poorest overall in mineral resources of all the world's continents.
- Europe has a wide variety of languages, nationalities, political organizations, and standard of living.
- Europe, in general, has a low mortality rate. Life expectancy is age 70 or older.
- Western Europe is dominated by market economies.
- Agriculture employs less than one-fifth of the work force.
- European mineral industries are based largely on coal.
- Europe accounts for approximately one-half of all international trade.
- Parliamentary democracies function in all the countries of western and northern Europe.
- Europe still has a number of monarchies and principalities: United Kingdom, Monaco, and Spain are some examples.

SOME INTERESTING EUROPEAN PERSONALITIES

Napoleon Bonaparte	Copernicus
Giuseppe Garibaldi	Wolfgang Amadeus Mozart
Queen Isabella	Otto von Bismarck
Prince Henry, the Navigator	James Cook
Charlemagne	Galileo
Vladimir Lenin	Frederic Chopin
Joseph Stalin	Raoul Wallenberg
Adolf Hitler	Sir Isaac Newton
Benito Mussolini	Vasco de Gama
Winston Churchill	Alexander the Great
Charles de Gaulle	Marco Polo
Klemens Metternich	Boris Yeltsin
Peter the Great	Alcuin
Marie Curie	Elizabeth I of England
Charles Darwin	Josef Broz (Marshal Tito)

TEACHER-DIRECTED ACTIVITIES FOR STUDENTS

1. Europe is a small continent but one of great diversity, as illustrated by the many cultures, religions, ethnic groups, and languages that can be found there. List these differences by country and see if any geographical patterns emerge. Note the significant differences within a particular culture or ethnic group (e.g., Irish Catholics and Protestants, blond blue-eyed Italians, Islamic Albanians, etc.).

2. Using a current map of Europe, identify the landlocked nations on the continent and discuss how that may have influenced their history and status in Europe.

3. Continental Europe still has several nations with royal families ruling their respective countries. List these nations and then discern how these differ from other nations that have elected governments.

4. Review the significant political and geographic changes that have occurred in Europe during the past several years and discuss how this has affected not only Europe but the world. Also discuss other changes that might occur during the next decade in Europe and how those changes could affect you personally.

5. Many European immigrants who came to the United States clustered for security, protection, and help in their transition into the "new world." Identify the areas in the United States that still have large concentrations of so-called "hyphenated-Americans."

   Russian-Americans _____

   Polish-Americans _____

   Greek-Americans _____

   Italian-Americans _____

   Slavic-Americans _____

   Portuguese-Americans _____

   Irish-Americans _____

   Scandinavian-Americans _____

   German-Americans _____

6. Review the flags of the nations in Europe and select those that, in your opinion, are the most unique, most colorful, and have interesting design.

North America

Area: 9,360,000 square miles; 16 percent of earth's surface
Population: 427,000,000; 11 percent of the total world population
Political Divisions: 23 independent nations, 14 dependencies
Biggest Nation: Canada, 3,849,674 square miles
Smallest Nation: St. Christopher-Nevis, 101 square miles
Northern-Most Nation: Canada

Southern-Most Nation: Panama
Eastern-Most Nation: Canada
Western-Most Nation: United States of America
Coastline: 190,000 miles
Highest Elevation: Mt. McKinley (Alaska), 20,320 feet
Lowest Elevation: Death Valley (California), −282 feet below sea level
Principal Rivers: Mississippi-Missouri, Columbia, St. Lawrence, Ohio,
   Rio Grande (Rio Bravo), Fraser, Mackenzie, Colorado
Principal Lakes: Great Lakes (Superior, Huron, Erie, Michigan, Ontario),
   Great Salt, Great Bear, Great Slave
Principal Mountain Ranges: Rocky, Appalachian, Cascade, Alaskan
Principal Deserts: Chihuahuan, Mojave, Sonoran
Largest City: Mexico City, Mexico
Principal Languages: Spanish, French, English

INDEPENDENT NATIONS OF NORTH AMERICA

Name	Sq. Miles	Population	Capital	Date of Independence
Antigua and Barbuda	171	64,000	St. John's	1981
Bahamas	5,380	247,000	Nassau	1973
Barbados	166	262,000	Bridgetown	1966
Belize	8,867	180,000	Belmopan	1981
Canada	3,849,674	27,100,000	Ottawa	1931
Costa Rica	19,575	3,302,000	San José	1838
Cuba	42,804	10,626,000	Havana	1898
Dominica	290	85,000	Roseau	1978
Dominican Republic	18,816	6,824,000	Santo Domingo	1844
El Salvador	8,260	5,309,000	San Salvador	1840
Grenada	133	87,000	Saint George's	1974
Guatemala	42,042	9,035,000	Guatemala City	1838
Haiti	10,714	6,216,000	Port-au-Prince	1804
Honduras	43,277	4,952,000	Tegucigalpa	1838
Jamaica	4,244	2,484,000	Kingston	1962
Mexico	756,136	87,870,000	Mexico City	1821
Nicaragua	50,200	3,745,000	Managua	1838
Panama	30,134	2,370,000	Panama City	1903
St. Kitts and Nevis	101	40,000	Basseterre	1983
St. Vincent and Grenadines	150	112,000	Kingstown	1979
Trinidad and Tobago	1,980	1,333,000	Port-of-Spain	1962
United States	3,450,120	260,498,000	Washington, DC	1788

DEPENDENT NATIONS OF NORTH AMERICA

Name	Sq. Miles	Population	Status
Anguilla	356	7,000	British dependency
Aruba	75	63,000	Affiliated with Netherlands
Bermuda	21	58,000	British dependency
Cayman Islands	100	26,000	British dependency
Greenland	840,000	55,000	Province of Denmark
Guadeloupe	658	347,000	Overseas Dept. of France
Martinique	425	340,000	Overseas Dept. of France
Montserrat	102	13,000	British dependency
Netherlands Antilles	310	185,000	Affiliated with Netherlands
Puerto Rico	3,515	3,552,000	US Commonwealth
St. Pierre and Miquelon	93	6,000	Overseas Dept. of France
Turks and Caicos Islands	166	10,000	British dependency
Virgin Islandsd (US)	132	111,000	US-organized unincorporated territory
Virgin Islands (British)	59	12,000	Brtitish dependency

SOME INTERESTING FACTS ABOUT NORTH AMERICA
- The Great Lakes form the largest body of fresh water in the world and, with their connecting waterways, they are the largest inland water transportation system in the world.

- The Yellowstone area contains the greatest concentration of geysers in the world; 140 vent the earth's inner heat in an area of less than one square mile. It can also claim to be the world's largest geyser field, with some 300 geysers in all. The volcanic eruption 600,000 years ago that resulted in the Yellowstone caldera is also unrivaled geologically.
- The longest unfortified border in the world (possibly in history) is the border between the United States and Canada.
- North America contains the world's largest island—Greenland.
- The North American climate is the most varied of any continent. The ice-covered plains of the north differ dramatically from the Caribbean beaches in the south. This makes for the most varied plant life of any continent, from lichens and mosses in the Arctic to plush tropical rain forests in the steamy heat of the Tropics.
- Mammals unique to North America are the bobcat, bison, coyote, pocket gopher, prairie dog, pronghorn, and ringtail.
- California's giant sequoias are the world's largest living things.
- North America is endowed with more than its relative share of the world's mineral resources, especially those that modern industry is dependent on: coal, petroleum, natural gas, and iron.
- The longest and widest mountain chain on earth is the North American Cordillera (the Rockies and other smaller western mountains).
- The greatest tidal variation anywhere occurs in Canada's Bay of Fundy (difference between high and low tides can be 53 feet).
- The Everglades contain one of the largest Mangrove forests on earth.
- Mammoth Cave is the longest cave system known in the world.

SOME INTERESTING HISTORICAL FIGURES

Lief Erickson	Robert Lasalle
Montezuma	W. L. Mackenzie
Christopher Columbus	Daniel Boone
Henry Hudson	Father Marquette
George Vancouver	Diego Riveria
Sir Walter Raleigh	Ponce de leon
Hernando Cortes	Octavio Paz
Walter Reed	James Hill
Benito Juarez	Tomas Estrada Palma
Sir John Macdonald	George Marshall
John Jacob Astor	Fidel Castro
Maximilian	Jim Bridger

TEACHER-DIRECTED ACTIVITIES FOR STUDENTS

1. Using an atlas, identify the 10 largest cities (by population) in North America.
2. Make a list of unique things about the North American continent. Choose one of these features and prepare a report (written or oral) to be shared in class.
3. Review immigration patterns to the continent and identify the sites where various ethnic, racial, or religious groups have tended to settle. Draw some conclusions about future immigration to North America and how it could affect the continent?

4. Discuss the "melting pot" and "salad bowl" theories regarding North American immigration. Which term better describes the history of the continent? How might it affect our collective continental future?

5. For an art project, reproduce the national flags of each nation and then share how flags represent a country's history.

6. Listen to the music and lyrics of selected national anthems and then discuss what national anthems are and what they are intended to do for the citizens of a nation.

South America

Area: 6,875,000 square miles; 12 percent of the world's land
Population: 302,000,000; 6.7 percent of the total world population
Political Divisions: 12 independent nations, 2 dependent nations
Biggest Nation: Brazil
Smallest Nation: Suriname
Northern-Most Nation: Colombia

Southern-Most Nation: Chile
Eastern-Most Nation: Brazil
Western-Most Nation: Ecuador
Coastline: 20,000 miles
Highest Elevation: Aconcagua, Argentina, 22,831 feet
Lowest Elevation: Valdes peninsula, Argentina, −131 feet below sea level
Principal Rivers: Amazon, Madeira, Magdalena, Orinoco, Paraguay
Principal Lakes: Maracaibo, Mirim, Poopo, Titicaca
Principal Mountain Ranges: Andes, Brazilian Highlands, Guiana Highlands
Principal Deserts: Atacama, Patagonia
Largest City: Sao Paulo, Brazil
Principal Languages: Spanish, Portuguese, English

INDEPENDENT NATIONS OF SOUTH AMERICA

Name	Sq. Miles	Population 1991 (approx.)	Capital	Date of Independence
Argentina	1,072,070	32,729,000	Buenos Aires	1816
Bolivia	424,165	6,706,000	LaPaz; Sucre	1825
Brazil	3,286,487	15,250,000	Brasilia	1822
Chile	292,135	13,082,000	Santiago	1818
Colombia	440,831	33,070,000	Bogotá	1819
Ecuador	109,484	10,506,000	Quito	1830
Guyana	83,000	765,000	Georgetown	1966
Paraguay	157,048	4,665,000	Asuncion	1811
Peru	496,225	21,905,000	Lima	1821
Suriname	63,067	396,000	Paramaribo	1975
Uruguay	68,037	3,063,000	Montevideo	1828
Venezuela	352,145	19,098,000	Caracas	1830

DEPENDENT NATIONS OF SOUTH AMERICA

Name	Sq. Miles	Population	Status
Falkland Islands	4,700	2,000	British Crown Colony
French Guiana	35,135	97,000	Overseas Dept. France

SOME INTERESTING FACTS ABOUT SOUTH AMERICA
- The continent contains the longest, continuous mountain range in the world above sea level. The Andes stretch 4,500 miles north and south on the continent.
- South America has a greater variety of plant life than any other continent in the world. For example, there are more than 2,500 different types of trees on the South American continent.
- Angel Falls in Venezuela has the longest drop in the world—3,212 feet.
- Next to the Himalayas (in Asia), the Andes are the highest mountain range in the world.
- Both the equator and Tropic of Capricorn pass through South America.
- Roman Catholicism is the dominant religion.
- A tremendously diversity in animal life lives on the continent, such as anaconda, piranha, llamas, vampire bats, and penguins.
- There are three dominant languages: Spanish, English, and Portuguese.

SOME INTERESTING HISTORICAL FIGURES

Christopher Columbus   Jose de San Martin
Amerigo Vespucci   Pedro Cabraz
Ferdinand Magellan   Francisco de Mirandis
Francisco Pizarro   Bernardo O'Higgins
Simon Bolivar   Antonio Jose de Sucre
Juan Peron   Jose Enrique Rodo
Evan Peron   Javier Perez de Cuellar
Jose Maria Velasco   Jose Gervasio Artigas
Gaspar Rodriguez de Francia

TEACHER-DIRECTED ACTIVITIES FOR STUDENTS

1. Study the map below and then answer the following questions.

The Lower 48 States of the United States Placed Over a Map of South America

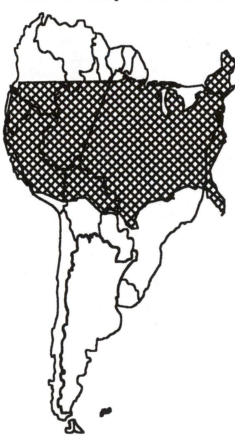

   a. How much bigger is South America, in square miles, than the United States?

   b. Name the islands to the East of Argentina. To whom do they belong?

   c. Which is the largest South American country? Which is the largest U.S. continental state?

   d. Draw in the equator and the Tropic of Capricorn. Which of these passes through South America? Which through the 48 continental states?

   e. Name two animals found in South America that are not found in the United States.

2. Learn how to say the following in Spanish or in Portuguese:

   Hello
   Goodbye
   Friend
   Where do you live?
   I live in the United States.

3. Plan a seven-day trip down the Amazon River. Using almanacs, atlases, and other sources, trace your route, identify ports of call and points of interest, and list the encounters or experiences with which you wish to be involved. Keep a diary of your imaginary journey.

4. Review the continent's potential and discuss the problems as South Americans prepare to enter the twenty-first century.
5. Discuss the unique geographic shape of Chile. Identify some of the problems the Chileans experience in communication, travel, and governance.
6. Using almanacs and encyclopedias, look up and learn the derivation of each country's name (e.g., *Ecuador* refers to the equator which passes directly through the nation).

MAP, ATLAS, ALMANAC, AND GLOBE ACTIVITIES _____

MAP AND GLOBE ACTIVITIES

1. Using the following map, identify the following:

North	Caribbean Sea
South	Amazon River
East	Nile River
West	Mississippi River
Equator	Yangtze River
Tropic of Cancer	Ob-Irtysh Rivers
Tropic of Capricorn	Seoul, Korea
Prime Meridian	Mexico City, Mexico
International Date Line	Cairo, Egypt
Atlantic Ocean	Sao Paulo, Brazil
Pacific Ocean	Shanghai, China
Indian Ocean	Los Angeles, California
Mediterranean Sea	New York, New York
Arabian Sea	London, Great Britain
Gulf of Mexico	Moscow, Russia
Caspian Sea	Mt. Everest (Nepal-China)
Sea of Okhotsk	Godwin-Austen (K–2) (India)
Black Sea	Kanchenjunga (Nepal-India)
China Sea	Nanga Parbat (India)
Bering Sea	Tirich Mir (Pakistan)

2. With yellow and blue markers, draw the following:

   Equator
   Tropic of Cancer
   Tropic of Capricorn
   Prime Meridian
   International Date Line

3. Make maps of routes to your school.
4. Make maps of the classroom, a room in your home, the school, the community.
5. Create maps of imaginary places. Where could the cities be located? What vegetation and animals could be found there? What kind of climate could it have?
6. Make models of your classroom, the school, the neighborhood, the community, the state.
7. Using an outline map of an area in your community, go for a walk in the area and map what you see on the walk.
8. Draw maps from written or verbal descriptions.
9. Decide on the best route to take to get to certain places.
10. Explore different kinds of maps. What does each tell you? What type of map would be best to tell you what industries are located in a particular place, what the population is, what the climate is like, and what agricultural products are grown?
11. Collect stamps and place them on their country of origin.
12. Create riddles for various geographic locations and see if you can find them on a map.

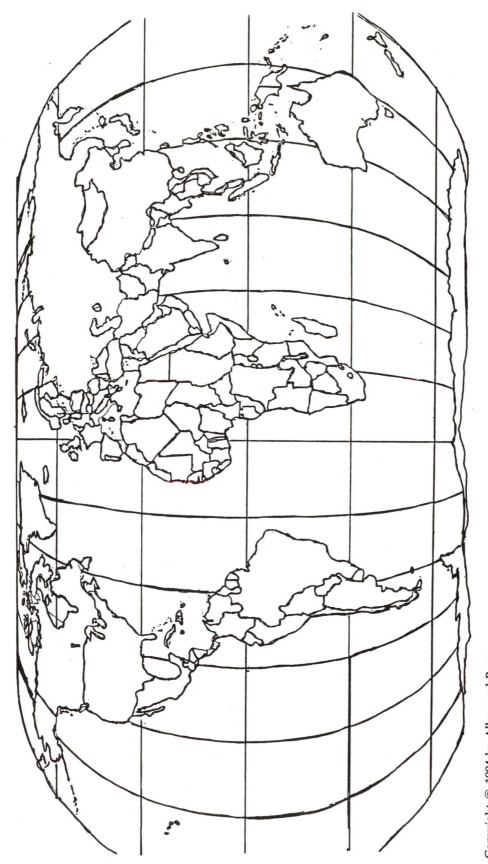

13. Study a map of a given area and predict what it might look like in 1, 10, and 100 years from now.
14. Create maps or models of what you would consider perfect classrooms, communities, or cities.
15. Make land-use maps of your community.
16. Collect pictures of foods that you eat and locate their places of origin on a world map.
17. Locate on a map the city where you were born. Identify also the birthplace of your parent(s), grandparent(s), or guardian(s).
18. Collect pictures of various places in the world and place them on a world map.
19. Make models, draw pictures, or write descriptions or stories about various landform features and locate them on a map (e.g., Grand Canyon or Mississippi River).
20. Whenever a place is mentioned in a story, a textbook, or in current events, locate that place on the map or globe.
21. Plan a hot-air balloon trip around the world.

    Establish:
    a. Route (countries, passports, airspace)
    b. Itinerary (time airborne, stops, U.S. embassies)
    c. Supplies (food, clothing, etc.)
    d. Amount of money needed (rate of exchange)
    e. The cultures and peoples you will probably meet (language, food, customs)

    Keep a log of the trip.
    Find pictures of the nations to be visited.
    Write tourist bureaus for information.
    Visit travel agencies for information.
    Interview people in your community from other nations before you embark on your trip.
    Using last year's school pictures, make a passport for your travels.

ATLAS AND ALMANAC ACTIVITIES

Using your world atlas almanac, answer the questions listed below.

1. Which is the only continent that has all three major lines of latitude (Cancer, Equator, and Capricorn) passing through it? (a) Africa, (b) South America, (c) Asia, (d) North America.
2. The most western capital city of Europe is: (a) London, (b) Paris, (c) Washington, DC, (d) Portugal, (e) Reykjavik.
3. Which continent has the highest mountains? (a) Africa, (b) South America, (c) Australia, (d) Asia, (e) North America.
4. If you were having lunch in Kuala Lumpur, you would be in: (a) Malaysia, (b) Borneo, (c) Cambodia, (d) New Guinea.
5. Which of the following nations is not in the Western hemisphere? (a) the United States of America, (b) Mexico, (c) Chile, (d) Australia.
6. The city furthest west is: (a) Montreal, (b) Quito, (c) New York, (d) Bogota.
7. The city furthest south is: (a) Mexico City, (b) Havana, (c) Calcutta, (d) Hong Kong.

8. The distance from Vancouver, British Columbia, to Yokohama is about: (a) 5,600 miles, (b) 6,200 miles, (c) 4,300 miles, (d) 7,100 miles.
9. Through which one of these countries does the Tropic of Capricorn pass? (a) Mexico, (b) Syria, (c) Brazil, (d) Ecuador.
10. The International Date Line passes through which of these countries? (a) Australia, (b) New Zealand, (c) CIS, (d) USA, (e) none of these.
11. Which one of these European cities has a population of less than 1,000,000? (a) Madrid, (b) Naples, (c) Istanbul, (d) Lisbon.
12. Which one of these statements is false? (a) Mount Logan in Canada is nearly three times the height of Mount Kosciusko in Australia. (b) Mount Logan is Canada's highest mountain. (c) The color used to show heights over 16,000 feet is a dark brown. (d) Mount Kosciusko is located in the state of New South Wales.
13. Which of these statements is false? (a) Churchill, Manitoba, is closer by sea to Liverpool, England, than is New York. (b) San Francisco is closer to Honolulu than is Los Angeles. (c) The Arctic Circle passes through Great Bear Lake. (d) Honolulu is farther west than Nome, Alaska.
14. Most of the country of Libya has a population density that may be described as: (a) almost uninhabited, (b) moderately populated, (c) thickly populated, (d) densely populated.
15. Which one of these countries has the greatest percentage of waste land? (a) Canada, (b) Australia, (c) New Zealand, (d) Egypt.
16. Which one of these countries has the largest population? (a) Canada, (b) China, (c) Nigeria, (d) Republic of South Africa.
17. Which one of these countries has the greatest percentage of its area in permanent pasture and meadow? (a) Canada, (b) Australia, (c) Switzerland, (d) New Zealand.
18. Which of the following countries does not belong to the British Commonwealth of nations? (a) Malaya, (b) Malawi, (c) Guyana, (d) Guinea.
19. Which coast of Britain receives the most annual rainfall? (a) west, (b) north, (c) east, (d) south.
20. If you were at Pretoria, you would be in: (a) Canada, (b) France, (c) South Africa, (d) Australia.
21. If you were hyaving dinner in Greece and were paying your bill, you would use: (a) pesos, (b) dollars, (c) rupees, (d) drachmas.
22. If you flew south out of Detroit, Michigan, USA, the first "foreign" country you would fly over would be: (a) Cuba, (b) Mexico, (c) Honduras, (d) Canada.
23. Which of these countries has a smaller population than Washington, DC? (a) Monaco, (b) Vatican City, (c) Liechtenstein, (d) all of the above.
24. How many countries have no coastline? (a) 30, (b) 50, (c) 70, (d) 100.
25. Switzerland has how many official languages? (a) one, (b) two, (c) three, (d) four.
26. Excluding the Commonwealth of Independent States, which country has the most land area in Europe? (a) Germany, (b) France, (c) Italy, (d) Great Britain.
27. The second largest nation (land mass) in the world is: (a) the United States, (b) Brazil, (c) Canada, (d) Australia.
28. The largest island in the world is: (a) Australia, (b) New Guinea, (c) Greenland, (d) none of these.
29. The following areas are called Archipelagos: (a) Japan, (b) Hawaii, (c) Philippine Islands, (d) all of these.
30. The latitude and longitude of your hometown is _____.

31. Name the *countries* (national political states) with the following latitude and longitude. List capital cities of those countries.

Latitude	Longitude	Country	Capital
40 N	30 E	_____	_____
23 N	90 E	_____	_____
3 S	77 W	_____	_____
42 S	147 E	_____	_____

32. Most of North America is between _____ longitudes

and _____ latitudes.

33. The latitude and longitude of both the North Pole and the South Pole are:

a. Magnetic North Pole _____ and _____.

b. Magnetic South Pole _____ and _____.

34. How many time zones are in the CIS? (a) 13, (b) 11, (c) 4, (d) 9.

35. What city in the United States is so located that you call Tokyo and London on the same business day? (a) Denver, (b) Kansas City, (c) Chicago, (d) Las Vegas.

36. Lines of latitude are how many miles apart? (a) 61, (b) 74, (c) 69, (d) 49.

37. The circumference of the earth is about: (a) 30,000 miles, (b) 40,000 miles, (c) 25,000 miles, (d) 60,000 miles.

38. In what exact direction do you travel when you go through the Panama Canal from the Caribbean Sea to the Pacific Ocean? (a) northwest to southwest, (b) northeast to southwest, (c) southwest to southeast, (d) northwest to northeast.

39. How many sovereign nations do the following continents have?

a. Antarctica _____

b. Africa _____

c. Europe _____

d. Australia _____

e. North America _____

f. Asia _____

40. Identify and name the countries found at the following latitude/longitude destinations.

a. lat. 40°N; long. 100°W _____

b. lat. 20°N; long. 100°W _____

c. lat. 40°N; long. 100°E _____

d. lat. 20°N; long. 100°E _____

e. lat. 30°S; long. 60°W _____

f. lat. 60°N; long. 30°E _____

g. lat. 30°N; long. 60°E _____

h. lat. 35°N; long. 140°E _____

i. lat. 35°S; long. 140°E _____

j. lat. 50&N; long. 10°E _____

k. lat. 52°N; long. 10°W _____

l. lat. 20°N; long. 50°E _____

m. lat. 15°S; long. 30°E _____

ATLAS AND ALMANAC EXERCISE ANSWER SHEET

1. c	**16.** b
2. e	**17.** a
3. 3	**18.** d
4. a	**19.** c
5. d	**20.** c
6. b	**21.** d
7. a	**22.** d
8. c	**23.** d
9. c	**24.** a
10. e	**25.** d
11. e	**26.** b
12. c	**27.** c
13. d	**28.** c
14. a	**29.** d
15. d	**30.** (will vary)

31. Turkey   Ankara
Bangladesh   Dhaka
Peru   Lima
Australia   Canberra

32. 20°W–180°W and 82°N–7°N

33. a. It is very difficult to figure the exact location. See encyclopedias for explanations.
b. 138°E and 68°S

34. a

35. a

36. c

37. c

38. c

39. a. 0
b. 52
c. 36 (not including new CIS states)
d. 1
e. 23
f. CIS
g. Iran
h. Japan
i. Australia
j. Germany
k. Ireland
l. Saudi Arabia
m. Zambia

MAP, GLOBE, AND ATLAS ACTIVITIES FOR THE UNITED STATES OF AMERICA _____

MAP ACTIVITIES

Activity 1: Using a map of the United States, identify and list the following physical features and information:

1. The Great Lakes
2. The Rocky Mountains
3. The Allegheny Mountains
4. Pacific Coast Cascades
5. The Great Smokies
6. Mexican Border
7. Alaska Border
8. Pacific Ocean
9. Atlantic Ocean
10. Gulf of Mexico
11. The Great Salt Lake
12. Florida Peninsula
13. Death Valley
14. Mt. McKinley
15. Mt. St. Helens
16. Mississippi River
17. Missouri River
18. Columbia River
19. Rio Grande
20. St. Lawrence River
21. Red River
22. Colorado River
23. Mount Waialeale
24. The Bering Strait
25. Great Plains
26. Kodiak Island
27. Island of Hawaii
28. Mt. Whitney
29. Continental Divide
30. Yukon River
31. Haleakala
32. The Bahamas
33. Mauna Loa
34. Gulf of California
35. Alaska Peninsula

Activity 2: Using a map of the United States (including Alaska and Hawaii), identify and illustrate the following:

1. The geographical center of the North American Continent (Rugby, North Dakota)
2. The major lines of latitude and longitude.
3. The size in miles of the 48 states, Alaska and Hawaii, and the total square miles.
4. The latitude and longitude of your region, state, and community.
5. The size (in miles) of your state.

Activity 3: Using a map of the 50 states, identify and locate some of the fastest growing cities in the United States. Likewise, identify and locate those cities that have lost population over the past decade.

Growing
(Color code, green)
1. Huntington Beach, California
2. Anchorage, Alaska
3. San Jose, California
4. Austin, Texas
5. Anaheim, California
6. Las Vegas, Nevada
7. Albuquerque, New Mexico
8. Phoenix, Arizona
9. Honolulu, Hawaii
10. San Diego, California
11. San Antonio, Texas
12. Miami, Florida

Losing Population
(Color code, red)
1. Dayton, Ohio
2. St. Louis, Missouri
3. Cleveland, Ohio
4. Minneapolis, Minnesota
5. Buffalo, New York
6. Atlanta, Georgia
7. Pittsburgh, Pennsylvania
8. Gary, Indiana
9. Cincinnati, Ohio
10. Ft. Worth, Texas
11. Chicago, Illinois
12. Milwaukee, Wisconsin

QUESTIONS FOR DISCUSSION, RESEARCH, OR SPECULATION
1. What trends do you see in these population shifts?
2. What might be some reasons?
3. How does it impact an area?
4. What are the ramifications for the future if these trends continue?
5. Hypothesize about the future of your community.

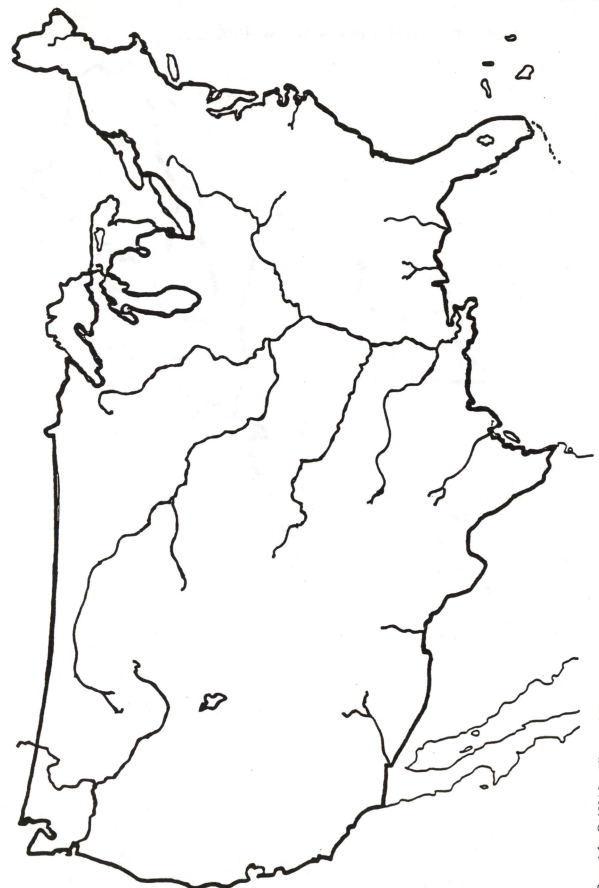

REGIONAL MAPS OF THE UNITED STATES OF AMERICA _____

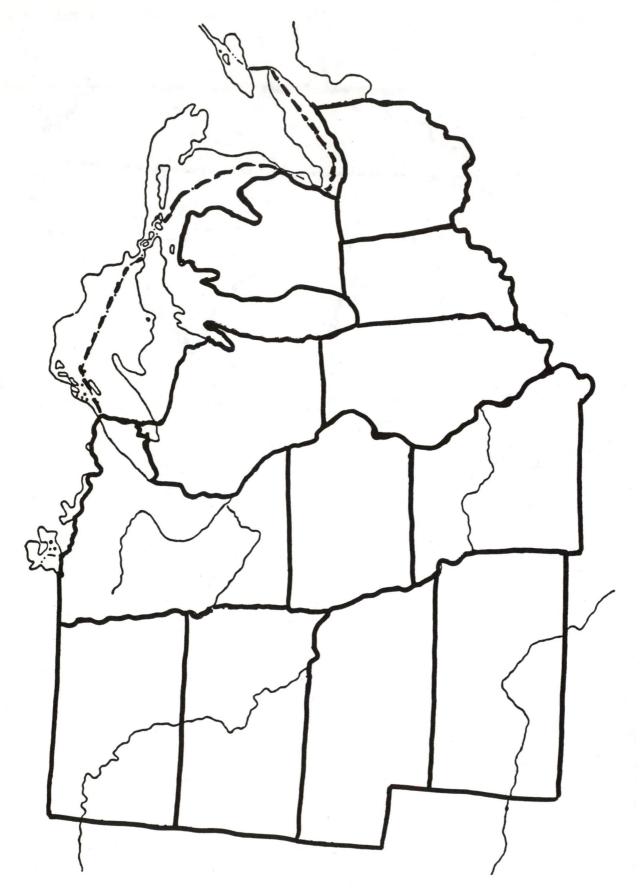

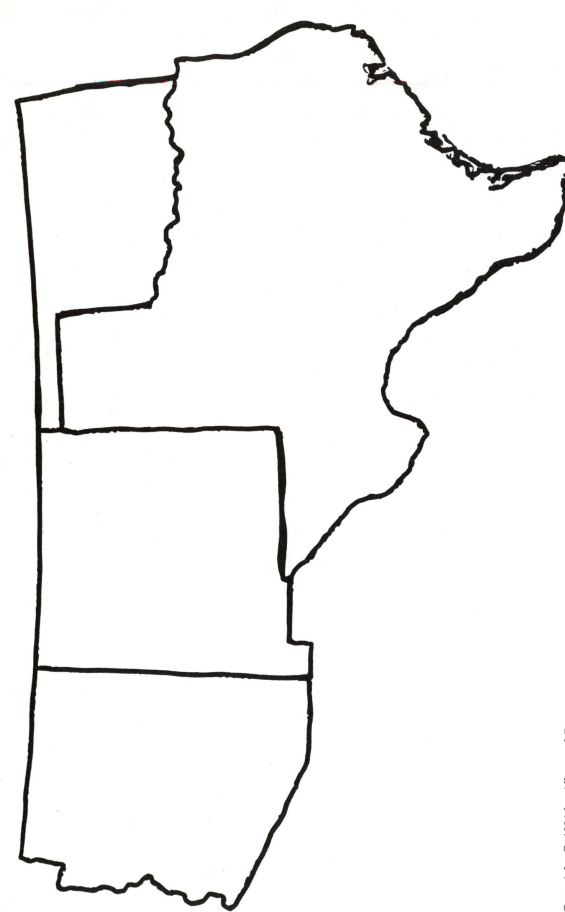

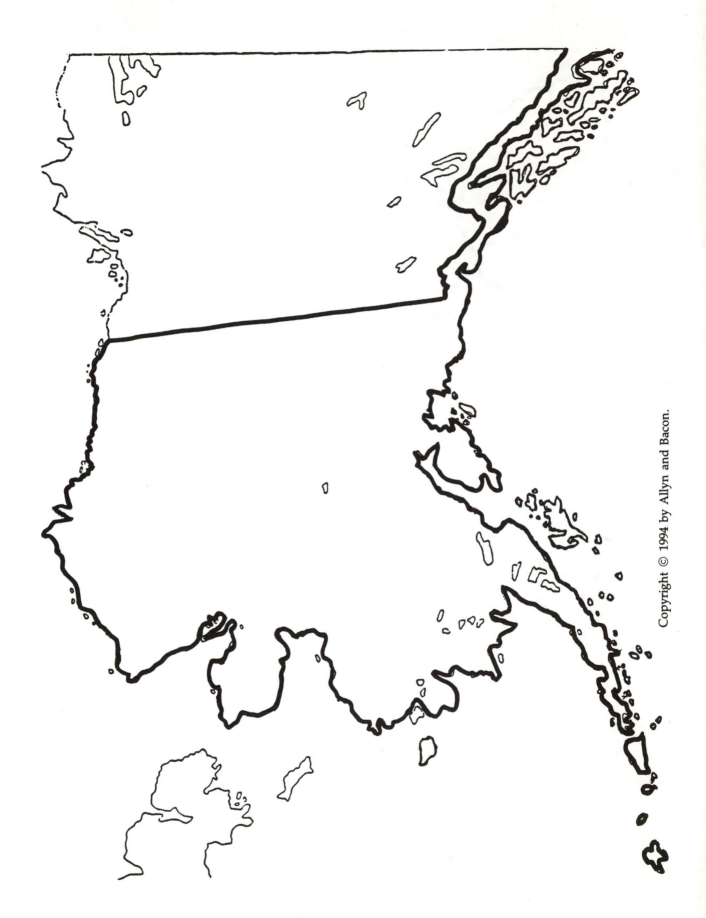

MAP ACTIVITIES (REGIONAL MAPS)

1. Utilizing atlases, almanacs, and the regional maps provided in this chapter, do the following:
   - Identify the states in a given region and locate their respective capital cities.
   - Identify what other states or nations border the states in the region being studied.
   - Identify, if any, lakes, rivers, or other natural boundaries that serve as political boundaries between areas.
   - Make a list of those states that have mostly straight borders and those that do not.
   - List the special and/or unique features in each region or states in that region.

2. The following questions are for discussions:
   - Why are the states in the west generally larger in land size than those in the east?
   - Where are the largest centers of population? Why?
   - Except for California, why are the largest population centers east of the Mississippi River?
   - Why do some states have no straight borders while others have all straight borders?
   - What, if any, are the language differences between the various regions? Why is that so?
   - Where are the largest concentrations of Black-American, Hispanic-American, Native-American, and Asian-American populations? Why?
   - What are the largest and smallest (population), the highest and lowest (elevation), the biggest and smallest (square mile), and the oldest and newest capital cities in the United States? How does this compare with other capitals like Ottawa, Mexico City, Tokyo, London, and Cairo?

WORLD MAPS
Africa

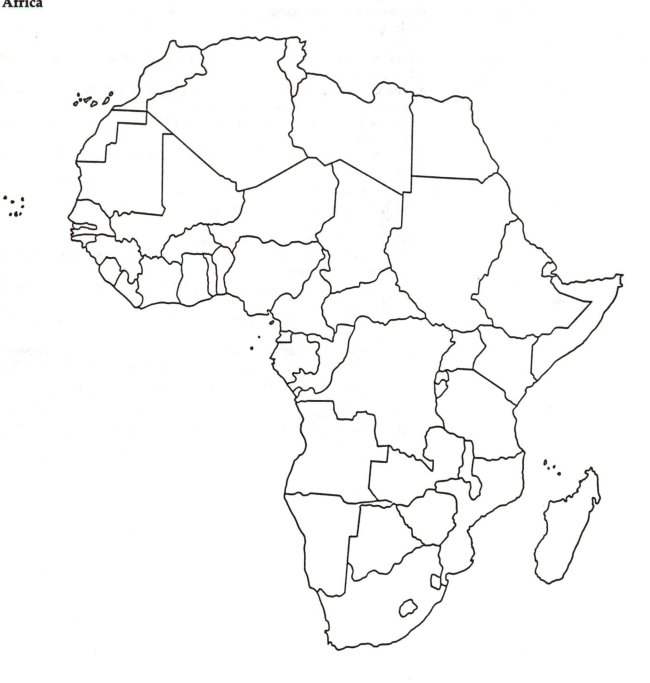

Antarctica

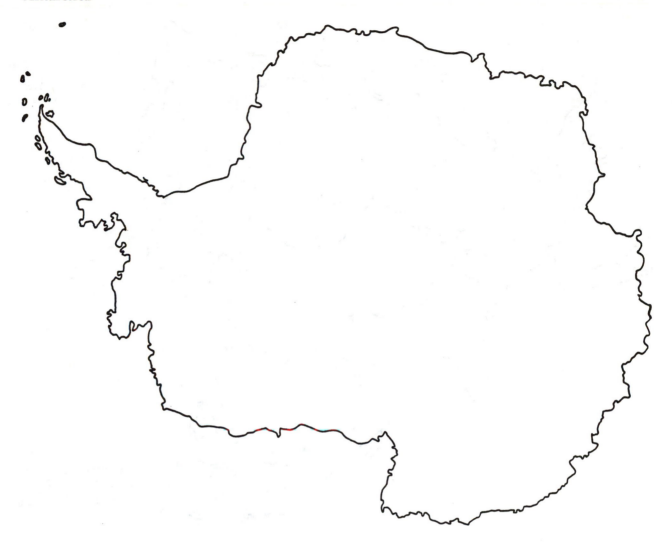

Asia

Australia

Europe

North America

South America

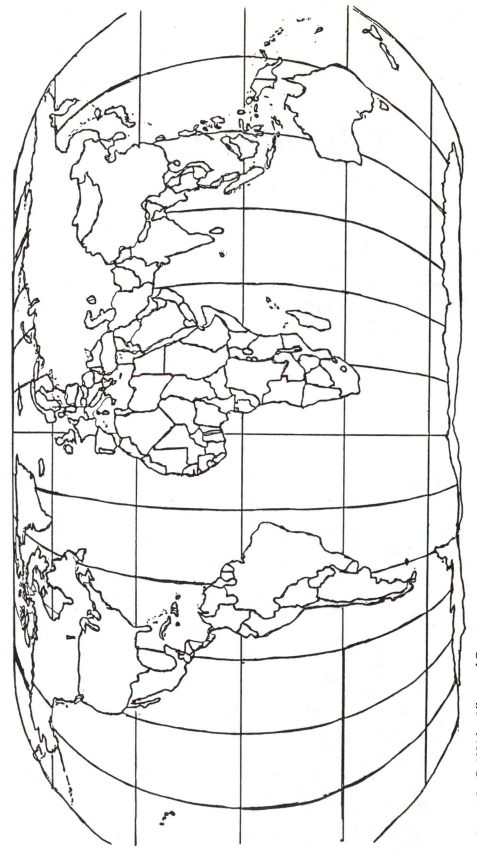

CHAPTER 3

Global and Multicultural Education

A person's feet should be planted in his own country but his eyes should survey the world—G. SANTAYANA

GLOBAL EDUCATION FOR THE TWENTY-FIRST CENTURY: SURVIVING IN THE GLOBAL VILLAGE

As the twenty-first century rapidly approaches, we Americans are becoming increasingly concerned that our schools are not adequately preparing students for the challenges of living in what has been termed the "Global Village." In spite of the numerous lessons of history, as well as the urging of professional organizations like the American Association of Colleges for Teacher Education (AACTE), the American Association of State Colleges and Universities (AASCU), and the National Council for the Accreditation of Teacher Education (NCATE), our national commitment and progress in developing a global perspective in teacher education programs has been tediously slow.

Global interdependence is a reality in ways unparalleled in human history. This is clearly evidenced by the expansion of economic, ecological, political, environmental, and technological networking of the past decade. In tomorrow's world these linkages will create an even greater need for global awareness and understanding as we endeavor to survive and save our planet.

We Americans, accept it or not, find ourselves increasingly more dependent on our global neighbors. Sadly, we also find that our knowledge and understanding of our global neighbors is essentially nonexistent. Too often our images of other lands and its people have been created for us by the media. In short, we are a people globally and culturally illiterate who find it increasingly difficult to understand or cope in a rapidly changing world. But change we must if we are to survive, let alone succeed, in the next millennium. Consequently, the question is not *Should we* but rather *How do we* affect change and how long will it take?

Change, and all that comes with it, is a difficult and threatening proposition and is often cloaked in political and emotional trappings. So it is with global education! In this instance it is a matter of resolving the "Americanism" versus the "globalism" controversy — that is, addressing and responding to those segments of our population who believe that global education is an international conspiracy intending to subvert American ideals and values. Globalism is the politicized concept of a new world order; global education refers to an educational process intent on making people aware of other cultures and people. It is comparing apples and oranges; what we are addressing here is *global education, not globalism!*

The major thrust of global education is to expand children's knowledge about the world in which they live. It is to celebrate the similarities and differences of many cultures, including our own. Thinking globally simply means making students globally literate in our modern world. It is also essential that students are encouraged to become more proactive and begin the process of both identifying and resolving the issues and problems confronting humankind. Global education programs should raise student consciousness about cultural differences and make them more aware of the diversity of ideas and practices found in all human societies. It should also allow them an opportunity to compare their own personal culture and global perspectives with others who also inhabit this planet.

Ideally, global education for our school population should be the best of all worlds — a well-balanced program that fosters wider international awareness and teaches students an appreciation of this nation's leadership in a complex world community. These concepts do not have to be in conflict; they can coexist academically and intellectually in the school curriculum. To do less not only cheats our children of a rich education but also deprives them of the knowledge and skills necessary for success — perhaps even survival — in the "global village."

Understanding and resolution begin with education. The following are some general goals and proposals for a well-balanced global education program:

GOALS
1. To stimulate a student's concepts of cultural awareness.
2. To understand cultural awareness is as much about "we and us" as it is about "they and them."
3. To recognize that it is naive to think or assume that there is only one appropriate way to act toward all human beings.
4. To understand that when we travel to other nations (or even other neighborhoods), we must adjust our behavior and thinking as we expect others to do when they visit our nation (or neighborhood).
5. To promote an awareness of other people, cultures, and attitudes that exist both nationally and globally.
6. To understand there are several ways humans express cultural and ethnic differences. Among others, they include stereotyping, ethnocentrism, prejudice, and discrimination.
7. To preserve American ideals and values and to understand our nation's current and future roles in the global community.

To achieve a more relevant global education program, educators must first reorder their thinking regarding social studies content and instruction. Certainly, history and geography will remain at the core of the curriculum, but a greater infusion (especially at the elementary level) with humanities-oriented subjects like literature, music, and art is essential in achieving global awareness and understanding with children in this age group. Even a casual review of new social studies textbooks and other learning materials clearly illustrates that tomorrow's curriculum directs students to think globally. The content, classroom lessons, and activities are all designed to make young students globally aware and knowledgeable about the many people and cultures with whom they share this planet and their daily lives.

In order to make global education a reality in schools for the twenty-first century, the following must occur:

1. Provide better training for classroom teachers:
   - More courses in history, geography, and global education
   - Instruction on how to infuse social studies with other areas of study (e.g., folk literature with geography, music with history)
2. Create more relevant learning materials (textbooks, learning units, and electronic learning devices).
3. Focus more content and information on non-Western cultures (e.g., Asian, African, and Middle Eastern).
4. Focus more content and information on other areas in the Western hemisphere (e.g., Central and South America).
5. Recognize the role of the United States in global issues—past, present, and future.

The primary goals are to educate both teachers and students to start thinking globally!

GLOBAL EDUCATION REFERENCES AND RESOURCES

"A World of Interconnections." Humphrey Tonkin and Jane Edwards, *Phi Delta Kappan, 62* (10), June 1981.

Center for Teaching International Relations (CTIR). University of Denver, Denver, CO 80208.

East Asia Resource Center, 302 Thomson Hall, DR-05, University of Washington, Seattle, WA 98195.

Educating Americans for Tomorrow's World: State Initiatives in International Education. National Governors Association, Hall of the States, 444 North Capitol Street, Washington, DC 20001-1572.

"Education for a World in Change." David C. King, *Intercom, 96/97.* Available from Global Perspectives in Education Inc., 45 John Street, Suite 1200, New York, NY 10038.

Getting Started in Global Education. National Association of Elementary School Principals, 1801 North Moore Street, Arlington, VA 22209.

"Global Education." Richard Remy (ed.), *Theory Into Practice, 21* (3), Summer 1982. Ohio State University, 149 Arps Hall, 1945 N. High Street, Columbus, OH 43210.

"Global Education: In Bounds or Out?" The Ad Hoc Committee on Global Education, *Social Education, 51* (4), April/May 1987.

"The Global Network." Andrew Smith (ed.), *Curriculum Review, 24* (2), November/December 1987.

Global Perspectives in Education, 218 East 18th Street, New York, NY 10003. Ask about the Information Exchange Network that helps educators share their resources, information, and ideas.

"Global Perspectives in Education." Steven L. Lamy (ed.), *Educational Research Quarterly, 8* (4), Special Issue, 1983. Available from CTIR, University of Denver, Denver, CO 80208.

Information Center on Children's Cultures, U.S. Committee for UNICEF, 331 E. 38th Street, New York, NY 10016.

Internationalizing Your School. Frank H. Rosengren, Marylee Crofts Wiley, and David S. Wiley, 1983. National Council on Foreign Language and International Studies, 45 John Street, Suite 1200, New York, NY 10038.

Near East Resource Center, 219 Denny Hall, DH-20, University of Washington, Seattle, WA 98195.

Population Education Activities for the Classroom. J. M. Schultz and H. L. Coon (eds.). ERIC/Center for Science, Mathematics and Environmental Education, The Ohio State University, 1200 Chambers Road, Columbus, OH 43210.

The Population Reference Bureau, Inc. 1337 Connecticut Avenue, N.W., Washington, DC 20036. Many excellent resources are available, including the Data Sheet. Their Population Handbook has a summary of demographic techniques and sample problems related to the Data Sheets. They also publish useful teaching modules and bulletins.

Project Learning Tree. American Forest Institute, 1619 Massachusetts Avenue N.W., Washington, DC 20036.

Project WILD. Salina Star Route, Boulder, CO 80302.

Promising Practices in Global Education: A Handbook With Case Studies. Robert Freeman (ed.), Occasional Paper No. 2. National Council on Foreign Language and International Studies, 45 John Street, Suite 1200, New York, NY 10038.

"Report on International Education." Council of Chief State School Officers, 379 Hall of the States, 400 N. Capitol Street N.W., Washington, DC 20001.

Russia and East European Area Center, 504 Thomson Hall, DR-05, University of Washington, Seattle, WA 98195.

South Asia Resource Center, 303 Thomson Hall, DR-05, University of Washington, Seattle, WA 98195.

Strengthening International Studies in Schools: A Directory of Organizations. Social Studies Development Center, 2805 E. 10th Street, Indiana University, Bloomington, IN 47407.

Superintendent of Public Instruction, Office for Multicultural and Equity Education, Old Capitol Building, Olympia, WA 98504.

Teaching about the Child and World Environment. U.S. Committee for UNICEF, 331 E. 38th Street, New York, NY 10016.

Teaching about Interdependence in a Peaceful World. U.S. Committee for UNICEF, 331 E. 38th Street, New York, NY 10016.

Teaching about Spaceship Earth. The Center for Global Perspectives in Education, 218 E. 18th Street, New York, NY 10003.

Teaching About the World. Merry Merryfield, 1990. Teacher Education Program with a Global Perspective. Mersham Center, Ohio State University, Columbus, OH 43210.

UNICEF Committee of Greater Seattle, 2217 4th Avenue, Seattle, WA 98121.

United Nations, New York, NY 10017.

United Nations Association, 1314 N.E. 43rd, Seattle, WA 98105.

The United States Prepares for It's Future. Report of the Study Commission on Global Education. Available from Global Perspectives in Education Inc., 45 John Street, Suite 1200, New York, NY 10038.

GLOBAL EDUCATION ACTIVITIES FOR STUDENTS _____

Continental Notebooks

Utilizing almanacs, encyclopedias, and atlases, create a Continental Notebook that will include information on countries in each of the seven continents. Use the following information sheet and place it in a three-ring notebook for group and/or individual use.

- Official name of country _____

On a world map, identify and shade in the continent on which the country is located. (map outline provided by teacher)	On the appropriate continental map, shade in the nation being studied. (map provided by teacher)
Map 1	Map 2

- Draw and color the nation's flag in the space below.

- National symbol is _____

• Brief historical background of the nation

• Major cultural and ethnic groups

• Population (1990) _____

• Capital city _____

• Other important cities

• Type of government _____

• Current head of state _____

• Official language(s) _____

• Major religion(s) _____

• Natural resources _____

• Major industries _____

• Exports _____

• Imports _____

• Name of currency _____

• Neighbors on the continent _____

- U.S. Embassy address _____
- U.S. Ambassador _____
- List some things you have learned from your research.

From Afghanistan to Zimbabwe—Cultural Differences and Customs from Around the World

- Many people shake hands when greeting or meeting one another, but this is *not* a universal custom. Some people do not want their "space" invaded and will use other gestures as a greeting.
- If a foreign national extends a hand to shake, take it and apply the same pressure he or she does—don't crush the hand!
- Typically, "Good morning," "Good afternoon" and "Good evening" are always acceptable forms of greeting. Personal questions like "How are you?" should be avoided.
- Some cultures perceive American friendliness as pushy or even rude. Be cool and react as others react to you—carefully and thoughtfully.
- Tipping is not acceptable in China.
- In Bulgaria, head gestures that go with yes and no are opposite to ours in the United States.
- Unlike many Arab nations, alcohol is acceptable in Iraq.
- In Greece, older citizens are revered and honored.
- Bargain and agree to the fare before you get into a cab in Sierra Leone (as well as some other countries).
- The Japanese begin and end personal visitations with head bows.
- If invited to a home in Germany, bring flowers.
- In Moslem countries you eat your meals with your right hand only.
- The people of Thailand do not touch another person's head—they believe the head to be the "seat of the soul"!
- In Turkey, women do not cross their legs when they sit.
- If invited to dinner in Uganda, bring chocolates.
- Only people of the same sex may shake hands or hug in Moslem countries—this does not happen between people of the opposite sex.
- In many Asian countries you remove your shoes before entering a home or holy place.
- In Thailand you do not sit with the soles of your shoes showing.
- Avoid bringing gifts of liquor into a Moslem home.

- Ask before taking pictures of people in China.
- Punctuality is very important in many nations.
- Be careful using hand gestures like "OK," thumb up, or "V" for victory—they have bad connotations in some places.

TEACHER-DIRECTED ACTIVITIES FOR STUDENTS

1. List some cultural things that are unique to Americans and discuss how even these are different in various regions of the United States.
2. Discuss how you could find out about the customs of another country if you were going there to visit.
3. Identify and list some ways you could be a good representative of the United States as you travel and/or meet people in different cultures.
4. Identify similarities and differences Washington state may have with another country that is located on the same latitude.
5. Review printed advertisements from other countries, identifying similarities and differences with U.S. advertisements. Create an ad.
6. Read non-Western literature and explore common human themes, and include how they intend to resolve global issues and problems.
7. Learn lullabies, rhymes, songs, or folktales from other countries and share them with one another.
8. Write letters to a pen pal in another country and invite guests to speak about their native countries.
9. Interview senior citizens in your community and chronicle their memories of their lifetimes.
10. Identify a product used by Americans. Trace where it came from and how it got to your hometown.
11. Identify and trace the origins of ethnic expressions popular in our culture.
12. Brainstorm a list of contributions in science, medicine, and mathematics from other cultures that have influenced and impacted our society.
13. Study local problems such as hunger and homelessness and compare your findings to world conditions.
14. Develop a list of careers associated with international business and trade. Identify and discuss skills required for the listed jobs and potential for growth.
15. Convert U.S. dollars into the currency of another country. If positive, go to a bank and secure some currency from that country.
16. Study the metric system. Develop measurements for a hypothetical house that is to be built.
17. Check labels on clothing and identify the point of origin.
18. Study one or more of your state's ethnic communities. Identify reasons for the group's immigration, their early history, and their current situation.
19. Participate in a letter/audio/video exchange with students from other nations.
20. Select a language to learn words, phrases, and cultural information.
21. Select music from another culture. Research it and share the information with other students.
22. Learn folk dances and teach other students how to perform them.
23. Host a cultural fair that includes the music, dancing, literature, and ethnic foods of a specific culture.
24. Discuss environmental and geographic issues that affect all nations.
25. Identify what you would have to do to be able to live and work in another country for a one- or two-year period.
26. List the items you must have with you if you were a tourist visiting another nation.

MULTICULTURAL EDUCATION

The United States of America is and always has been a pluralistic society. From the very beginning, there were national, political boundaries on this continent. The native populations were themselves characterized by great diversity and had differing concepts and practices regarding religious, socioeconomic, caste, and gender issues. When Europeans found their way to the Western hemisphere, the modality of the North American continent dramatically changed and has continued to do so with each new wave of immigration.

Even though we are reminded daily of our diversity, we firmly cling to the notion that the melting pot is still boiling and that it serves to erase differences and to acculturate the society. The notion persists that we who live in this country speak the same language, dress similarly, and enjoy the same foods and entertainment—that we are all the same. By simply identifying ourselves as "Americans," we tend to ignore our racial, ethnic, cultural, and social identities. We are Americans and most of us are proud of that fact, but we may also take pride in our individual and personal heritages.

Schools can play a major role in efforts to teach acceptance and mutual respect for cultural diversity. Without question, schools are the most logical places to begin the educational process of discovery and acquisition of knowledge in multicultural education. Educators must be trained, the curriculum must be redefined and reflect diversity, and learning materials must illustrate culturally diverse people in positive and meaningful roles.

Multicultural education should be total school and school district effort. Rather than a day or week set aside on the school calendar to teach about racism or to celebrate cultural diversity, the entire curriculum and personnel (teachers, administrators, special educators, counselors, speech correctionists, and support staffs) have vital roles in a multicultural education program. The curriculum, learning materials, teaching strategies, and district philosophy must all reflect multiculturalism and promote a genuine respect for all forms of diversity.

Some of the goals for a comprehensive multicultural program are the following:

> Understanding multiple historical perspectives
> Developing cultural consciousness
> Developing intercultural competence
> Combatting racism, prejudice, and discrimination
> Raising awareness of the state of the planet and global dynamics
> Developing social action skills
> Blending the goals of multicultural and global education

In developing and implementing curriculum models, educators must:

> Develop personal perspectives on teaching and learning
> Develop rationales
> Develop instruction strategies
> Select and evaluate materials and resources

To realize these goals, we must first achieve a multicultural perspective. An understanding of our own ethnicity and culture, as well as those of our fellow citizens both nationally and globally, is essential. These goals are not designed to allow us to sit in judgment of other people or cultures, nor are they to create a tolerance or empathy; rather, they are designed to promote awareness and understanding of the similarities and differences among all people. Once realized, we can begin the serious assault on the more divisive forces like sexism, racism, prejudice, and discrimination.

Another rationale for development of a multicultural education in our schools is the fact that our society is rapidly changing. Currently, 25 percent of all school-age children attending school belong to an ethnic minority. By the year 2000, it is estimated that numbers will increase to something over 30 percent. Unfortunately, very few classroom teachers today are adequately prepared to work effectively in a culturally diverse classroom, let alone teach about multiculturalism.

Finally, it is important that we also consider another issue of multiculturalism—global education. Until recently, multicultural education focused primarily on specific ethnic groups within one society. But our rapidly shrinking world and increasing interdependence among all nations—particularly as we cope with global issues related to environment, ecology, human rights, and a scarcity of natural resources—have broadened our scope to include global perspectives. Consequently, instruction in and about global education becomes equally important in K–8 education.

The following are examples of classroom activities that can expand students' knowledge and understandings of both multicultural and global education.

TEACHER-DIRECTED ACTIVITIES FOR STUDENTS

1. Each week introduce new vocabulary terms to students. For example:

Culture	Stereotyping
Race/Racism	Racio-Ethnic
Religion	Disadvantaged
Ethnicity/Ethnic Groups	Social Class
Minority/Minority Groups	Anglo Americans
Gender	African Americans
Prejudice	Native Americans
Discrimination	Hispanic Americans
Genocide	Asian Americans
Hate	Multicultural

2. Find examples of how these concepts may have affected history as well as your lives.
3. Using books, new magazines, and television programs, find examples of some of the above mentioned concepts.
4. Read *Anne Frank* and discuss the concepts of religion, hate, discrimination, ethnic groups, and genocide.
5. List all the things you dislike or "hate" and explain why you feel so strongly about each item on your list. Discuss with the class the concept of prejudice and that all humans do have prejudices. Further, identify ways in which you might overcome your prejudices.
6. Identify and examine your attitudes, experiences, and behaviors when you feel discriminated against.
7. List ways in which people might overcome racism.
8. Compile a list of people, places, and things that are or have been discriminated against. Discuss how victims of hate oppression might feel and react.
9. List all your favorite foods. Using a world map, identify their place of origin.
10. Discuss and list the things that all people have in common.

11. Read (or listen to) stories about children from other cultures or ethnic groups. Compile a list of how you are similar to the children you have learned about.

Children's Books

The following resources may be used by educators in developing multicultural awareness and perspective. They may also aid in developing units on multicultural education.

After careful and thoughtful consideration, the author decided to focus on only four groups of people: Native Americans, Hispanic Americans, African Americans, and Asian Americans. This decision does not negate the importance of other cultures, but time and space considerations made it essential to limit the number of resources. Additionally, the author believes the aforementioned groups will continue to be the populous groups in the K–12 school system for the rest of this decade and probably well into the twenty-first century.

ASIAN AMERICANS

Baron, Virginia Olsen, ed. *Sunset in a Spider Web: Sijo Poetry of Ancient Korea.* Translated by Chung Seuk Park, illustrated by Minja Park Kim. New York: Holt, Rinehart & Winston, 1974.

Behn, Harry, trans. *Cricket Songs: Japanese Haiku.* New York: Harcourt Brace Jovanovich, 1964.

Behn, Harry, trans. *More Cricket Songs: Japanese Haiku.* New York: Harcourt Brace Jovanovich, 1971.

Chang, Diana. "Saying Yes." In *Asian-American Heritage: An Anthology of Prose and Poetry.* Edited by David Hsin-Fu Wand. New York: Washington Square Press, 1974.

Davis, Daniel S. *Behind Barbed Wire: The Imprisonment of Japanese Americans During World War II.* New York: Dutton, 1982.

DeJong, Meindert. *The House of Sixty Fathers.* Illustrated by Maurice Sendak. 1956. Reprint. New York: Harper & Row, 1987.

Fritz, Jean. *China Homecoming.* New York: Putnam's, 1985.

Fritz, Jean. *Homesick: My Own Story.* Illustrated by Margot Tomes. New York: Putnam's, 1982.

Issa, Yayu, Kikaku et al., eds. *Don't Tell the Scarecrow: And Other Japanese Poems.* Illustrated by Talivaldis Stubis. New York: Four Winds, 1969.

Lee, Jeanne M. *Toad is the Uncle of Heaven: A Vietnamese Folk Tale.* New York: Holt, Rinehart & Winston, 1985.

Lord, Bette Bao. *In the Year of the Boar and Jackie Robinson.* Illustrated by Marc Simont. New York: Harper & Row, 1984.

Louie, Ai-Ling. *Yeh-Shen: A Cinderella Story from China.* Illustrated by Ed Young. New York: Philomel, 1982.

McHugh, Elisabet. *Karen and Vicki.* New York: Greenwillow, 1984.

McHugh, Elisabet. *Karen's Sister.* New York: Greenwillow, 1983.

McHugh, Elisabet. *Raising a Mother Isn't Easy.* New York: Greenwillow, 1983.

Meltzer, Milton. *The Chinese Americans.* New York: Crowell, 1980.

Nhuong Huynh, Quang. *The Land I Lost: Adventures of a Boy in Vietnam.* Illustrated by Vo-Dinh Mai. New York: Harper & Row, 1982.

Sadler, Catherine Edwards. *Heaven's Reward: Fairy Tales from China.* Illustrated by Cheng Mung Yun. New York: Atheneum, 1985.

Sadler, Catherine Edwards. *Treasure Mountain: Folktales from Southern China.* Illustrated by Cheng Mung Yun. New York: Atheneum, 1982.

Uchida, Yoshiko. *The Best Bad Thing.* New York: Atheneum, McElderry, 1983.

Uchida, Yoshiko. *The Dancing Kettle and Other Japanese Folktales.* New York: Harcourt Brace, 1949.

Uchida, Yoshiko. *The Happiest Ending.* New York: Atheneum, McElderry, 1985.

Uchida, Yoshiko. *In-Between Miya.* Berkeley, Calif.: Creative Arts Books, 1967.

Uchida, Yoshiko. *A Jar of Dreams.* New York: Atheneum, McElderry, 1981.

Uchida, Yoshiko. *Journey Home.* New York: Atheneum, McElderry, 1978.

Uchida, Yoshiko. *Journey to Topaz.* Berkeley, Calif.: Creative Arts, 1985.

Uchida, Yoshiko. *The Magic Listening Cap: More Folktales from Japan.* New York: Harcourt Brace Jovanovich, 1965.

Uchida, Yoshiko. *Samurai of Gold Hill.* Berkeley, Calif.: Creative Arts, 1985.

Uchida, Yoshiko. *The Sea of Gold and Other Tales from Japan.* New York: Scribner's, 1965.

Uchida, Yoshiko. *The Two Foolish Cats.* Illustrated by Margot Zemach. New York: Atheneum, McElderry, 1987.

Watkins, Yoko Kawashima. *So Far from the Bamboo Grove.* New York: Lothrop, Lee & Shepard, 1986.

Yagawa, Sumiko. *The Crane Wife.* Translated by Katherine Paterson, illustrated by Suekichi Akaba. New York: Morrow, 1981.

Yep, Laurence. *Child of the Owl.* New York: Harper & Row, 1977.

Yep, Laurence. *Mountain Light.* New York: Harper & Row, 1985.

Yep, Laurence. *The Serpent's Children.* New York: Harper & Row, 1984.

AFRICAN AMERICANS

Aardema, Verna. *Bimwili and the Zimwi.* Illustrated by Susan Meddaugh. New York: Dial, 1985.

Aardema, Verna. *The Bingananee and the Tree Toad.* Illustrated by Ellen Weiss. New York: Warne, 1983.

Aardema, Verna. *Bringing the Rain to Kapiti Plain.* Illustrated by Beatiz Vidal. New York: Dial, 1981.

Aardema, Verna. *Oh, Kojo! How Could You!* Illustrated by Marc Brown. New York: Dial, 1984.

Adoff, Arnold. *All the Colors of the Race.* Illustrated by John Steptoe. New York: Lothrop, Lee & Shepard, 1982.

Adoff, Arnold. *Big Sister Tells Me That I'm Black.* New York: Holt, Rinehart & Winston, 1976.

Adoff, Arnold. *I Am the Darker Brother.* New York: Macmillan, 1968.

Adoff, Arnold. *My Black Me.* New York: Button, 1974.

Adoff, Arnold. *The Poetry of Black America.* New York: Lothrop, Lee & Shepard, 1981.

Bryan, Ashley. *Beat the Story Drum, Pum-Pum.* New York: Atheneum, 1980.

Bryan, Ashley. *The Dancing Granny.* New York: Atheneum, 1977.

Bryan, Ashley, ed. *I Greet the Dawn: Poems by Paul Laurence Dunbar.* New York: Atheneum, 1978.

Bryan, Ashley. *I'm Going to Sing: Black American Spirituals.* Vol. 2. New York: Atheneum, 1982.

Bryan, Ashley. *Lion and The Ostrich Chicks.* New York: Atheneum, 1986.

Bryan, Ashley. *The Ox of the Wonderful Horns and Other African Folktales.* New York: Atheneum, 1971.

Bryan, Ashley. *Walk Together Children: Black American Spirituals.* Vol. 1. New York: Atheneum, 1974.

Clifton, Lucille. *Amifika*. Illustrated by Thomas Di Grazia. New York: Dutton, 1977.

Clifton, Lucille. *Everett Anderson's Goodbye*. Illustrated by Ann Grifalconi. New York: Holt, Rinehart & Winston, 1983.

Clifton, Lucille. *My Friend Jacob*. Illustrated by Thomas Di Grazia. New York: Dutton, 1980.

Collier, James Lincoln. *Louis Armstrong: An American Success Story*. New York: Macmillan, 1985.

Cornell, Jean G. *Ralph Bunche: Champion of Peace*. New York.

Courlander, Harold, & Herzog, George. *The Cow-Tail Switch and Other West African Stories*. Illustrated by Madye Lee Chastain. New York: Holt, Rinehart & Winston, 1986.

Fenderson, Lewis H. *Thurgood Marchall: Fighter for Justice*. New York: McGraw-Hill, 1969.

Greenfield, Eloise. *Africa Dream*. New York: Harper & Row, 1977.

Greenfield, Eloise. *First Pink Light*. New York: Crowell, 1976.

Greenfield, Eloise. *Mary McLeod Bethune*. New York: Crowell, 1977.

Greenfield, Eloise. *Me and Neesie*. New York: Harper & Row, 1984.

Greenfield, Eloise. *Rosa Parks*. New York: Crowell, 1973.

Guy, Rosa. *Mother Crocodile*. Illustrated by John Steptoe. New York: Delacorte, 1981.

Hamilton, Virginia. *Dustland*. New York: Greenwillow, 1980.

Hamilton, Virginia. *The Gathering*. New York: Greenwillow, 1980.

Hamilton, Virginia. *Junius Over Far*. New York: Harper & Row, 1985.

Hamilton, Virginia. *A Little Love*. New York: Philomel, 1984.

Hamilton, Virginia. *The Mystery of Drear House*. New York: Greenwillow, 1987.

Hamilton, Virginia. *"The People Could Fly" American Black Folktales*. Illustrated by Leo and Diane Dillon. New York: Knopf, 1985.

Hamilton, Virginia. *Sweet Whispers, Brother Rush*. New York: Putman's, 1982.

Hamilton, Virginia. *Willie Bea and the Time the Martians Landed*. New York: Greenwillow, 1983.

Harris, Joel. *Jump: The Adventures of Brer Rabbit*. Edited by Van D. Parks and Malcolm Jones, illustrated by Barry Moser. San Diego: Harcourt Brace Jovanovich, 1986.

Harris, Joel. *Jump Again! More Adventures of Brer Rabbit*. Adapted and illustrated by Barry Moser. San Diego: Harcourt Brace Jovanovich, 1987.

Haskins, James. *Black Music in America: A History Through its People*. New York: Crowell, 1987.

Haskins, James. *Black Theater in America*. New York: Crowell, 1982.

Haskins, James. *Diana Ross: Star Supreme*. Illustrated by Jim Spence. New York: Viking, 1985.

Haskins, James. *Fighting Shirley Chisholm*. New York: Dial, 1975.

Haskins, James. *From Lew Alcindor to Kareem Abdul-Jabbar*. New York: Lothrop, Lee & Shepard, 1979.

Haskins, James. *Katherine Dunham*. New York: Putnam's, 1982.

Haskins, James. *Space Challenger: The Story of Guion Bluford*. Minneapolis: Carolrhoda, 1984.

Haskins, James, & Benson, Kathleen. *The Sixties Reader*. New York: Viking, 1986.

Jaquith, Priscilla. *Bo Rabbit Smart for True: Folktales from the Gullah*. Illustrated by Ed Young. New York: Philomel, 1981.

Keats, Ezra Jack. *John Henry: Am American Legend*. New York: Pantheon, 1965.

Keats, Ezra Jack. *The Tales of Uncle Remus: The Adventures of Frer Rabbit*. Illustrated by Jerry Pinkney. New York: Dial, 1987.

Keats, Ezra Jack. *To Be a Slave.* Illustrated by Tom Feelings. New York: Dial, 1968.

McDermott, Gerald. *Anansi the Spider: A Tale from the Ashanti.* New York: Holt, Rinehart & Winston, 1972.

McKissack, Patricia. *Paul Laurence Dunbar: A Poet to Remember.* Chicago: Children's Press, 1984.

Mathis, Sharon Bell. *The Hundred Penny Box.* New York: Viking, 1975.

Meltzer, Milton. *Mary McLeod Bethune: Voice of Black Hope.* Illustrated by Stephen Marchesi. New York: Viking, 1987.

Myers, Walter Dean. *Crystal.* New York: Viking, 1987.

Myers, Walter Dean. *Fast Sam, Cool Clyde and Stuff.* New York: Viking, 1975.

Myers, Walter Dean. *Hoops.* New York: Delacorte, 1981.

Myers, Walter Dean. *The Legend of Tarik.* New York: Scholastic, 1982.

Myers, Walter Dean. *Motown and Didi.* New York: Viking, 1984.

Myers, Walter Dean. *The Nicholas Factor.* New York: Viking, 1983.

Myers, Walter Dean. *Won't Know Till I Get There.* New York: Viking, 1982.

Steptoe, John. *Mufaro's Beautiful Daughters.* New York: Greenwillow, 1987.

Steptoe, John. *Stevie.* New York: Harper & Row, 1969.

Walker, Alice. *Langston Hughes, American Poet.* New York: Crowell, 1974.

Williams, Sylvia. *Leontyne Price: Opera Superstar.* Chicago: Children's Press, 1984.

HISPANIC AMERICANS

Ancona, George. *Bababas: From Manolo to Margie.* New York: Clarion, 1982.

Belpre, Pura. *Once in Puerto Rico.* Illustrated by Christine Price. New York: Warne, 1973.

Belpre, Pura. *The Rainbow-Colored Horse.* Illustrated by Antonio Martorell. New York: Warne, 1978.

Blackmore, Vivian, retel. *Why Corn Is Golden: Stories About Plants.* Illustrated by Susana Martinez-Ostos. Boston: Little, Brown, 1984.

Brenner, Barbara. *Mystery of the Plumed Serpent.* Illustrated by Blanche Sims. New York: Knopf, 1981.

Brown, Tricia. *Hello Amigos!* Photography by Fran Oritz. New York: Holt, Rinehart & Winston, 1986.

Cruz, Martel. *Yagua Days.* Illustrated by Jerry Pinkney. New York: Dial, 1987.

de Gerez, Toni, trans. *My Song Is a Piece of Jade: Poems of Ancient Mexico in English and Spanish.* Illustrated by William Stark. Boston: Little, Brown, 1984.

dePaola, Tomie. *The Lady of Guadalupe.* New York: Holiday House, 1980.

de Treviño, Elizabeth Borten. *I, Juan de Pareja.* New York: Farrar, Straus & Giroux, 1965.

Griego, Margot C., et al., *Tortillitas Para Mama and Other Spanish Nursery Rhymes.* Illustrated by Barbara Cooney. New York: Holt, Rinehart & Winston, 1981.

Holguin, Jiminez, Puncel, Emma Morales, & Puncel, Conchita Morales. *Para Chiquitines.* New York: Bowker, 1969.

Meltzer, Milton. *The Hispanic Americans.* Photography by Morrie Camhi and Catherine Noren. New York: Crowell, 1982.

Mohr, Nicholasa. *Felita.* Illustrated by Ray Cruz. New York: Dial, 1979.

Mohr, Nicholasa. *Going Home.* New York: Dial, 1986.

Schon, Isabel, ed. *Doña Blanca and Other Hispanic Nursery Rhymes and Games.* Minneapolis: Denison, 1983.

NATIVE AMERICANS

Baker, Olaf. *Where the Buffaloes Begin.* Illustrated by Stephen Gammell. New York: Warne, 1981.

Baylor, Byrd. *And It Is Still that Way: Legends Told by Arizona Indian Children.* New York: Scribner's, 1976.

Baylor, Byrd. *Before You Came This Way.* New York: Dutton, 1969.

Baylor, Byrd. *The Other Way to Listen.* Illustrated by Peter Parnell. New York: Scribner's, 1978.

Baylor, Byrd. *When Clay Sings.* Illustrated by Tom Bahti. New York: Scribner's, 1972.

Bierhorst, John. *Doctor Coyote: A Native American Aesop's Fables.* Illustrated by Wendy Watson. New York: Macmillan, 1987.

Bierhorst, John. *The Girl Who Married a Ghost and Other Tales from the North American Indian.* Photography by Edward Curtis. New York: Four Winds, 1977.

Bierhorst, John. *In the Trail of the Wind: American Indian Poems and Rituals Orations.* New York: Farrar Straus & Giroux, 1971.

Bierhorst, John. *The Naked Bear: Folktales of the Iroquois.* Illustrated by Dirk Zimmer. New York: Morrow, 1987.

Bierhorst, John. *The Mythology of North America.* New York: Morrow, 1985.

Bierhorst, John. *The Ring in the Prairie: A Shawnee Legend.* Illustrated by Leo and Diane Dillon. New York: Dial, 1970.

Bierhorst, John. *The Sacred Path: Spells, Prayers and Power Songs of the American Indians.* New York: Morrow, 1983.

Clark, Ann Nolan. *In My Mother's House.* Illustrated by Velino Herrera. New York: Viking, 1969.

Cleaver, Elizabeth. *The Enchanted Caribou.* New York: Oxford University Press, 1985.

Courlander, Harold. *People of the Short Blue Corn: Tales and Legends of the Hopi Indians.* Illustrated by Enrico Arno. New York: Harcourt Brace Jovanovich, 1970.

dePaola, Tomie. *The Legend of the Bluebonnets.* New York: Putnam's, 1983.

Freedman, Russell. *Children of the Wild West.* New York: Clarion, 1983.

Freedman, Russell. *Indian Chiefs.* New York: Holiday House, 1987.

Fritz, Jean. *The Double Life of Pocahontas.* Illustrated by Ed Young. New York: Putnam's, 1983.

Goble, Paul. *Buffalo Woman.* New York: Bradbury, 1984.

Goble, Paul. *Death of the Iron Horse.* New York: Bradbury, 1987.

Goble, Paul. *The Gift of the Sacred Dog.* New York: Bradbury, 1980.

Goble, Paul. *The Girl Who Loved Wild Horses.* New York: Bradbury, 1978.

Goble, Paul. *The Great Race of the Birds and Animals.* New York: Bradbury, 1985.

Goble, Paul. *Star Boy.* New York: Bradbury, 1983.

Gorsline, Douglas. *North American Indians.* New York: Random House, 1978.

Harlan, Judith. *American Indians today: Issues and Conflicts.* New York: Watts, 1987.

Harris, Christie. *Mouse Woman and the Vanished Princesses.* Illustrated by Douglas Tait. New York: Atheneum, 1976.

Harris, Christie. *Once More Upon a Totem.* Illustrated by Douglas Tait. New York: Atheneum, 1973.

Highwater, Jamake. *Anpao: An American Indian Odyssey.* Illustrated by Fritz Scholder. Philadelphia: Lippincott, 1977.

Hirschfelder, Arlene. *Happily May I Walk: American Indians and Alaska Native Today.* New York: Scribner's, 1986.

Hobbs, Will. *Bearstone.* New York: Atheneum, 1989.

Houston, James. *Songs of the Dream People: Chants and Images from the Indians and Eskimos of North America.* New York: Atheneum, McElderry, 1972.

Kroeber, Theodora. *Ishi: Last of His Tribe.* Illustrated by Ruth Robbins. Boston: Parnassus, 1964.

Lewis, Richard. *I Breathe a New Song: Poems of the Eskimo*. Illustrated by Oonark. New York: Simon & Schuster, 1971.

McDermott, Gerald. *Arrow to the Sun: A Pueblo Indian Tale*. New York: Viking, 1974.

Monroe, Jean Guard, & Williamson, Ray A. *The Dance in the Sky: Native American Star Myths*. Illustrated by Edgar Stewart. Boston: Houghton Mifflin, 1987.

Richter, Conrad. *A country of Strangers*. New York: Knopf, 1966.

Siberell, Anne. *The Whale in the Sky*. New York: Dutton, 1982.

Steptoe, John. *The Story of Jumping Mouse*. New York: Lothrop, Lee & Shepard, 1984.

Tunis, Edwin. *Indians*, rev. ed. New York: Harper & Row, 1978.

Wheeler, M. J. *First Came the Indians*. Illustrated by James Houston. New York: Atheneum, McElderry, 1983.

Wood, Nancy. *Many Winters*. Illustrated by Frank Howell. New York: Doubleday, 1974.

Wosmek, Frances. *A Brown Bird Singing*. New York: Lothrop, Lee & Shepard, 1986.

MORE INFORMATION, RESOURCES, AND ACTIVITIES FOR STUDENTS _____

A World of Inventions

We live in a world filled with wondrous things! Automobiles, television, computers, jet airplanes, and electric lights, just to mention a very few. Have you ever wondered how things came about or where they came from? If so, this exercise is designed to teach you about where some things came from and how virtually all cultures have contributed to the many and wonderful things we enjoy and take for granted.

INVENTION	PLACE OF ORIGIN	APPROXIMATE TIME
Antibiotics	USA	1952
Bread	Sumeria	300 B.C.
Bricks	Sumeria	300 B.C.
Calendar	Egypt	300 B.C.
Clocks	Egypt	300 B.C.
Computers	Great Britain	1834
Alphabet	Egypt	300 B.C.
Telegraph	France	1794
Color television	USA	1928
Elevator	Greece	230
Gas engines	Great Britain	1838
Newspapers	China	740
Vitamins	East Dutch Indies	1888
Jet airplanes	Germany	1942
Canned food	France	1795
Soda pop	USA	1890
Peanut butter	USA	1901
Polio vaccine	USA	1953
Talking movies	USA	1929
Monotheistic religion	Middle East	4000 B.C.
Coins	Lydia (Turkey)	500 B.C.
Penicillin	Great Britain	1929
Paper	China	712
Barometer	Italy	1643
Rifles	Great Britain	1525
Paper money	China	845
Gunpowder	China	1000
Bicycle	Scotland	1839
Telescope	Holland	1600
Radio	USA	1900
Automobile	France	1870
Telephone	USA	1876
Television	Germany	1884
Photography	France	1826
Numbers	Egypt	3000 B.C.
Bifocal glasses	USA	1783
Revolver	USA	1835
False teeth	USA	1822
Sewing machine	USA	1846
Seismology	Great Britain	1660
Processed steel	Great Britain	1856
Ice machines	USA	1873

Paved highways	Mayan	2000 B.C.
Candy	Egypt	3000 B.C.
Popcorn	North/South America	400 B.C.
Writing	Sumeria	3500 B.C.

ACTIVITIES

1. Create a time line and place on it what you believe to be the 10 most significant inventions.
2. Locate on a world map where those inventions were developed.
3. Pick a discovery and discuss or write about its impact on the world community.
4. Pick an invention and list the ways it impacts your personal life.
5. Hypothesize about inventions that may be coming by the year 2000 and beyond.

Great Religions of the World

Listed below are some of the world's great religions and philosophies. By definition, a religion is the service and worship in God or the supernatural. It is a commitment or devotion to a faith or observance. A philosophy, by definition, is a search for general understanding of values and reality by mostly speculative rather than observational means. For example, Taoism is a philosophy rather than a religion per se because its followers seek a simple, unassertive life filled with good fortune, deeds, and a long life of happiness.

All religions and philosophies, however, do have several things in common, like values, morality, and a belief in a supernatural world. As you learn about each, examine the differences as well as the similarities they possess.

1. Zoroastrianism
2. Deism
3. Judaism
4. Islam
5. Buddhism
6. Confucianism
7. Hinduism
8. Taoism
9. Shintoism
10. Christianity
    a) Catholicism
       1) Eastern Orthodox
       2) Roman Catholic
    b) Baptists
    c) Methodists
    d) Presbyterianism
    e) Lutheranism
    f) Calvinism
    g) Episcopalianism
    h) Later Day Saints (Mormons)
    i) Society of Friends (Quakers)
    j) Amish
    k) Mennonites
    l) Jehovah Witness
    m) Christian Scientist

ACTIVITIES

1. On a world map, identify (color code) the major concentrations of the great religions and philosophies. Then discuss the reasons for these concentrations and perhaps future movements.
2. List the largest (by population) religions in the world. Identify the fastest and slowest growing of these. Explain the phenomenon.
3. Review the basic similarities of Christianity and why there are so many different sects.
4. Define the following:

Religion	Hell	Orthodox	Heaven	Spirit
Philosophy	Faith	Supernatural	Values	Sect
Nirvana	Soul	Reincarnation	Morality	

Planet Earth

ACTIVITIES

Using the "Planet Earth" illustration or a large reproduction, do the following activities either individually or as a group project:

1. Identify and list ways to environmentally save our planet (see top example).
2. Identify and list some of the various races, nationalities, ethnicities, and religions that make up the population of our planet (see bottom example).
3. Clip magazine or newspaper articles that spotlight stories from around the globe and that have a specific theme (e.g., the environment, natural disasters). then discuss the concept of "global community" and how world events directly and/or indirectly impact your life.

PLANET EARTH

Poles
Catholics
Bolivians
Kenyans
Blacks
INDIANS
Dutch
Jews
Hindus
Anglos
THAI'S
AMERICANS
Egyptians
Japanese
French
Moslems
Greeks
Korean
Irish
Mexicans
Pakistani
Nigerians
ASIANS

PLANET EARTH

Stop Pollution
Save the Rain Forest
Recycle
SAVE THE WHALES
Save the ozone layer
Clean a Stream

Interesting World Figures

1. Marie Curie	39. Hans Christian Andersen
2. Mohandas Gandhi	40. Galileo
3. Rosseau	41. Peter Tchaikovsky
4. Charles Darwin	42. Edmund Haley
5. Karl Marx	43. Elizabeth B. Browning
6. Salvador Dali	44. Mohammed
7. Confucius	45. Catherine the Great
8. Pierre C. L'Enfant	46. Buddha
9. Leonardo da Vinci	47. Vladimir Lenin
10. Michelangelo	48. Eva Peron
11. Florence Nightingale	49. Golda Meier
12. Napoleon Bonaparte	50. Ayatollah Khomenei
13. Simon Bolivar	51. Indira Ghandi
14. Sir Isaac Newton	52. Margaret Thatcher
15. Anwar Sadat	53. Paul McCartney
16. Benito Juarez	54. Pierre Trudeau
17. Socrates	55. Fidel Castro
18. Marquis de Lafayette	56. Mao Tse Tung
19. Sir Winston Churchill	57. Prince Henry, the navigator
20. Christopher Columbus	58. Benjamin Disraeli
21. Charles de Gaulle	59. Chiang Kai-Shek
22. Gerardus Mercator	60. Chou En-lai
23. Captain James Cook	61. Anton Von Leeuwenhoek
24. Joseph Lister	62. Elizabeth I of England
25. Jan Christian Smuts	63. Guiseppi Garibaldi
26. Ho Chi Minh	64. Dag Hammarskjold
27. Julius Caesar	65. Mustafa Kemal
28. Raoul Wallenberg	66. Nikita Khrushchev
29. Jacques Cousteau	67. Auguste Rodin
30. Wolfgang Mozart	68. Frederick Froebel
31. Valentia Tereshkova	69. Paul Gaugin
32. Copernicus	70. William Shakespeare
33. Yuri Gagarin	71. Sir Arthur Conan Doyle
34. Amerigo Vespucci	72. Jenny Lind
35. Rembrandt	73. Sir Edmund Hillary
36. Louis Pasteur	74. George Orwell
37. Paul Cezanne	75. Dr. Sun Yat-Sen
38. Ferdinand Magellan	

ACTIVITIES

1. Select a person from the list.
   a. Read an autobiography or biography of his or her life and identify in which country and on what continent he or she live(d).
   b. On a world map, identify the country of birth of all the personalities listed. Then research a person from the above list and highlight the significant events of his or her life on a mobil, paper shape, or bulletin board.
   c. Create a play or simulation about the life of one of these people.
   d. Review what the world was like during the time this person lived (other famous people, art, literature, etc.).
   e. Create a time line of the major events during this person's life.

CHAPTER 4

Our American Heritage

This country will not be a good place for any of us to live in unless we make it a good place for all of us to live in. —T. ROOSEVELT

THE PLEDGE OF ALLEGIANCE

I pledge allegiance to the flag of the United States of America and to the Republic for which it stands, one nation, under God, indivisible, with liberty and justice for all.

The Pledge of Allegiance first appeared in print on September 8, 1892, in *The Youth's Companion,* an educational publication. It's author, Francis Bellamy, assistant editor of the publication, wrote it to commemorate the celebration of Columbus Day—the 400th anniversary of the navigator's voyage to the Western hemisphere. The words achieved instant popularity and the pledge was quickly transformed into an annual Columbus Day tradition and then into a daily classroom ritual.

Wording of the pledge has undergone two major alterations. In 1923, the words "my flag" were replaced by "the flag of the United States of America," and in 1954, President Eisenhower signed a bill adding the words "under God" to the text. In 1942, Congress made the Pledge of Allegiance part of its code for honoring the flag of the United States of America.

Most states once required pupils to say the pledge as part of the daily school ritual. Some students refused, resulting in several court cases that finally were decided by the U.S. Supreme Court, which upheld an individual's right to refuse to recite the pledge. Interestingly, with the exception of Nazi Germany, which made it obligatory for all Germans to pledge allegiance to the nation and Adolf Hitler, only the United States of America has had an obligatory pledge of allegiance.

VOCABULARY BUILDER
Pledge: A promise to perform
Allegiance: Loyalty
Republic: Democratic form of government
Liberty: Freedom
Justice: Fairness
Indivisible: Not to be divided
Nation: A community of people with national boundaries and similar
    interests

TEACHER-DIRECTED ACTIVITIES FOR STUDENTS
1. Discuss why some people would refuse to recite the pledge.
2. Review the constitutional right that allows people to refuse saying the
   pledge or to burn the flag. Describe your feelings about this.
3. Analyze the pledge and suggest other words or ideas that might be included in the future.

THE DECLARATION OF INDEPENDENCE

After several years of frustration and disappointment, many American Col-
onists became convinced that they had no recourse but to declare their independence from Great Britain and establish the "United States of America."

In the summer of 1776, 56 members of the Second Continental Congress
met in Philadelphia, Pennsylvania, to address the issue of independence for
the thirteen colonies. On June 7, Richard Henry Lee of Virginia addressed the
delegates and proposed that the Colonies declare themselves free and independent from Great Britain. A committee consisting of Thomas Jefferson, John
Adams, Benjamin Franklin, Robert R. Livingston, and Roger Sherman was appointed to create a written document proclaiming American independence.
The Committee asked Jefferson to write the document, which he did in a one-
week period.

After some editorial changes, the document was presented to the entire
delegation for approval. Again, there was some debated and minor changes,
but finally it was approved unanimously by the 56 delegates on July 4, 1776.
John Hancock of Massachusetts and Chair of the Continental Congress was
the first to sign, stating that he wanted to write his name in letters large enough
so that King George III would not have to use his spectacles to read it!

The Declaration of Independence can be divided into four parts: (a) the
Preamble, (2) the Declaration of Rights, (3) Bill of Indictment, and (4) Statement of Independence.

The Preamble   This statement explains why the document was written.

The Declaration of Rights   This is the most famous and widely cited portion
of the document.

> We hold these truths to be self evident, that all men are created equal, that they
> are endowed by their creator with certain unalienable rights, that among these
> are Life, Liberty and the Pursuit of Happiness.

Bill of Indictment   This states that the American Colonies can no longer endure the abuses of the British government and must become removed from

that government. It also accused King George III of inflicting the abuses to subjugate the Colonies and to gain total and complete control over them.

Statement of Independence   This states simply that because all previous appeals have failed, the colonies are now establishing and stating their independence of the crown.

SIGNERS OF THE DECLARATION OF INDEPENDENCE

Connecticut
Samuel Huntington
Roger Sherman
William Williams
Oliver Wolcott

Delaware
Thomas McKean
George Read
Caesar Rodney

Georgia
Button Gwinnett
Lyman Hall
George Walton

Maryland
Charles Carroll
Samuel Chase
William Paca
Thomas Stone
Lewis Morris

Massachusetts
John Adams
Samuel Adams
Elbridge Gerry
John Hancock
Robert Treat Paine

New Hampshire
Josiah Butler
Matthew Thornton
William Whipple

New Jersey
Abraham Clark
John Hart
Francis Hopkinson
Richard Stockton
John Witherspoon

New York
William Floyd
Francis Lewis
Philip Livingston
Lewis Morris

North Carolina
Joseph Hewes
William Hooper
John Penn

Pennsylvania
George Clymer
Benjamin Franklin
Robert Morris
John Morton
George Ross
Benjamin Rush
James Smith
George Taylor
James Wilson

Rhode Island
William Ellery
Stephen Hopkins

South Carolina
Thomas Heyward, Jr.
Thomas Lynch, Jr.
Arthur Middleton
Edward Rutledge

Virginia
Carter Braxton
Benjamin Harrison
Thomas Jefferson
Richard Henry Lee
Francis Lightfoot Lee
Thomas Nelson, Jr.
George Wythe

INTERESTING FACTS ABOUT THE DECLARATION OF INDEPENDENCE

1. It is one of the most significant and important documents *ever* written in the history of the world! It simply but profoundly states that if a government fails in its purpose, the people have a right to establish a new government. It is a revolutionary notion in history and the seed of future world revolutions.

2. Thomas Jefferson wrote the actual document based on the ideas and writings of John Locke—an Englishman!
3. The document was passed without one dissenting vote.
4. July 4, 1776, is considered the birthday of the United States of America.
5. Delegates Thomas Jefferson and John Adams, writing Committee members and future presidents, both died on July 4, 1826—50 years after the adoption of the Declaration of Independence.
6. The Declaration of Independence along with the Bill of Rights and the Constitution of the United States are on permanent display at the National Archives Building in Washington, DC.

TEACHER-DIRECTED ACTIVITIES FOR STUDENTS

1. Review the Declaration of Independence and highlight significant phrases and/or concepts. Apply those to our basic rights in our contemporary world.
2. Build vocabulary by defining such terms as *declaration, independence, unalienable,* and so on.
3. Discuss the irony of the deaths of John Adams and Thomas Jefferson.
4. From the list of delegates, identify those who went on to make other contributions.
5. Discuss why some colonies sent large groups while others sent only a few delegates.

THE CONSTITUTION OF THE UNITED STATES OF AMERICA

The United States Constitution is the basic law of the American people. It outlines the role and responsibilities of our national government and the rights guaranteed to each and every American citizen.

BACKGROUND INFORMATION

May 1787	Constitutional Convention opens in Philadelphia, Pennsylvania. George Washington is elected as the chairman of the group meeting in Independence Hall.
July 26	A basic plan is sent to the Committee of Detail for a first draft to be written.
Sept. 12	The Committee on Style (James Madison, Alexander Hamilton, Gouverneur Morris) presents a final draft to the delegates.
Sept. 17	Of the 55 delegates, 39 sign the final draft.
June 21 1788	New Hampshire becomes the ninth state to accept the Constitution, making it the law of the land.

INTERESTING FACTS ABOUT THE CONSTITUTION

1. Gouverneur Morris actually wrote the document, even though James Madison was called the "Father of the Constitution."
2. Only two signers, George Washington (1788–1796) and James Madison (1808–1816), became Presidents of the United States of America.
3. The original document is in the National Archives Building in Washington, DC.

4. Four delegates also signed the Declaration of Independence in 1776.
5. Massachusetts sent the most delegates to the Convention.

Preamble

> We the people of the United States, in order to form a more perfect union, establish justice, insure domestic tranquility, provide for the common defense, promote the general welfare, and secure the Blessings of Liberty to ourselves and our Posterity, do ordain and establish this Constitution for the United States of America.

A *preamble* is an introduction that clearly states the reasons for an idea or document. The purpose of the Preamble of the Constitution was to tell the world that newly freed Americans truly believed that the people have the power to establish and change a government. It also declared that they were going to write a document that would establish the laws of the land that would protect their individual and collective freedoms. They also intended that these rights and freedoms were to be guaranteed to Americans for all time!

The Constitution

The delegates were so afraid of creating a government that would put all the power into one person's hands, that they wrote the Constitution with a system of checks and balances. In other words, they divided the power of the government into three segments: the elected representatives, the President, and the Supreme Court. This would ensure that no King or Queen would ever rule the United States, and that each branch of government needed the other to function. These sections were called articles and the idea of each section is now discussed.

Article I Legislative Branch

Section 1   Congress

All the power to make laws is given to a Congress made up of a Senate and a House of Representatives.

Section 2   House of Representatives

1. The House of Representatives will be made up of members chosen every two years by a vote of the people. In each state, voters will be those who are already allowed to vote in state elections.
2. Representatives must be at least 25 years old and citizens of the United States. They must live in the state in which they are elected.
3. The number of Representatives from a state will be based on the size of the population from that state. Indians not taxed will not be counted, and a slave will be counted as three-fifths of a person.
4. In case of a vacancy, a special state election will be held.
5. Members of the House of Representatives will choose their own officers. Also, they alone will have the power of impeachment.

Section 3   Senate

1. The Senate of the United States will be made up of two senators from each state. They will be chosen by their state legislatures. Senators will be elected to six-year terms.
2. One-third of the Senate will be chosen every two years. When a vacancy occurs, the state legislature will choose someone to fill the vacancy. If the legislature is in recess, the state governor can appoint someone to serve temporarily.
3. Senators must be at least 30 years old and citizens of the United States. They must live in the state in which they are elected.
4. The Vice President of the United States shall be President of the Senate. He (or she) shall vote only in case of a tie.
5. Senators shall choose all senate officers except the President of the Senate.
6. The Senate will try any federal official who is impeached. The Chief Justice (of the Supreme Court) will preside. Conviction will require agreement by two-thirds of those present.
7. Individuals who are impeached and convicted may be removed from office and are disqualified from holding other offices under the United States. Convicted individuals are subject to trial and punishment under the law.

Section 4   Rules for Both Houses

1. Election procedures for members of Congress will be decided by each state.
2. Congress shall meet at least once a year.

Section 5   Rules for Each House

1. In case of an election challenge, the House and the Senate will judge the election and qualification of their own members. A majority of each is necessary to do business.
2. Each House will determine its own procedures.
3. Each House will keep and publish a record of its proceedings.
4. Neither House may adjourn for more than three days without the consent of the other.

Section 6   Privileges and Restrictions

1. Senators and Representatives shall be paid for their services. They cannot be arrested while Congress is in session, nor be questioned outside Congress for speeches made there.
2. No Senator or Representative shall be appointed to any civil office while serving in Congress.

Section 7   Method of Passing Laws

1. All tax bills must come from the House of Representatives.
2. Every bill passed by the House and Senate must be signed by the President. If he (or she) refuses, and the bill is reconsidered and approved by two-thirds of each House, it will become law.
3. All orders and resolutions requiring approval by the House and Senate shall also require approval by the President.

Section 8   Powers Granted to Congress

Congress can:

1. Set and collect taxes.
2. Borrow money.
3. Regulate foreign and interstate trade.
4. Pass naturalization and bankruptcy laws.
5. Coin money.
6. Punish those who counterfeit United States money.
7. Establish a postal service.
8. Issue patents and copyrights.
9. Establish courts lower in rank than the Supreme Court.
10. Punish crimes committed at sea.
11. Declare war.
12. Maintain an army.
13. Maintain a navy.
14. Regulate the army and navy.
15. Call out a state's militia.
16. Share with the states control of the militia.
17. Make laws for the District of Columbia.
18. Make any laws necessary to do any of the above.

Section 9   Powers Denied the National Government

1. Congress may not prohibit the states from importing any person (in other words, slave) they desire until the year 1808.
2. No one can be held or imprisoned without charges being brought, unless when during rebellion or invasion the public safety requires it.
3. No one person shall be declared guilty of a crime by action of Congress. No one can be guilty for an action which was made a crime after the action was done.
4. Direct taxes will be in proportion to the population.
5. No taxes will be placed on articles exported from one state to another.
6. The ports in every state will be treated equally, and states shall not require ships from another state to pay duties.
7. Money from the treasury can be taken out only by law. Treasury records shall be published.
8. The United States will not give out titles of nobility. No federal office holder can accept any kind of gift from another country unless Congress approves.

Section 10   Powers Denied the States

States shall not:

1. Make treaties.
2. Coin money.
3. Pass laws declaring specific individuals guilty of crimes.
4. Try individuals for actions that were declared crimes after the action was done.
5. Grant titles of nobility.
6. Charge duties except to cover the cost of necessary inspections.
7. Have armies or navies in peacetime, and shall not make military agreements with other states or countries. They will not make war unless actually invaded or are in such danger that they cannot delay.

Article II   Executive Branch

Section 1   President and Vice President

1. The President will be the executive officer of the United States. He (or she) and the Vice President shall be elected to four-year terms.
2. Each state will appoint electors to meet in the state to vote for President and Vice President. The number of electors from each state shall equal the state's number of Senators and Representatives. Each elector will vote for two people. Their votes shall be sealed and sent to the President of the Senate. The person having the most votes shall be President. In a tie, the House of Representatives will decide. The person having the second highest number of votes will be Vice President.
3. Congress will set the day for the electors to vote.
4. To be eligible for the office of President, a person must be a natural-born citizen of the United States, at least 35 years old, and have lived in the United States at least 14 years.
5. If the President is removed, dies, resigns, or is unable to fulfill his (or her) responsibilities, the Vice President will serve as Chief Executive. If neither can serve, Congress will appoint a President to finish the term.
6. The President will be paid for his (or her) services, but his (or her) salary may not be changed while he (or she) is in office.
7. Before entering office, an elected President must take this oath: "I do solemnly swear that I will faithfully execute the office of President of the United States, and will, to the best of my ability, preserve, protect and defend the Constitution of the United States."

Section 2   Powers of the President

1. The President shall be the Commander in Chief of the armed forces. He (or she) can require written reports from the heads of the executive departments. He (or she) can grant pardons for offenses against the United States.
2. The President can, with Senate approval, make treaties, appoint Ambassadors and Supreme Court Judges, and fill other positions established by law.

Section 3   Duties of the President

The President shall make regular reports to Congress on the state of the union, shall recommend to them laws that he (or she) thinks should be passed, and can call them into special session. He (or she) shall faithfully enforce the laws of the United States.

Section 4   Impeachment

Any officer of the United States shall be removed from office if impeached and convicted of treason, bribery, or other crimes.

Article III   Judicial Branch

Section 1   Federal Courts

Judicial matters shall be in the hands of a Supreme Court and other federal courts created by Congress. The judges shall hold their offices during their good behavior and they shall be compensated for their work.

Section 2 Authority of the Federal Courts

1. Federal courts will handle all legal questions arising under this Constitution and under federal laws. Controversies between two or more states and between a state and citizens of another state will be handled by federal courts.
2. Cases affecting ambassadors, ministers and consuls, and those in which a state is a party, will go directly to the Supreme Court. In all other cases under its authority, the Supreme Court will have power to review the actions of lower courts.
3. All crimes (except in cases of impeachment) shall be tried by jury and the trial shall be held in the state where the crime was committed.

Section 3 Treason

1. "Treason" means only "making war against the United States" or "supporting the enemy."
2. Congress shall declare the punishment for treason.

Article IV The States

Section 1 Official Acts

The official acts of each state shall be honored in all other states.

Section 2 Privileges of Citizens

1. The citizens in each of the states shall have the same rights.
2. Persons charged with crimes who flee to another state shall be returned.
3. Persons who owe others their labor and flee to another state shall be returned.

Section 3 New States and Territories

1. New states may be admitted to the Union by Congress.
2. Congress shall control all United States territory and property.

Section 4 Guarantees to the States

Congress guarantees to every state a republican form of government, and shall protect them against invasion. If asked by a state, Congress will also provide protection against internal violence.

Article V Method of Amendment

This Constitution can be amended in this way: Two-thirds of the Senate and of the House of Representatives can propose changes, or two-thirds of the states can request that a convention meet to make changes. Changes from either of these two sources become a part of the Constitution when they have been approved by three-fourths of the states.

Article VI General Provisions

1. Debts owed by the Confederation will remain unchanged under this Constitution.
2. This Constitution shall be the highest law of the land.
3. All state and federal officers must swear to uphold this Constitution. No office holder shall ever be required to pass a religious test.

Article VII   Ratification

This Constitution will go into effect when it has been ratified by nine states. Rhode Island was the thirteenth state to ratify the Constitution on May 29, 1790.

The Bill of Rights

Background Information

When Thomas Jefferson, who was serving as our ambassador to France and thus not at the Constitutional Convention, read the Constitution, he was greatly impressed. He did believe, however, that people's individual rights needed to be listed and clearly defined so that each citizen would understand his or her guaranteed rights. Consequently, Jefferson proposed adding 12 amendments that would enumerate these rights. Of the 12, 10 were accepted and became the first amendments (the Bill of Rights) to the U.S. Constitution on December 15, 1791. A simplified version appears below.

Amendment I

The government cannot make laws that would interfere with religion. It cannot deny free speech or a free press. It also assures people the right to peaceful assemble.

Amendment II

Each citizen has the right to keep and/or carry weapons.

Amendment III

In peacetime, no soldier shall be placed in a person's home without the owner's consent.

Amendment IV

People cannot be searched, or their property seized before a warrant has been issued to do so. This protects both people and their possessions.

Amendment V

Each citizen has the right of due process of the laws. No person can be forced to be a witness against himself or herself and cannot be tried twice for the same crime.

Amendment VI

In criminal prosecutions, the accused shall be given the right to a fair and speedy trial and be provided counsel for his or her defense.

Amendment VII

Civil suits where the amount contested exceeds $20 shall be by jury rather than judged on by the rules of common law.

Amendment VIII

Excessive bail, fines, nor cruel and unusual punishments shall be inflicted.

Amendment IX

The listing of specific rights in the Constitution does not mean that other specific rights are taken away or changed.

Amendment X

Powers not delegated to the United States by the Constitution, nor prohibited by it to the states, are reserved to the states respectively, or to the people who live in these states.

TEACHER-DIRECTED ACTIVITIES FOR STUDENTS

1. Review the history of the Bill of Rights. Who was the author? Why were they added? How do they effect our daily lives?
2. Create a classroom Bill of Rights designed to identify and protect individual rights.
3. Select one of the first 10 amendments to the Constitution and list the ways it affects us.
4. Take a field trip to a district court or ask a judge to visit the classroom. Discuss how our rights are protected by the legal system.
5. Have a mock trial with an issue to be resolved in class. You and your classmates play certain roles such as judge, jury, attorneys, bailiff, defendants, and prosecutors.
6. Debate a national issue like gun control or school prayer.
7. Discuss the vocabulary of the Bill of Rights and how it has been interpreted differently throughout history.

Amendments XI–XXVII

Amendment XI (Jan. 8, 1798)

It is impossible for a citizen of one state to sue another in federal court. However, individuals can still sue state authorities in federal court for depriving them of their constitutional rights.

Amendment XII (Sept. 25, 1804)

The appointment of the President and the Vice President will be made by the President of the Senate on the basis of a majority count of all the votes sent in by the different states. The Vice President must be constitutionally eligible for election to the position of President.

Amendment XIII (Dec. 18, 1865)

Slavery shall not exist in the United States. Involuntary servitude may only be carried out as punishment for a crime.

Amendment XIV (July 18, 1868)

1. All persons born or naturalized in the United States are citizens of the United States and the state in which they reside. All the privileges of the basic Constitution will be accorded them.
2. Representatives shall be apportioned among the states according to their respective numbers of males over the age of 21.

3. No United States citizen who has been involved in insurrection or rebellion against the United States may stand for election to any government position.
4. The United States public debt may not be questioned. However, all debts claimed against the United States shall be held illegal and void.

Amendment XV   (March 30, 1870)

Race, color, nor previous condition of servitude could bar a male, over the age of 21, from voting in the United States.

Amendment XVI   (Feb. 25, 1913)

Congress has the power to lay and collect taxes on income without consensus from the individual states.

Amendment XVII   (May 31, 1913)

The Senate shall be composed of two Senators from each state. If a position falls vacant, the legislature of the state may make a temporary appointment until the people fill the vacancy by election.

Amendment XVIII   (Jan. 29, 1919)

The manufacture, sale, or transportation of alcohol is prohibited.

Amendment XIX   (Aug. 26, 1920)

The right to vote is extended to women.

Amendment XX (Jan. 23, 1933)

The terms of the President and the Vice President shall end at noon on the 20th day of January and the terms of senators and representatives at noon on the 3rd January of the years in which such terms would have ended.

Amendment XXI   (Dec. 5, 1933)

The eighteenth amendment is repealed. Each state must ratify the amendment within seven years from the date of submission.

Amendment XXII   (March 1, 1951)

No person shall be elected President more than twice. This amendment must be ratified by three-quarters of the states.

Amendment XXIII   (March 29, 1961)

The district constituting the seat of government shall appoint electors of the President and Vice President as well as Senators and Representatives.

Amendment XXIV   (Jan. 23, 1964)

The failure to pay taxes cannot prohibit a citizen from voting.

Amendment XXV   (Feb. 10, 1967)

1. The Vice President will become President on the removal of the President from office or by death or by resignation.

2. The President will nominate a Vice President if there is a vacancy until such time that both Houses of Congress confirm the appointment.
3. If the President is unable to carry out his (or her) duties, the Vice President will assume such duties.
4. The President shall resume his (or her) duties if no inability exists unless the Vice President and a majority of other principal officers give a written declaration that they feel the President is incapable of carrying out such duties. Thereupon, Congress will decide the issue within 21 days after the receipt of the written declaration. Either the President will resume his (or her) duties or the Vice President will continue to discharge the duties.

Amendment XXVI   (June 30, 1971)

The right to vote is extended to all 18-year-old citizens.

Amendment XXVII   (May 19, 1992)

No law varying the compensation for the services of Senators or Representatives shall take effect until an election of Representatives has intervened.

SOME INTERESTING FACTS ABOUT THE U.S. CONSTITUTION

1. The Assembly Room at the Pennsylvania State House (now called Independence Hall) is where the Declaration of Independence (1776), the Articles of Confederation (1781), and the United States Constitution (1787) were all signed.
2. The final document was signed by the delegates on September 17, 1787.
3. James Madison is called the "Father of the Constitution" because he kept records of the debates and was an influential delegate, but Governor Morris actually wrote the document.
4. Rhode Island refused to send delegates because they were opposed to having a federal government meddle in the state's affairs.
5. George Clymer, Benjamin Franklin, Robbert Morris, George Read, Roger Sherman, and James Wilson signed both the Declaration of Independence and the U.S. Constitution.
6. George Washington and James Madison were the only two signers to become U.S. Presidents.
7. Three delegates refused to sign the document: Elbridge Gerry, George Mason, and Edmund Randolph.
8. Delegates signed in geographical order from North to South: New Hampshire, Massachusetts, Connecticut, New York, New Jersey, Pennsylvania, Delaware, Maryland, Virginia, North Carolina, South Carolina, and Georgia.
9. Delaware was the first state to ratify the Constitution on December 7, 1787 — three months after the delegates signed.
10. There were 39 delegates who signed the Constitution. They were:

George Washington	Charles Pinckney
Benjamin Franklin	John Rutledge
James Madison, Jr.	Pierce Butler
Alexander Hamilton	Roger Sherman
Gouverneur Morris	William S. Johnson
Robert Morris	James McHenry
James Wilson	George Read
Charles C. Pinckney	Richard Bassett

Richard D. Spaight
William Blount
Hugh Williamson
Daniel of St. Thomas Jenifer
Rufus King
Nathaniel Gorham
Jonathan Dayton
Daniel Carroll
William Few
Abraham Baldwin
John Langdon
Nicholas Gilman

William Livingston
William Paterson
Thomas Mifflin
George Clymer
Thomas FitzSimons
Jared Ingersoll
Gunning Bedford, Jr.
Jacob Broom
John Dickinson
John Blair*
David Brearley
William Jackson†

11. The original document is on display at the National Archives building in Washington, DC.

AT-A-GLANCE INDEX TO THE CONSTITUTION OF THE UNITED STATES OF AMERICA

Subject	Article or Amendment	Subject	Article or Amendment
Advice and consent	Article II, Section 2	Legislative branch	Article I
Amendment	Article V	National debt	Article VI
Appointment	Article II, Section 2	Pocket veto	Article I, Section 7
Assembly, Right of Bill	Amendment 1	Poll tax	Amendment 24
Bill of Rights	Amendments 1 to 10		
Church and state	Article VI	President	Article II
	Amendment 1		Amendment 12
Citizenship	Amendment 14		Amendment 22
Civil rights	Amendment 14	Presidential succession	Article II, Section 1
	Amendment 15		Amendment 20
Commander in chief	Article II, Section 2		Amendment 25
Commerce clause	Article I, Section 8	Prohibition	Amendment 18
Congress	Article I		Amendment 21
	Amendment 12	Ratification	Article V
Congressional Record	Article I, Section 5	Right of assembly	Amendment 1
Court	Article III	Search warrant	Amendment 4
Double jeopardy	Amendment 5	Senate	Article I
Due process of law	Amendment 5		Amendment 12
	Amendment 14		Amendment 17
Electoral College	Article II, Section 1	Slavery	Amendment 13
	Amendment 12		Amendment 14
	Amendment 23	State	Article IV
Ex post facto	Article I, Section 9	State of the Union message	Article II, Section 3
Executive branch	Article II		
Extradition	Article IV, Section 2	States' rights	Amendment 10
Freedom of religion	Amendment 1	Supremacy clause	Article VI
Freedom of speech	Amendment 1	Supreme Court	Article III
Freedom of the press	Amendment 1	Treason	Article III, Section 3
House of Representatives	Article I, Section 6	Trial	Amendment 5
Immunity, Congressional	Article I, Section 6	Vice President	Article II, Sections 1, 5
Impeachment	Article I, Section 2		Amendment 12
	Article I, Section 3		Amendment 20

*John Dickinson was absent but had someone sign for him.
†William Jackson was the secretary of the convention but not an official delegate.

	Article II, Section 4		Amendment 25
Income tax	Article I, Section 9	Voting	Amendment 14
	Amendment 16		Amendment 15
Judicial branch	Article III		Amendment 19
Judicial review	Article III, Section 2		Amendment 23
Jury and trial by jury	Article III, Section 2		Amendment 24
	Amendment 6		Amendment 26
	Amendment 7	Washington, D.C.	Amendment 23
Lame duck amendment	Amendment 20	Woman suffrage	Amendment 19

TEACHER-DIRECTED ACTIVITIES FOR STUDENTS

1. Read and discuss the Preamble to the U.S. Constitution. Why is there a Preamble and what does it mean?
2. Review the three major sections of the Constitution and discuss the writers' concern regarding separation of powers.
3. Research the history of the Constitution and its authors.
4. Discuss why the Constitution has been able to survive and function for over 200 years when others have not.
5. Read biographies or autobiographies of the men who wrote the document.
6. Discuss the reasons why the United States has had to add 17 amendments (since the Bill of Rights) to the Constitution over the course of our history.
7. Select one amendment and research its history and impact on our legal system.
8. Review and list those amendments that are directly linked to civil rights.
9. What other nations have written constitutions? Do they also have a written list of people's rights?
10. Speculate on any future amendments to the U.S. Constitution.

THE UNITED STATES OF AMERICA: INFORMATION AND EXERCISES

WHEN DID YOUR STATE JOIN THE UNION?

Rank	State	Entered Union
1	Delaware	December 7, 1787
2	Pennsylvania	December 12, 1787
3	New Jersey	December 18, 1787
4	Georgia	January 2, 1788
5	Connecticut	January 9, 1788
6	Massachusetts	February 6, 1788
7	Maryland	April 28, 1788
8	South Carolina	May 23, 1788
9	New Hampshire	June 21, 1788
10	Virginia	June 25, 1788
11	New York	July 26, 1788
12	North Carolina	November 21, 1789
13	Rhode Island	May 29, 1790
14	Vermont	March 4, 1791

WHEN DID YOUR STATE JOIN THE UNION? (Continued)

Rank	State	Entered Union
15	Kentucky	June 1, 1792
16	Tennessee	June 1796
17	Ohio	March 1, 1803
18	Louisiana	April 30, 1812
19	Indiana	December 11, 1816
20	Mississippi	December 10, 1817
21	Illinois	December 3, 1818
22	Alabama	December 14, 1819
23	Maine	March 15, 1820
24	Missouri	August 10, 1821
25	Arkansas	June 15, 1836
26	Michigan	January 26, 1837
27	Florida	March 3, 1845
28	Texas	December 29, 1845
29	Iowa	December 28, 1846
30	Wisconsin	May 29, 1848
31	California	September 9, 1850
32	Minnesota	May 11, 1858
33	Oregon	February 14, 1859
34	Kansas	January 29, 1861
35	West Virginia	June 20, 1863
36	Nevada	October 31, 1864
37	Nebraska	March 1, 1867
38	Colorado	August 1, 1876
39	North Dakota	November 2, 1889
40	South Dakota	November 2, 1889
41	Montana	November 8, 1889
42	Washington	November 11, 1889
43	Idaho	July 3, 1890
44	Wyoming	July 10, 1890
45	Utah	January 4, 1896
46	Oklahoma	November 16, 1907
47	New Mexico	January 6, 1912
48	Arizona	February 14, 1912
49	Alaska	January 3, 1959
50	Hawaii	August 21, 1959

Presidents and Vice Presidents of the United States of America

1. George Washington (Virginia)   John Adams
   (no party)
   March 4, 1789–March 3, 1793
   March 4, 1793–March 3, 1797

2. John Adams (Massachusetts)   Thomas Jefferson
   (Federalist)
   March 4, 1797–March 3, 1801

3. Thomas Jefferson (Virginia)   Aaron Burr
   (Democrat/Republican)
   March 4, 1801–March 3, 1805
   March 4, 1805–March 3, 1809

 4. James Madison (Virginia)   George Clinton
     (Democrat/Republican)
     March 4, 1809–March 3, 1813
     March 4, 1813–March 3, 1817   Elbridge Gerry

 5. James Monroe (Virginia)   Daniel D. Tompkins
     (Democrat/Republican)
     March 4, 1817–March 3, 1821
     March 4, 1821–March 3, 1825

 6. John Quincy Adams (Massachusetts)   John C. Calhoun
     (Democrat/Republican)
     March 4, 1825–March 3, 1829

 7. Andrew Jackson (Tennessee)   John C. Calhoun
     (Democrat)
     March 4, 1829–March 3, 1833
     March 4, 1833–March 3, 1837

 8. Martin Van Buren (New York)   Richard M. Johnson
     (Democrat)
     March 4, 1837–March 3, 1841

 9. *William Henry Harrison (Ohio)   John Tyler
     (Whig)
     March 4, 1841–April 4, 1841

10. John Tyler (Virginia)
     (Whig)
     April 6, 1841–March 3, 1845

11. James Polk (Tennessee)   George M. Dallas
     (Democrat)
     March 4, 1845–March 3, 1849

12. Zachary Taylor (Louisiana)   Millard Fillmore
     (Whig)
     March 4, 1849–July 9, 1850

13. Millard Fillmore (New York)
     (Whig)
     July 10, 1850–March 3, 1853

14. Franklin Pierce (New Hampshire)   William R. King
     (Democrat)
     March 4, 1853–March 3, 1857

15. James Buchanan (Pennsylvania)   John C. Breckinridge
     (Democrat)
     March 4, 1857–March 3, 1861

16. *Abraham Lincoln (Illinois)   Hannibal Hamlin
     (Republican)
     March 4, 1861–March 3, 1865
     March 4, 1865–April 14, 1865   Andrew Johnson

17. Andrew Johnson (Tennessee)
     (Democrat)
     April 15, 1865–March 3, 1869

18. Ulysses S. Grant (Illinois)   Schuyler Colfax
     (Republican)
     March 4, 1869–March 3, 1873
     March 4, 1873–March 3, 1877

19. Rutherford B. Hayes (Ohio)   William A. Wheeler
    (Republican)
    March 4, 1877–March 3, 1881

20. *James A. Garfield (Ohio)   Chester A. Arthur
    (Republican)
    March 4, 1881–Sept. 19, 1881

21. Chester A. Arthur (New York)
    (Republican)
    Sept. 20, 1881–March 3, 1885

22. Grover Cleveland (New York)   Thomas A. Hendricks
    (Democrat)
    March 4, 1885–March 3, 1889

23. Benjamin Harrison (Indiana)   Levi P. Morton
    (Republican)
    March 4, 1889–March 3, 1893

24. **Grover Cleveland (New York)   Adlai E. Stevenson
    (Democrat)
    March 4, 1893–March 3, 1897

25. *William McKinley (Ohio)   Garret A. Hobart
    (Republican)
    March 4, 1897–March 3, 1901
    March 4, 1901–Sept. 14, 1901   Theodore Roosevelt

26. Theodore Roosevelt (New York)   Charles Fairbanks
    (Republican)
    Sept. 14, 1901–March 3, 1905
    March 4, 1905–March 3, 1909

27. William H. Taft (Ohio)   James S. Sherman
    (Republican)
    March 4, 1909–March 3, 1913

28. *Woodrow Wilson (New Jersey)   Thomas R. Marshall
    (Democrat)
    March 4, 1913–March 3, 1921

29. Warren G. Harding (Ohio)   Calvin Coolidge
    (Republican)
    March 4, 1921–August 2, 1923

30. Calvin Coolidge (Massachusetts)   Charles Dawes
    (Republican)
    August 3, 1923–March 3, 1925
    March 4, 1925–March 3, 1929

31. Herbert C. Hoover (California)   Charles Curtis
    (Republican)
    March 4, 1929–March 3, 1933

32. *Franklin D. Roosevelt (New York)   John N. Garner
    (Democrat)
    March 4, 1933–Jan. 20, 1937
    Jan. 20, 1937–Jan. 20, 1941
    Jan. 20, 1941–Jan. 20, 1945   Henry A. Wallace
    Jan. 20, 1945–April 12, 1945   Harry S. Truman

33. Harry S. Truman (Missouri)
    (Democrat)

April 12, 1945–Jan. 20, 1949	
Jan. 20, 1946–Jan. 20, 1953	Alben William Barkley
34. Dwight D. Eisenhower (New York) (Republican)	Richard M. Nixon
Jan. 20, 1953–Jan. 20, 1957	
Jan. 20, 1957–Jan. 20, 1961	
35. *John F. Kennedy (Massachusetts) (Democrat)	Lyndon B. Johnson
Jan. 20, 1961–Nov. 22, 1963	
36. Lyndon B. Johnson (Texas) (Democrat)	
Nov. 22, 1963–Jan. 20, 1965	
Jan. 20, 1965–Jan. 20, 1969	Hubert H. Humphrey
37. Richard Nixon (New York) (Republican)	Spiro T. Agnew
Jan. 20, 1969–Jan. 20, 1973	
Jan. 20, 1973–August 9, 1974	
38. Gerald R. Ford (Michigan) (Republican)	Nelson A. Rockefeller
August 9, 1974–Jan. 20, 1977	
39. James Earl Carter (Georgia) (Democrat)	Walter F. Mondale
Jan. 20, 1977–Jan. 20, 1981	
40. Ronald Reagan (California) (Republican)	George Bush
Jan. 5, 1981–Jan. 3, 1985	
Jan. 3, 1985–Jan. 19, 1989	
41. George Bush (Texas) (Republican)	Dan Quayle
Jan. 20, 1989–Jan. 19, 1993	
42. William Clinton (Arkansas) (Democrat)	Albert Gore, Jr.
Jan. 20, 1993–Present	

Presidential Oath

I do solemnly swear (or affirm) that I will faithfully execute the office of President of the United States, and will to the best of my ability, preserve, protect, and defend the Constitution of the United States.

*Died in office.
**Only President to serve two terms in office nonconsecutively.

THE STATES IN REVIEW

State	Capital	Nickname	Flower	Bird
Alabama	Montgomery	Heart of Dixie	Camellia	Yellowhammer
Alaska	Juneau	The Last Frontier	Forget-Me-Not	Willow Ptarmigan
Arizona	Phoenix	Grand Canyon State	Seguaro Cactus Blossom	Cactus Wren
Arkansas	Little Rock	Land of Opportunity	Apple Blossom	Mockingbird
California	Sacramento	Golden State	Golden Poppy	California Valley Quail
Colorado	Denver	Centennial State	Rocky Mt. Columbine	Lark Bunting
Connecticut	Hartford	Constitution State	Mt. Laurel	American Robin
Delaware	Dover	First State	Peach Blossom	Blue Hen Chicken
Florida	Tallahassee	Sunshine State	Orange Blossom	Mockingbird
Georgia	Atlanta	Empire State of the South	Cherokee Rose	Brown Thrasher
Hawaii	Honolulu	Aloha State	Hibiscus	Hawaiian Goose
Idaho	Boise	Gem State	Syringa	Mountain Bluebird
Illinois	Springfield	Prairie State	Native Violet	Cardinal
Indiana	Indianapolis	Hoosier State	Peony	Cardinal
Iowa	Des Moines	Hawkeye State	Wild Rose	Eastern Goldfinch
Kansas	Topeka	Sunflower State	Sunflower	Western Meadowlark
Kentucky	Frankfort	Blue Grass State	Golden Rod	Kentucky Cardinal
Louisiana	Baton Rouge	Pelican State	Magnolia	Brown Pelican
Maine	Augusta	Pine Tree State	White Pinecone Tassel	Chickadee
Maryland	Annapolis	Old Line State	Black-eyed Susan	Baltimore Oriole
Massachusetts	Boston	Bay State	Mayflower	Chickadee
Michigan	Lansing	Great Lake State	Apple Blossom	Robin
Minnesota	St. Paul	Gopher State	Pink and White Lady's Slipper	Common Loon
Mississippi	Jackson	Magnolia State	Magnolia	Mockingbird
Missouri	Jefferson city	Show Me State	Hawthorn	Bluebird
Montana	Helena	Treasure State	Bitterroot	Western Meadowlark
Nebraska	Lincoln	Cornhusker State	Golden Rod	Western Meadowlark
Nevada	Carson City	Silver State	Sagebrush	Mountain Bluebird
New Hampshire	Concord	Granite State	Purple Lilac	Purple Finch
New Jersey	Trenton	Garden State	Purple Violet	Eastern Goldfinch
New Mexico	Sante Fe	Land of Enchantment	Yucca	Roadrunner
New York	Albany	Empire State	Rose	Bluebird
North Carolina	Raleigh	Tarheel State	Dogwood	Cardinal
North Dakota	Bismark	Peace Garden State	Wild Prairie Rose	Western Meadowlark
Ohio	Columbus	Buckeye State	Scarlet Carnation	Cardinal
Oklahoma	Oklahoma City	Sooner State	Mistletoe	Scissortailed Flycatcher
Oregon	Salem	Beaver State	Oregon Grape	Western Meadowlark

State	Capital	Nickname	Flower	Bird
Pennsylvania	Harrisburg	Keystone State	Mt. Laurel	Ruffed Grouse
Rhode Island	Providence	Ocean State	Violet	Rhode Island Red
South Carolina	Columbia	Palmetto State	Carolina Jessamine	Carolina Wren
South Dakota	Pierre	Sunshine State	Pasque Flower	Ringnecked Pheasant
Tennessee	Nashville	Volunteer State	Iris	Mockingbird
Texas	Austin	Lone Star State	Bluebonnet	Mockingbird
Utah	Salt Lake City	Beehive State	Sage Lily	Sea Gull
Vermont	Montpelier	Green Mountain State	Red Clover	Hermit Thrush
Virginia	Richmond	Old Dominion	Flowering Dogwood	Cardinal
Washington	Olympia	Evergreen State	Western Rhododendron	Willow Goldfinch
West Virginia	Charleston	Mountain State	Rhododendron	Cardinal
Wisconsin	Madison	Badger State	Wood Violet	Robin
Wyoming	Cheyenne	Equality State	Indian Paintbrush	Meadowlark

TEACHER-DIRECTED ACTIVITIES FOR STUDENTS

1. Using the map provided, identify the states and their respective capital cities.
2. Identify the largest and smallest (population) capital cities.
3. List the capital cities that were named for American presidents.
4. Why are some state capitals at or near the center of the state while others are not?
5. Why are the states generally bigger in the west than in the east?
6. List the biggest cities that are not capital cities in the following states:

   a. Washington _____

   b. California _____

   c. New York _____

   d. Missouri _____

   e. Florida _____

   f. Michigan _____

   g. Texas _____

   h. Illinois _____

   i. Nevada _____

   j. Oregon _____

   Can you find any others?

The Flag of the United States of America

History

The United States flag, the "Stars and Stripes," was officially adopted on June 14, 1777 (now celebrated as Flag Day). The Continental Congress stated, "The flag of the United States be 13 stripes alternate red and white, that the union be 13 stars white in a blue field representing a new constellation."

However, after Vermont and Kentucky joined the union (1795), two more stripes and two more stars were added. At this rate our flag would either keep growing in size or the stripes would become very small. In 1818, the decision was made to keep the 13 stripes permanently, representing the first 13 colonies, and to add stars to indicate the current number of states in the union. There were many variations in the number of points on the stars, in the shades of red and blue, and in the width to length part of the flag until 1912, when a standardized design and color was established.

Importance of Flags to a Nation

Flags have great importance to the nations they represent. The flag of the United States of America is red, white, and blue. The symbolism of the colors is "red is hardiness and courage, white for purity and innocence, and blue for vigilance, perseverance and justice."

Every nation proudly displays its flag for special occasions, holidays, and events. We also see national flags at the Olympic Games or other sporting events where athletes from various nations perform.

SOME INTERESTING FACTS ABOUT OUR FLAG

1. No one knows for certain who designed or who made the first American flag. Congressman Francis Hopkinson claimed that he designed the flag, but traditionally Betsy Ross is credited with sewing the first U.S. flag for George Washington. Although Betsy Ross was a seamstress who had made flags, there is no proof that she actually made the original "Stars and Stripes."

2. The flag of 1777 had no official arrangement for the stars. The most popular design had alternating rows of 3-2-3-2-3.

3. The flag of 1795 had 15 stripes and 15 stars for each state.

4. The flag of 1861, used in the Civil War, had 34 stars for all the states, including the recently seceded southern states.

5. The 48-star flag served as the national flag the longest of any of our flags, from 1912 to 1959.

6. There is no legal or other official authority for assigning the stars in the flag to certain states. There is, however, a popular wish to give each state a definite star, according to the order in which it ratified the Constitution or entered the Union, with the stripes similarly designated for the 13 original colonies. Can you locate your state's star?

TEACHER-DIRECTED ACTIVITIES FOR STUDENTS

1. Using an encyclopedia, review how our national flag has changed during the past 200 years.

2. Design a flag for the United States of America if we would add two new states to the union.

3. List how many other nations in the world have red, white, and blue on their flag.

4. Look at other national flags to see if you can discover something about that country from the color(s) and/or symbol(s) being shown on their respective flags.

HOW WE HAVE GROWN—U.S. CENSUS FIGURES

1610	350 (estimated)
1780	2,780,000 (estimated)
1800	5,308,483
1860	31,443,321
1900	75,994,575
1940	131,669,275
1950	150,697,361
1960	179,323,175
1970	203,302,031
1980	226,545,805
1990	248,709,873

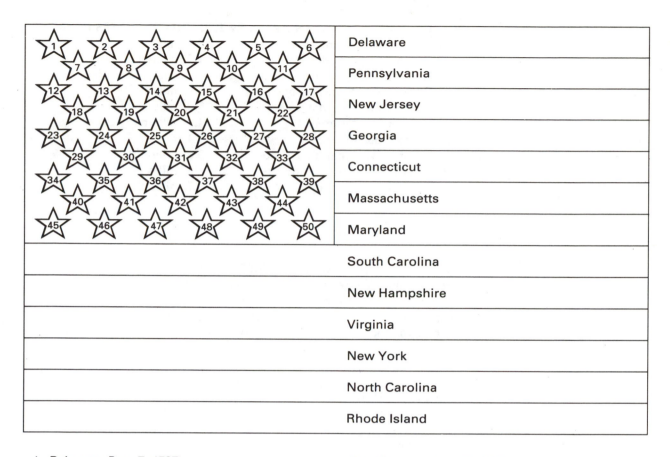

	Delaware
	Pennsylvania
	New Jersey
	Georgia
	Connecticut
	Massachusetts
	Maryland
South Carolina
New Hampshire
Virginia
New York
North Carolina
Rhode Island

1. Delaware, Dec. 7, 1787
2. Pennsylvania, Dec. 12, 1787
3. New Jersey, Dec. 18, 1787
4. Georgia, Jan. 2, 1788
5. Connecticut, Jan. 9, 1788
6. Massachusetts, Feb. 6, 1788
7. Maryland, April 28, 1788
8. South Carolina, May 23, 1788
9. New Hampshire, June 21, 1788
10. Virginia, June 26, 1788
11. New York, July 26, 1788
12. North Carolina, Nov. 21, 1789
13. Rhode Island, May 19, 1790
14. Vermont, March 4, 1791
15. Kentucky, June 1, 1792
16. Tennessee, June 1, 1796
17. Ohio, March 1, 1803
18. Louisiana, April 30, 1812
19. Indiana, Dec. 11, 1816
20. Mississippi, Dec. 10, 1817
21. Illinois, Dec. 3, 1818
22. Alabama, Dec. 14, 1819
23. Maine, March 15, 1820
24. Missouri, Aug. 10, 1821
25. Arkansas, June 15, 1836

26. Michigan, Jan. 26, 1837
27. Florida, March 3, 1845
28. Texas, Dec. 29, 1845
29. Iowa, Dec. 28, 1846
30. Wisconsin, May 29, 1848
31. California, Sept. 9, 1850
32. Minnesota, May 11, 1858
33. Oregon, Feb. 14, 1858
34. Kansas, Jan. 29, 1861
35. West Virginia, June 20, 1863
36. Nevada, Oct. 31, 1864
37. Nebraska, March 1, 1867
38. Colorado, Aug. 1, 1876
39. North Dakota, Nov. 2, 1889
40. South Dakota, Nov. 2, 1889
41. Montana, Nov. 8, 1889
42. Washington, Nov. 11, 1889
43. Idaho, July 3, 1890
44. Wyoming, July 10, 1890
45. Utah, Jan. 4, 1896
46. Oklahoma, Nov. 16, 1907
47. New Mexico, Jan. 6, 1912
48. Arizona, Feb. 14, 1912
49. Alaska, Jan. 3, 1959
50. Hawaii, Aug. 21, 1959

LARGEST METROPOLITAN AREAS IN THE UNITED STATES (1990)

1.	Greater New York area	18.1 million
2.	Greater Los Angeles area	14.5 million
3.	Greater Chicago area	8.1 million
4.	Greater San Francisco area	6.2 million
5.	Greater Philadelphia area	5.9 million
6.	Greater Detroit area	4.7 million
7.	Greater Boston area	4.1 million
8.	Greater Washington, DC area	3.9 million
9.	Greater Dallas-Ft. Worth area	3.8 million
10.	Greater Houston area	3.7 million

SEVENTY-FIVE INTERESTING AMERICANS

Henry David Thoreau	Wilbur Wright
William H. McGuffey	F. Scott Fitzgerald
Rosa Parks	Charles Lindberg
Thomas Paine	Thomas Nast
Ben Franklin	Bret Harte
Sally Ride	Daniel Webster
Crispus Attucks	Jackie Robinson
Edward R. Murrow	Irving Berlin
Sam Houston	Elizabeth Peabody
Neil Armstrong	Mark Twain (Samuel Clemens)
James Audubon	Mathew Henson
Marcus Whitman	Clara Barton
Jonas Salk	Ralph Nader
Louisa May Alcott	Eleanor Roosevelt
Clare Booth Luce	Jim Thorpe
Merriweather Lewis	Brigham Young
William Clark	Jane Addams
Thomas Edison	Elvis Presley
Martin Luther King, Jr.	Linus Pauling
Patrick Henry	Marian Anderson
Henry Ford	Dolly Madison
Thomas Eakins	Harriet Beecher Stowe
Nathan Hale	D. W. Griffith
Norman Rockwell	Josephine Baker
Rachel Carson	Phineas T. Barnum
Amelia Earhart	Julia Childs
George Washington Carver	Jackson Pollock
Susan B. Anthony	Paul Robeson
Harriet Tubman	Robert E. Lee
Willa Cather	Earl Warren
Haym Solomon	Douglas MacArthur
Dr. Robert Ballard	Charles Curtis
Robert Frost	James Fenimore Cooper
Frank Lloyd Wright	Oveta Culp Hobby
Washington Irving	Emily Dickinson
John Philip Sousa	Cesar Chavez
Frederick Douglass	Clarence Darrow
Orville Wright	

TEACHER-DIRECTED ACTIVITIES FOR STUDENTS
1. Select a person from the preceding list.
   a. Read an autobiography or biography.
   b. Research a person and highlight the significant events of his or her life on a mobil, paper shape, or bulletin board.
   c. Create a play or simulation about the life of one of these personalities.
   d. Review what the world was like during the time this person lived (other famous people, art, literature, etc.).
   e. Create a time line of the major events during the person's life.

AMERICA GOES TO WAR

American Revolutionary War (1775–1783)
War of 1812 (1812–1815)
Mexican War (1846–1848)
American Civil War (1861–1865)
Spanish-American War (1898)
World War I (1917–1918)
World War II (1941–1945)
Korean War (1950–1953)
Vietnam (1965–1975)
Grenada (1983)
Panama (1989)
Gulf War (1991)

TEACHER-DIRECTED ACTIVITIES FOR STUDENTS
1. Discuss the concept of war and how it affects history, geography, and politics.
2. Discuss how "localized" wars are different from world wars.
3. Identify and list America's allies and enemies for each war in which we were involved.
4. Review the reasons why nations go to war and discuss why war is sometimes unavoidable.
5. Identify some places where future wars might take place and discuss America's role, if any, in these potential conflicts areas.
6. Obtain recordings of such songs as "Over There," "Pack Up Your Troubles," "Don't Sit Under the Apple Tree," "Praise the Lord and Pass the Ammunition," and "You're in the Army Mr. Jones." Arrange to have copies made of the lyrics and have a sing-a-long. Then discuss the patriotic music and its importance during war.
7. Divide into groups and find a song from one of the wars or conflicts in which the United States of America has participated. Respond to the following questions:
   a. What was the national mood at the time the music was popular?
   b. Were the lyrics reflective of national values and attitudes?
   c. Why was the song written and which audience?
8. Read the poem "The Dead Drummer-Boy."

"THE DEAD DRUMMER-BOY"

'Midst tangled roots that lined the wild ravine,
　Where the fierce fight raged hottest through the day,
And where the dead in scattered heaps were seen,
Amid the darkling forests' shade and sheen,
　Speechless in death he lay.

The setting sun, which glanced athwart the place
　In slanting lines, like amber-tinted rain,
Fell sidewise on the drummer's upturned face,
Where Death had left his gory finger's trace
　In one bright crimson stain.

The silken fringes of his once bright eye
　Lay like a shadow on his cheek so fair;
His lips were parted by a long-drawn sigh,
That with his soul had mounted to the sky
　On some wild martial air.

No more his hand the fierce tattoo shall beat,
　The shrill reveille, or the long-roll's call,
Or sound the charge, when in the smoke and heat
Of fiery onset foe with foe shall meet,
　And gallant men shall fall.

Yet maybe in some happy home, that one—
　A mother—reading from the list of dead,
Shall chance to view the name of her dear son,
And move her lips to say, "God's will be done!"
　And bow in grief her head.

But more than this what tongue shall tell his story?
　Perhaps his boyish longings were for fame?
He lived, he died; and so, *memento mori*—
Enough if on the page of War and Glory
　Some hand has writ his name.

Anonymous

After reading this poem, discuss the following questions:
a. To which war does this poem refer?
b. Does the poem glorify war?
c. Why were young boys involved in war?
d. How did this war change the United States of America?
e. How has war changed from this period to now?
f. What other poems have been written about war and how do they reflect a national attitude?

9. Look through newspapers and review political cartoons that were published during America's involvement in a war. Discuss the attitude of the cartoon and what it was trying to communicate.

10. Throughout recorded history war has not always been a popular way of settling disputes between nations. Research newspapers for political cartoons or editorials or research music history for "protest" songs to illustrate this attitude.

11. Discuss the evolution of war from "throwing rocks" to nuclear weapons. What are the ramifications for each of us in the future?

NATIVE-AMERICAN POPULATIONS IN 1492

TEACHER-DIRECTED ACTIVITIES FOR STUDENTS

1. Examine the number of different Native-American peoples that existed when Columbus reached the new world in 1492 (see illustration). How many still exist today? Discuss what happened to the others.

2. Discuss whether the term *Indian* is a correct or even appropriate term when referring to the native populations of North and South America.

3. Identify the Native-American population that lives or lived in your area. If still in the area, invite a spokesperson to your classroom for a discussion of his or her history and culture. If no native population still lives in your area, try and discover what happened to them.

4. Compare and contrast the similarities and differences of native populations across continental America. Pay special attention to their traditional dress, customs, language, art, and religion.

5. Research what other areas of the world had native populations before the age of discovery and exploration. How were they similar to America? What happened to them?

6. Discuss where, if any, there are native populations still living outside of the United States and what their future will look like as we approach the year 2000.

7. Research and discuss the Native-American reverence for earth philosophy. Draw some comparisons with other philosophies or doctrines currently popular.

8. List all the stereotypes you can regarding "Indians" and discuss the credibility of these viewpoints.

9. Speculate on how the United States of America would be different if it had settled by Asian peoples who landed on the West Coast. Would our attitudes and policies toward Native Americans be the same or different?

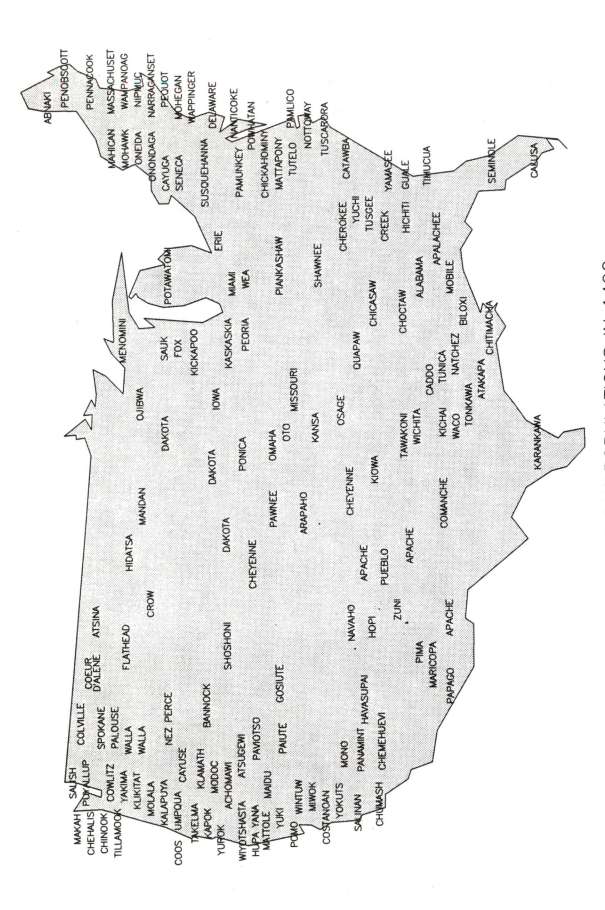

NATIVE AMERICAN POPULATIONS IN 1492

CHAPTER 5

Voices from the Past

If you want the present to be different from the past, study the past.
BARUCH SPINOZA

USING PRIMARY RESOURCES IN SOCIAL STUDIES EDUCATION

A primary resource is a source in its original form that comes from a person who was directly involved in an event and recorded his or her observations. Why are primary resources important? Students learn about the past and acquire historical perspective as they come into direct contact with people from the past. Imagine how exciting it is to be able to listen to the actual voice of Thomas Alva Edison describe how he invented the incandescent lightbulb or to read Clara Barton's notes on how the International Red Cross came into being. Think also of how greatly enriched the study of American history could be by having students read the words and impressions of people like Lewis and Clark as they chronicled in detail their 8,000-mile journey some 200 years ago.

Not only are such happenings exciting but they are very important factors in making history relevant and come alive for each of us. Academically, primary resources provide opportunities for students to go well beyond the textbook accounts of history and engage in more inquiry-oriented learning processes. Best of all, perhaps, is the easy access to a great variety of resources available to teachers and students. Listed here are some of those resources and a rationale for their employment in social studies education.

FIVE GOOD REASONS FOR USING PRIMARY RESOURCES

1. Primary source materials add the "meat" to the dry bones of history!
2. These materials enrich and enhance the basic information that is generally only briefly reviewed by traditional school textbooks.
3. Source materials bring students into direct contact with the people who lived and made history.
4. Source materials give students some insights into how social scientists gather information.
5. Source materials encourage students to engage in higher-level thinking skills such as analysis, synthesis, and evaluation.

SOME SUGGESTED RESOURCES
1. Library of Congress, Washington, DC
2. The Queens Printing House, Ottawa, Canada
3. Family collections:
   Diaries
   Letters
   Family histories
   Oral histories
   Family bibles
4. Newspapers
5. Autobiographies
6. Biographies
7. Local resource persons
8. Commercially produced source material kits
9. Library collections
10. Embassies

These are excellent resources, and, for a very small investment, teachers can build their own resource file. Teachers might also consider having resource and artifact drives in their communities. That is, teachers ask local residents to lend their family histories, bibles, letters, diaries, photos, and so on for classroom use. The eagerness and generosity of patrons and fellow citizens will be amazing.

The remainder of this chapter contains samplings of the kind of primary resources that may be used in the study of history. Included are a letter, a manuscript, and personal recollections of a significant event in history. When using primary resources, the following activities are suggested:

TEACHER-DIRECTED ACTIVITIES FOR STUDENTS
1. After reading a document, identify what event was being described and what you learned from the document.
2. Identify in which historical period the event happened. Then, using almanacs and encyclopedias, trace what other major events were going on at that same time in history.
3. Trace the life and times of the writer. See if you can discover what happened to the person or the event(s) being described.
4. How do we know that the document is "real" and not a fake? List some specific examples of "real" sources and fake sources.

EXCERPTS

This is part of a letter written by Christopher Columbus to Lord Raphael Sanchez, an official at the Spanish court of Ferdinand and Isabella after his first voyage to the "new world."

EXCERPTS FROM A CHRISTOPHER COLUMBUS LETTER

March 14, 1493

Knowing that it will give you pleasure to learn that I have brought my project to a successful end, I have decided to write you about all the events which occurred on my voyage.

Thirty-three days after my departure, I reached the Indian Sea, where I discovered many islands, thickly populated. I took possession of them in the name of our great King, by means of a public announcement. To the first of these islands

I gave the name of the blessed Savior (San Salvador), under whose protection I had reached this and other islands. To each island I gave a name, ordering that one should be called Santa Maria de la Concepcion, another Fernandina, the third Isabella, the fourth Juana (Cuba), and so on.

In all the islands there is no difference in the physical appearance of the inhabitants or in their manners or language. They all understand each other clearly, a fact which should help our glorious King reach what I assume is his main goal—the conversion of these people to a belief in Christ. . . .

As to the advantages to be gained from my voyage, with a little assistance from our great rulers, I can get them as much gold as they need, as much spice, cotton, and pitch as they can use, and as many men for the navy as Their Majesties require. I can bring back rhubarb and other kinds of drugs. In fact, I am sure that the men I left in the fort have already found some.

Therefore, let the King and Queen, our Princes, their happy kingdoms, and all the other provinces where Christ is worshipped give thanks to our Lord and Savior Jesus Christ, who has given us this great victory and much prosperity. Let there be parades and sacred feasts, and let the churches be decorated. Let Christ rejoice on earth as he rejoices in heaven at the thought of saving so many souls in so many nations that would otherwise have been lost. (From Brady, Marion, & Howard Brady. *Idea and Action in American History*, Prentice Hall, 1977, p. 14.)

Excerpts from Samuel Pepys's diary describes the "Great Fire of London," which virtually destroyed the city in August of 1666. Pepys was a retired naval officer who kept the only known complete diary of this period of history, giving us a true picture of Elizabethan England.

EXCERPTS FROM SAMUEL PEPYS'S DIARY

August 2, 1666

Some of our mayds sitting up late last night to get things ready against our feast to-day, Jane called us up about three in the morning, to tell us of a great fire they saw in the City. So I rose and slipped on my night-gowne, and went to her window, and thought it to be on the backside of Marke-lane at the farthest; but, being unused to such fires as followed, I thought it far enough off; and so went to bed again and to sleep. About seven rose again to dress myself, and there looked out at the window, and saw the fire not so much as it was and further off. So to my closett to set things to rights after yesterday's cleaning. By and by Jane comes and tells me that she hears that above 300 houses have been burned down to-night by the fire we saw, and that it is now burning down all Fish-street, by London Bridge. So I made myself ready presently, and walked to the Tower, and there got up upon one of the high places, Sir J. Robinson's little son going up with me; and there I did see the houses at that end of the bridge all on fire, and an infinite great fire on this and the other side the end of the bridge . . . the Lieutenant of the Tower, who tells me that it begun this morning in the King's baker's house in Pudding-lane, and that it hath burned St. Magnus's Church and most part of Fish Street. . . . Having staid, and in an hour's time seen the fire rage every way, and nobody, to my sight, endeavouring to quench it, but to remove their goods, and leave all to the fire. . . . So I was called for, and did tell the King and Duke of Yorke what I saw, and that unless his Majesty did command houses to be pulled down nothing could stop the fire. . . . At last met my Lord Mayor in Canning-street, like a man spent, with a handkercher about his neck. To the King's message he cried, like a fainting woman, "Lord! what can I do? I am spent; people will not obey me. I have been pulling down houses; but the fire overtakes us faster than we can do it." That he needed no more soldiers; and that, for himself, he must go and refresh himself, having been up all night. So he left me, and I him, and walked home, seeing people all almost distracted, and no manner of means used to quench the fire. The houses, too, so very thick therabouts, and full of matter for burning, as pitch and tarr, in Thames-street; and warehouses of oyle, and wines, and brandy, and other things. Here I saw

Mr. Issake Houblon, the handsome man, prettily dressed and dirty, at his door at Dowgate, receiving some of his brothers' things, whose house was on fire; and, as he says, have been removed twice already; and he doubts (as it soon proved) that they must be in a little time removed from his house also, which was a sad consideration. And to see the churches all filling with goods by people who themselves should have been quietly there at this time. By this time it was about twelve o'clock; and so home. . . . All over the Thames, with ones face in the wind, you were almost burned with a shower of fire drops. . . . So as houses were burned by the drops and flakes of fire, three or four, nay, five or six houses, one from another . . . we could endure no more upon the water, we to a little ale-house on the Bankside . . . and there staid till it was dark almost, and saw the fire grow; and, as it grew darker, appeared more and more . . . in corners . . . upon steeples . . . between churches and houses . . . it made me weep to see it. (From *The Diary of Samuel Pepys*. Vols. IV–VI, 1664–1667. Harcourt, Brace and Company, New York, 1924, pp. 392–396.)

These are excerpts from a pamphlet entitled "Common Sense" and written by Thomas Paine in 1776 exhorting his fellow citizens to seek independence from Great Britain.

"COMMON SENSE" BY THOMAS PAINE

In the following pages I offer nothing more than simple facts, plain arguments, and common sense. . . .

Some say that because America has done well under Great Britain in the past, her future happiness depends on continuing the relationship. Nothing could be more wrong. One might as well claim that because a child has done well on milk, it should never have meat.

Others say, "England has protected us." That she has defended our continent at our expense, as well as her own, is admitted. But she would have defended Turkey for the same reasons—trade and power.

"But Britain is our parent country," some say. Then that makes her behavior all the more shameful. Even brute animals do not devour their young, nor savages make war on their families. Europe, not England, is the parent of America. This new world has been a home for mistreated lovers of liberty from every part of Europe. They have come here, not from a mother's tender embraces, but to escape the cruelty of the monster.

Any connection with Great Britain tends to involve us in European wars and quarrels, and set us against nations which would otherwise be friendly. Since all of Europe is our market, we should not favor any one part of it.

It is only right and reasonable that we separate. The blood of the dead cries, "Tis time to part." Even the distance God has placed America from England is natural proof that rule of one by the other was not what Heaven intended.

But if you say you are still willing to overlook the wrongs England has done us, then I ask, "Has your house been burned? Has your property been destroyed before your eyes? Are your wife and children without a bed to lie on or bread to eat? Have you lost a parent or child by their hands and you are the heart-broken survivor?" If you have not, then you are not a judge of those who have. but if you have, and can still shake hands with the murderers, then whatever be your rank in life, you are a coward.

Every quiet method to settle our differences peacefully has failed. Our plans have been turned down scornfully. So, since nothing but fighting will work, for God's sake let us come to final separation.

George Washington's farewell address was a formal announcement to the nation he loved that he was not going to run for a third term. It was written in 1792, four years prior to its publication, by Washington and James Madison. At the end of his second term, Washington pulled out the address, dusted it off, and sent it to John Jay and Alexander Hamilton for their input and suggestions. After numerous edits, the address was published on September 19, 1796, in the *American Daily Advertiser* in Philadelphia.

The address represents the thoughts and character of George Washington. It is the "warnings of a parting friend." He stressed the need for a firm union and a strong central government, and warned against permanent alliances abroad. The farewell address also stressed the concept of isolationism, staying out of world affairs. The trend of isolationism dominated the U.S. foreign policy for most of its history. While there have been numerous disputes, the overall belief in isolationism held until the twentieth century.

GEORGE WASHINGTON'S FAREWELL ADDRESS

It is of infinite moment that you should properly estimate the immense value of your national union to your collective and individual happiness. . . . The name of American, which belongs to you in your national capacity, must always exalt the just pride of patriotism more than any appellation derived from local discriminations. . . . The very idea of the power and the right of the people to establish government presupposes the duty of every individual to obey the established government. . . . Let me . . . warn you in the most solemn manner against the baneful effects of the spirit of party generally. . . . A fire not to be quenched, it demands a uniform vigilance to prevent its bursting into a flame, lest, instead of warning, it should consume. . . .

Of all dispositions and habits which lead to political prosperity, religion and morality are indispensable supports. . . . Promote, them, as an object of primary importance, institutions for the general diffusion of knowledge. In proportion as the structure of a government gives force to public opinion, it is essential that public opinion should be enlightened. As a very important source of strength and security, cherish public credit. . . . Observe good faith and justice toward all nations. Cultivate peace and harmony with all. . . .

The nation which indulges toward another an habitual hatred or an habitual fondness is in some degree a slave. . . . The great rule of conduct for us in regard to foreign nations, is, in extending our commercial relations to have with them as little political connection as possible. . . .

The Monroe Doctrine established the basic position of U.S. foreign policy. It was formulated by President James Monroe and Secretary of State John Quincy Adams. The Doctrine, which was delivered by President Monroe to Congress on December 2, 1823, held two major clauses:

1. It warned that the United States would oppose establishment of any new European colony in the Americas.
2. Interference in the internal affairs of American nations by Europe would not be tolerated.

The Doctrine was meant to deal with the Russian threat in the Pacific Northwest and Spain's threat to recover Latin American colonies. It held no legal status and was virtually unenforceable. As these two threats died down, the Doctrine was basically forgotten. It was later revived by President James Polk when concern rose surrounding the annexation of Texas and the settlement of the Oregon Territory.

Through Polk's revival, the Doctrine was established as the cornerstone of U.S. foreign policy. It was called upon in later disputes—the Civil War; the 1895 dispute with Great Britain over the boundary of British Guiana; in 1902 when Great Britain, Germany, and Italy blockaded Venezuela to collect revenues owed to them; and in the 1962 controversy over Soviet long-range missiles in Cuba.

Although the Monroe Doctrine was established as the cornerstone of the U.S. foreign policy, it received little recognition from other countries. It was not until after World War II that the League of Nations officially recognized it. In 1940, under Franklin Roosevelt, as a result of the Nazi threat, the Doctrine received a new and democratic interpretation. An attack on any American republic was an attack on them all. It received formal adoption in 1941 when Congress made it a law. In a sense, the Doctrine did not obtain international recognition until the twentieth century.

The Monroe Doctrine has played a major role in U.S. foreign policy throughout history. Recognized legally by the world or not, it has been involved in and settled many disputes over foreign threats. Today, the United States still opposes European and Communist intervention in the Western hemisphere but it does not do so much on its own. Through cooperation with Latin America and Canada, the nations of America uphold the Doctrine.

THE MONROE DOCTRINE

The occasion has been judged proper for asserting as a principle in which the rights and interests of United States are involved, that the American continents, by the free and independent condition which they have assumed and maintain, are henceforth not to be considered as subjects for future colonization by any European powers. . . . The political system of the allied powers is essentially different in this respect from that of America. . . .

We owe it, therefore, to candor, and to the amicable relations existing between the United States and those powers, to declare that we should consider any attempt on their part to extend their system to any portion of this hemisphere as dangerous to our peace and safety. With the existing colonies or dependencies of any European power we have not interfered and shall not interfere. But with the governments who have declared their independence, and maintained it, and whose independence we have, on great consideration and on just principles, acknowledged, we could not view any interposition for the purpose of oppressing them, or controlling in any other manner their destiny, by any European power, in any other light than as the manifestation of an unfriendly disposition towards the United States. . . . Our policy in regard to Europe, which was adopted at an early stage of the wars which have so long agitated that quarter of the globe, nevertheless remains the same, which is, not to interfere in the internal concerns of any of its powers; to consider the government de facto as the legitimate government for us; to cultivate friendly relations with it, and to preserve those relations be a frank, firm, and manly policy, meeting, in all instances, the just claims of every power; submitting to injuries from none. But in regard to these continents circumstances are eminently and conspicuously different. It is impossible that the allied powers should extend their political system to any portion of either continent without endangering our peace and happiness; now can anyone believe that our southern brethren, if left to themselves, would adopt it of their own accord. It is equally impossible, therefore, that we should behold such interposition, in any form, with indifference.

President Abraham Lincoln delivered this speech on November 19, 1863, at the site of the Battle of Gettysburg in Pennsylvania to dedicate part of the battlefield as a cemetery for those who lost their lives during this significant battle.

Lincoln made five handwritten copies of the speech. He planned to read the second version and he held it in his hand while speaking. But he made some changes as he spoke. He added "under God" after the word *nation* in the last sentence.

Several reporters took down his words while he spoke. Lincoln signed only one copy of the address and this, the fifth version, is the one carved on a stone plaque in the Lincoln Memorial.

The Battle of Gettysburg was perhaps the single most important battle in the United States history. Out of the smoke, flame, and death, one of this country's greatest literary works was created by Abraham Lincoln. This speech served to set the stage by awakening those principles on which this country was founded. The Gettysburg Address set the tone for unifying our divided nation.

The Battle of Gettysburg was fought on July 1, 2, and 3 in 1863. Gettysburg is a small town located in southern Pennsylvania. The geography of the area consists of rolling hills and valleys. On July 1, 1863, two armies faced each other on opposing ridges. General George Meade commanded the northern army while General Robert E. Lee commanded the southern army. Over a three-day period 50,000 northern and southern troops would die. This high fatality so saddened Lincoln that five different speeches were written to commemorate this battle. It is stated that the final speech was completed on the back of an old envelope while Lincoln was traveling by train to Gettysburg.

On November 19, 1863, Gettysburg was dedicated as a national cemetery by Abraham Lincoln. Today Gettysburg is a national historical monument. This monument serves to remind us all not only of the men who died there but of Abraham Lincoln who unified a nation without malice toward anyone.

VOCABULARY

Score: An old English word that refers to the number 20.
Forth: To go forward in time. Syn. *forward*
Conceived: to form an idea. Syn. *visualized*
Liberty: The right to act in a manner of one's own choosing. Syn. *freedom*
Dedicated: To set apart for some special use. Syn. *commit*
Proposition: A plan suggested for acceptance. Syn. *propose*
Endure: To continue in existence. Syn. *continue*
Consecrate: To declare or set apart as sacred. Syn. *dedicate*
Detract: To take away a desirable part. Syn. *wriote off*
Hallow: To honor as being holy. Syn. *devote*
Honored: Glory, distinction. Syn. *respect*
Nobly: Showing greatness. Syn. *grand*
Devotion: Attached to an idea or person. Syn. *loyal*
Resolve: To make a decision. Syn. *decide*
Vain: Devoid of worth or value. Syn. *empty*

THE GETTYSBURG ADDRESS

Four score and seven years ago our fathers brought forth on this continent a new nation, conceived in liberty and dedicated to the proposition that all men are created equal.

Now we are engaged in a great civil war, testing whether that nation or any nation so conceived and so dedicated can long endure.

We are met on a great battle-field of that war. We have come to dedicate a portion of that field as a final resting place of those who here gave their lives that that nation might live.

It is altogether fitting and proper that we should do this. But, in a larger sense, we cannot dedicate, we cannot consecrate, we cannot hallow this ground. The brave men, living and dead, who struggled here have consecrated it far above our poor power to add or detract.

The world will little note nor long remember what we say here. But it can never forget what they did here.

It is for us the living, rather, to be dedicated here to the unfinished work which they who fought here have thus far so nobly advanced. It is rather for us to be here dedicated to the great task remaining before us, that from these honored dead we take increased devotion to that cause for which they gave the last full measure of devotion; that we here highly resolve that these dead shall not have died in vain; that this nation, under God, shall have a new birth of freedom, and that government of the people, by the people, and for the people shall not perish from the earth.

Today, Jim Migaki is an Associate Professor at Washington State University in Pullman, Washington. The following is his childhood recollection of December 7, 1941, the day the Japanese invaded Pearl Harbor.

A JAPANESE-AMERICAN REMEMBERS DECEMBER 7, 1941

My cousin's wedding was typical, traditional, and, to this child, boring. We had to sit in front pews even if we were the first ones at the church. "Sit still. Don't fidget. Want a Lifesaver?" Well, what could you do? The whole congregation was sitting behind you. Everybody in the community knew you (me) and you can't do anything that would embarrass the family. Besides, I didn't want to go to Hell and there was that possibility—even in church.

The recption after the wedding was a different story. It was in the "Round-Up Room" of the Desert Hotel, long-gone but fondly remembered. At the time, it seemed that a reception was the only good thing about marriage and weddings. Food, cake, ice cream, laughter, sliding around on the "Spangle"-slicked floor, music. Was there anything better? Sure! It was the brass banister on which my friends and I were sliding. It was during this activity that the police arrived. We stopped sliding on the banister immediately (I thought they were kidding about what would happen if we didn't behave).

It was later learned that the police, detectives, FBI men were not really invited guests. The silence that fell upon the room would nowadays demand the question: "Who's the fink that filed a noise complaint?" The conversations became whispered. There was crying again, but it was different and frightening, not happy and confusing as at the wedding. Some of the community leaders were escorted out of the room into waiting police cars. But, hey, this was exciting! They even had guns. It was better than listening to "Gangbusters" on the radio. Do all wedding receptions end this way? Why do we have to hurry home? What's Pearl Harbor? Bomb? War? Boy, weddings are really stupid!

Some of the details became clear on the way home. This was serious stuff. But as I was getting ready for bed, the usual routine was interrupted by the doorbell, followed by strange but polite voices. They were sorry to disturb us but they had to search the house. I peeked down the warm air vent in my bedroom floor and saw two men in the living room below me. Another one or two men were in the kitchen. It was still exciting, but the excitement of wonder and ignorance was now one of fear gelled by the reality of intrusion. They were coming upstairs. I'd better get in bed.

"Who's is all this?" "It's my brother's." "Oh, he must like science stuff" (whew, they didn't see my fireworks). "Who's is this?" "It's my brother's." "I'm afraid we'll have to take this. You'll get a receipt for it." (Maybe they found the fireworks, maybe they found the rockets or bombs I made. I'm in big trouble. Maybe they're taking my chemicals. Please, not my chemicals. I hate the Japanese. Why'd they have to bomb that place? Wait a minute, I'm Japanese. No, I'm American. Oh, oh, they're coming in here.)

"Hi, fella!" (Well, he knows I'm awake, no sense trying to fake it.) "Is this yours?" "Yes, my sister got it for me. I switched the speaker and put in earphone plugs." "Mind if I lsiten?" "OK." And what's this for?" "That's the ground. It goes out to the lightning arrestor and then to a pipe outside." "Oh, that's pretty nice, son. Thanks for letting me listen." (Yeah, but what did you take?) They looked around the other bedrooms and went downstairs. I must have fallen asleep. I don't know when they left.

"What did they take?" Breakfast was more interesting than usual. "What's on the radio? Hey, where's the radio?" "They took it." "What did they take that was mine?" "They took your B-B gun. They took our camera, too." "How come?" There were no satisfying answers, just many unanswered questions. For example: Why did they take the little radio on the refrigerator and leave mine?

School was pretty much normal. We learned about the bombing and I found out where Pearl Harbor was. My friends were still my friends and they seemed even friendlier as the days went by—some parents were a bit different.

Our family was not "relocated" and only a few persons from Spokane were "sent away." I guess "they" felt we were not a particular threat. Our lives were changed, though, and it was probably no different when love and hate are trying to coexist. Many of my experiences during the war period were not much changed or different from those of my Caucasian friends. My personal interpretations of similar experiences, however, were probably very much different.

I remember the father of one of my best friends: He was a successful (at least they had a nice home) businessman. At one time at his home, he asked how things were going. He mentioned how "his people" had been treated throughout history (they were Jewish). He made it a point to emphasize that I was welcome. I could "feel" what he was saying, but it didn't really sink in until years later.

There were other friends—and parents. One parent was an attorney. They had just moved to a "snob address" house. While playing with my friend and his dog, the father called my friend into another room. My friend came back with tears in his eyes. I thought he had been punished. He told me that I had to go home because his father didn't want me around the house. His father was "starting out" and didn't want to have people think his son was friendly with a Jap. We started playing at my house. Interestingly, even after fifty years, we still communicate and talk on the phone. We both ended up in higher education.

As the war went on, little incidents are remembered. One day, as I was riding my bike, a man yelled at me from the sidewalk: "Hey, kid, c'mere." I rode toward him—but not too close—and asked, "What?" "You a Chink or a Jap?" "I'm American," I answered. "Good fer you, kid. Here, take this. You Japs have it tough." He gave me a quarter. He was obviously drunk, but I didn't care. A quarter could buy five candy bars—if you could find any to buy.

Blackouts were inconvenient and a bit scary at first. There was also a curfew. Civil Defense tests were something else. Cubs and Scouts were asked to volunteer to be "victims" during a mock air attack. We were given specific locations near our homes where we were to be when the siren sounded. We had tags pinned on us. My tag said "burns, abrasions, phosphorous bomb." I sat on the corner until a man with an armband with "CD" in a triangle in a circle approached. He read my tag, wrote something in a small book, and walked off. A minute or so later, he and two other men came by. They talked about Scouts, Japs, kids, and the tag and treatments. They told me to go home. I was about two blocks from home but it was probably two or three hours before I got there.

What great fun this was! Everywhere was pitch black. No street lights, no house lights, only the occasional blade of light from a flashlight cutting through the blackness. You could hear people walking and talking, but the sounds came from nowhere. I knew every nook and cranny in the neighborhood. If I was a spy, I could blow up anything I wanted, run away in the dark or hide in one of the "secret places" that all kids have. Someone else must have had the same thoughts because I was never asked to volunteer again. Somewhere in my accumulation of junk, I probably still have that "Junior Warden" armband.

Houses had to have blackout curtains and most were black. No light was to be seen from the outside. This was to foil enemy bombers looking for targets. From the outside, though, you could still see an occasional spark from a chimney. Well, no matter, the enemy was too dumb to notice that.

From the inside of the house you got a different, gloomy, even morbid perspective. I used to wonder if the Ball and Dodd Funeral Home always looked like this. It wasn't far from our house (they have since moved from their prior location on Fourth and Jefferson).

An interesting rumor (there were many circulating) was that the Benewah Milk Bottle on Cedar between Third and Fourth (it's still there) was being used to hide an anti-aircraft cannon. This was proved to be false when a worker there let us look up through the ceiling where a light fixture could be lifted. The three of us in the store at the time never told anyone—the rumor was more fun than the truth. We even added to the story by telling others that the ladder on the side was for reaching the "spotter's" platform. This allowed someone to hide in the top of the bottle and watch for enemy aircraft. The spotter up there was, of course, a high-ranking officer from Geiger Army Air Force Base.

Before the war even started, our home was always crowded by "old" guys. This was most likely due to my mother's cooking and my five older sisters. Interestingly, many of these men were students at Washington State University (Washington State College at the time). After the war started, some volunteered, others were drafted, but they still appeared at infrequent times. Our house was/seemed to be a small USO for the Japanese-American service men in the area. Two of them eventually became brothers-in-law. Both were highly decorated, one in the 442nd, the other in the CBI Theater. The one in the China-Burma-India Theater got malaria in the jungles of Burma. (In later years I suggested to him that it [malaria] must have affected his brain. He transferred to the University of Washington and got his degree there.)

It was not unusual to have a houseful of servicemen on weekends. It was a most fruitful time for me. I was probably the only kid in the neighborhood who always had gum and candy—courtesy of the PX and K rations via the men who liked my mother's cooking and/or my sisters. Either way, I couldn't lose. If I wasn't happy, I could make life miserable for them. I was always happy.

The only real fight I ever got into during my school years resulted from a racial slur. During a football game, I caught a pass and was being chased by the opposing team members. One of them yelled, "Catch that Jap!" After the excitement of the touchdown, several players on both teams persuaded me and the other player into a fight—as kids often "persuade." He was actually getting the best of me until he ran off toward his house. I tackled him on the sidewalk and was pounding his head on the concrete when the coach arrived and broke us apart. The crowd disappeared as the coach arrived. After a lengthy lecture, the other fellow left for his house and the coach and I walked toward the school. We talked about the war, kids teasing about Japs, and nearly everything except football. That coach eventually became a junior high principal and I ended up teaching at his school many years later. The fight, however, was the only real overt violence experienced. The other fellow and I became friends in the next few days, but it was interesting to note that he was never really accepted by others as I was. He later became accepted and eventually established quite a record as a boat racer. I went on to car racing.

Most of the other events caused by the war were probably little different in their impact on Japanese Americans than on Caucasian Americans, excluding those who were relocated. There were the occasional signs "We don't serve Japs" in restaurant windows; the periodic sneers and whispered comments in public, but not much that really affected my life at the time.

Some of my friends were probably more sensitive to racism and prejudice than I was. One instance comes to mind: The Spokane schools had a weekly program called "The Spokane Rangers Are on the Air." They had try-outs for the elementary student part on the program. Three of us ended up as finalists for the part. The two of us who did not get the part were informed by some of our fellow students that I did not get it because I was Japanese and the other fellow didn't get it because he was Jewish. Actually, the best choice was made. The fellow who did get the part had the ability, and also his father was in the Air Force—the only parent of the three of us who was in the armed forces. It was a great choice. Besides, the issue of racism in our schools was never encountered. If anything, teachers and students seemed more supportive and sympathetic. When it did occur, it was always with persons who were strangers in more public situations. Even during the war it often seemed that Black Americans had it rougher than the Asian Americans. This was even expressed to me by some of my Black-American friends.

As stated at the beginning, this is written from the perspective of a child and a memory tinted with a bit of nostalgia. It is, however, as accurate as I remember it.

CHAPTER 6

Enriching Social Studies Instruction

Teaching of others, teacheth the teacher. —THOMAS FULLER

PATRIOTIC TO PROTEST: TEACHING SOCIAL STUDIES THROUGH MUSIC

Probably no other medium better illustrates a group's history and culture than does music. Certainly, literature, art, and architecture also reflect social, cultural, and historical attitudes, but music seems to be the most articulate narrative of the human condition throughout history. This is especially true in the study of American history. Virtually every generation, since the first permanent settlers arrived on this continent, has produced artisans who have poignantly captured and chronicled our national being in lyric and music. These composers and performers give us a clear picture of our national psyche—who we were, how we lived, and what we believed.

Aside from the more familiar popular and patriotic music of mainstream America, there were also those artists who gave us an intimate glimpse into the lives and times of the "other Americans" trying to cope and survive in a nation either aloof or hostile to their very presence. The many ethnic and social subcultures, frequently only glossed over in traditional history textbooks, had their respective music and traditions recorded and performed by artists who forever preserved their rich heritage and cultures. In many instances, these artisans became the historians of the politically and socially disenfranchised.

Fortunately, most of this music has survived and certainly much of what we now know about Black, Hispanic, and Native-American history and culture is directly traceable to the efforts of the musicians who preserved it. Most importantly for educators, the music affords us with a marvelous vehicle to enrich the teaching of history and provide students with an opportunity to experience and celebrate the rich social and cultural diversity that makes the United States of America a truly unique nation.

The following selections are but a few examples of the music that both illustrate our history as well as chronicle our ever-changing national character. Be it patriotic, ethnic, cultural, or protest, American music often defines American history and helps clarify our understanding of the past.

Included with some of the selections is background information, biographical sketches, and classroom-ready activities. The section also contains a bibliography for classroom use.

Patriotic Music

This is the music that inspires us and rekindles our national pride! Whether it be the national anthem or a rousing march by John Philip Sousa, we find our patriotism surging forward and experience a feeling of great pride in our nation, especially during those special times like the Fourth of July or the Olympic games. Listed below are a few of those songs.

"Yankee Doodle"

"Yankee Doodle" was probably written by an English army surgeon, Dr. Richard Schuckburg. Essentially, he wrote it to poke fun at the unrefined and untrained colonial American soldiers during the French and Indian Wars. The American colonials then picked up the tune and created their own verses to the music. When General Cornwallis surrendered, the victorious Americans sang "Yankee Doodle" as the defeated British army marched out of Yorktown while the British band played "The World Turned Upside Down."

"YANKEE DOODLE"
Father and I went down to camp,
Along with Captain Goodwin,
And there we saw the men and boys,
As thick and hasty puddin'

Chorus: Yankee Doodle keep it up
Yankee Doodle dandy
Mind the music and the step
And with the girls be handy

And there was Captain Washington,
Upon a slappin' stallion,
And giving orders to his men,
I guess there was a million

Chorus

And the feathers on his hat,
They looked so 'tarnal finy,
I wanted peskely to get
To give to my Jemina

Chorus

And then they had a swamping gun,
As big as a log of maple,
On a deuced little cart,
A load for father's cattle.

Chorus

"The Star-Spangled Banner"

Music by John Staford Smith, Words by Francis Scott Key

"The Star-Spangled Banner," as with so many of the patriotic songs and national anthems, was brought about from the struggle of people to be free. In the War of 1812, the United States was fighting to maintain its hard-earned independence from Great Britain. By 1814, the British forces had captured and burned the city of Washington DC. Their next goal was to seize and occupy the port of Baltimore, which provided access for the much needed food and supplies for American defenses. On September 13, 1814, the British sailed up chesapeake Bay, preparing to launch an attack against Fort McHenry, which guarded the entrance to Baltimore's harbor.

Francis Scott Key, a young lawyer, visited the admiral to the British fleet just prior to the battle. Under a flag of truce, Key requested the release of an American prisoner of war. The admiral was willing, but would allow no one to go ashore until the bombardment of Fort McHenry was completed. Throughout the day and night, Key watched the shelling from the deck of a ship in the attacking British fleet. "As the first rays of the sun appeared, he was immensely relieved to see 'Old Glory' still proudly flying over the battered fort." On the back of the letter, he wrote the beginning lines, "Oh, say can you see?" The poem was completed later that evening and was printed in *The Baltimore Patriot* under the title, "The Defense of Fort McHenry." Shortly afterward, the poem was sung to the tune of a popular English drinking song, "To Anacreon in Heaven." "The Star-Spangled Banner" was designated as the official national anthem of the United States by an Act of Congress in 1931.

Portions of "The Star-Spangled Banner" have been used as thematic material by other composers. When Arturo Toscanini revived "Hymn of the Nations" by Verdi during World War II, he added "The Star-Spangled Banner" to the national anthems of England, France, and Italy which Verdi had included in his score. The performance of this tremendous work can be heard on records or in film "Hymn of the Nations" produced by the United States Office of War Information.

The opening phrases of "The Star-Spangled Banner" were also used by Giacomo Puccini in his opera, *Madame Butterfly*. Additionally, Victor Herbert includes it as a climax to *American Fantasy*, a musical tribute to the United States, his adopted land.

"THE STAR-SPANGLED BANNER"

O say! can you see, by the dawn's early light,
What so proudly we hailed at the twilight's last gleaming?
Whose broad stripes and bright stars, through the perilous fight,
O'er the ramparts we watched, were so gallantly streaming!
And the rockets' red glare, the bombs bursting in air,
Gave proof through the night that our flag was still there.
O say, does that Star-Spangled Banner yet wave
O'er the land of the free and the home of the brave?

On the shore dimly seen through the mists of the deep,
Where the foe's haughty host in dread silence reposes,
What is that which the breeze, o'er the towering steep,
As it fitfully blows, half conceals, half discloses?
Now it catches the gleam of the morning's first beam,
In full glory reflected now shines on the stream;
'Tis the Star-Spangled Banner, O long may it wave
O'er the land of the free and the home of the brave!

O thus be it ever when free men shall stand
Between their loved homes and the war's desolation!
Blest with vict'ry and peace, may the heav'n rescued land
Praise the Pow'r that hath made and preserved us a nation,
Then conquer we must, when our cause it is just,
And this be our motto: "In God is our trust!"
And the Star-spangled Banner, In triumph shall wave
O'er the land of the free and the home of the brave!

"America"

Music by Henry Carey, Words by Samuel Frances Smith

The melody of "America" is credited to Henry Carey, a popular English composer and dramatist from the early eighteenth century.

Samuel Smith best shares how the words of "America" came to be written:

The hymn "America" was the fruit of examining a number of music books and songs for German public schools. . . . Falling in with the tune of one of them, now called "America," and being pleased with its simple and easy movement, I glanced at the German words, and seeing that they were patriotic, instantly felt the impulse to write a patriotic hymn of my own, to the same tune. Seizing a scrap of waste paper, I put upon it within half an hour the verses substantially as they stand today. I did not propose to write a national hymn. I did not know that I had done so. The whole matter passed out of my mind. A few weeks afterwards I sent to Mr. Mason some translations and other poems; this must have chanced to be among them. This occurred in February, 1832. To my surprise, I found later that he had incorporated it into the programme for the celebration of the Fourth of July, 1832, in Park Street Church, Boston. When this was composed I was profoundly impressed with the necessary relation between love of God and love of country; and I rejoice if the expression of my own sentiments and convictions still finds an answering chord in the hearts of my countrymen (Charles Leonhard, *Discovering Music Together*, Follett Educational Corporation, Chicago, 1967)

"AMERICA"
My country! 'tis of thee,
Sweet land of liberty,
Of thee I sing;
Land where my fathers died,
Land of the Pilgrim's pride,
From ev'ry mountain side
Let freedom ring.

My native country,
Land of the noble free,
Thy name I love,
I love thy rocks and rills,
Thy woods and templed hills;
My heart with rapture thrills
Like that above.

Let music swell the breeze,
And ring from all the trees,
Sweet Freedom's song;
Let mortal tongues awake,
Let all that breathe partake,
Let rocks their silence break,
The sound prolong.

Our fathers' God, to Thee,
Author of liberty,
To Thee we sing;
Long may our land be bright
With Freedom's holy light;
Protect us by Thy might,
Great God, our King!

"America, The Beautiful"

Music by Samuel A. Ward, Words by Katherine Lee Bates

In 1895, Katherine Bates, an English professor at Wellesley College, visited Pike's Peak in Colorado. She was so inspired by the "beauty of the vast expanse before her eyes" that she wrote this poem reflecting great pride in the grandeur and magnificence of our country.

Samuel Ward, an American composer, set the poem to music. "America, The Beautiful" was the first patriotic song for which both words and music were written by native-born Americans.

"AMERICA, THE BEAUTIFUL"
O beautiful for spacious skies,
For amber waves of grain,
For purple mountains majesties,
Above the fruited plain!
America! America!
God shed his grace on thee,
And crown thy good with brotherhood
From sea to shining sea!

O beautiful for pilgrim feet,
Whose stern impassioned stress
A thoroughfare for freedom beat
Across the wilderness!
America! America!
God mend thine every flaw,
Confirm thy soul in self-control,
Thy liberty in law!

O beautiful for heroes proved,
In liberating strife,
Who more than self their country loved,
And mercy more than life!
America! America!
May God Thy gold refine,
Till all success be nobleness,
And every gain divine!

O beautiful for patriot dream,
That sees beyond the years,
Thine alabaster cities gleam
Undimmed by human tears!
America! America!
God shed His grace on thee,
And crown thy good with brotherhood,
From sea to shining sea!

One could also include in this section the many songs by Irving Berlin, the patriotic "war" songs of World War I and II, as well as Woody Gutherie's "This Land Is Your Land." Indeed, an interesting and fun class project is to identify and collect patriotic music that was popular during our times of national crisis and discuss how music mirrors our national psyche.

Historical Music

Historical music is that music we associate with significant events in our collective national experiences, like wars and the immigration of thousands to our shores, essentially all our ancestors. The following pieces are some examples of historical music.

"Dixie"

Written by Daniel D. Emmett

Daniel Emmett was a member of a minstrel-show company and he wrote this song to be a closing number as a finale for the company. It was intended to be the closing act in which the entire cast would participate. It was an instant hit! Interestingly, when Abraham Lincoln ran for President in 1860, "Dixie" was the campaign song used against him by his opponents. During Lincoln's presidency (1861–1865), he banned the song from being played in the White House or at other state and social functions. It was only after his death in 1865 that "Dixie" was played in the District of Columbia.

"DIXIE"
I wish I was in the land of cotton
Old times there are not forgotten
Look away, look away, look away Dixieland.
In Dixieland where I was born in early on one frosty morning'
Look away, look away, look away, Dixieland.
There's buckwheat cakes and Indian batter.
Makes you fat or a little fatter
Look away, look away, look away, Dixieland.
Then hoe it down an scratch your gravel
To Dixieland I'm bound to travel,
Look away, look away, look away, Dixieland.

"Battle Hymn of the Republic"

Written by Julia Ward Howe

After visiting several military campsites around Washington, DC, in 1861, Julia Ward Howe was inspired to write a poem that was later entitled the "Battle Hymn of the Republic" by James Russell Lowe. Initially, however, the poem was sung to "John Brown's Body" and after it was published in *The Atlantic Monthly* in 1862, it became the most popular war song of the union forces. Howe was truly one of the most famous and respected women of her time. After the war between the states (1861–1865), she became very interested and active in social reform. She established the New England Women's Club and became the first president of the New England Woman Suffrage Association. She is also given credit for introducing the notion of "Mother's Day" in the United States.

"BATTLE HYMN OF THE REPUBLIC"
Mine eyes have seen the glory of the coming of the Lord,
He is tramping out the vintage where the grapes of wrath are stored,
He hath loosed the fateful lightning of his terrible swift sword,

He has sounded forth the trumpet that shall never retreat,
His is sifting out the hearts of men before his judgment seat,
Oh, be swift, my soul, to answer Him! Be jubilant, my feet
In the beauty of the lilies Christ was born across the sea,
With a glory in His bosom that transfigures you and me,
As he died to make men holy, let us die to make men free.

"Give Me Your Tired, Your Poor"

Music by Irving Berlin, Words by Emma Lazarus

The lyrics of the music are from the final lines of a poem written by Emma Lazarus and later inscribed on a tablet at the base of the Statue of Liberty which stands in New York harbor. The most familiar lines of her poem "Send those, the homeless, tempest-tost to me, I lift my lamp beside the golden door," have inspired generations of new Americans as they landed on our eastern shores, as well as Irving Berlin who put music to these words from Emma Lazarus.

Emma Lazarus wrote "The New Colossus" in 1883 to protest the violent anti-Jewish attacks that had taken place in Russia and started the great wave of Jewish immigrants to the United States of America.

The Statue of Liberty was designed by Frederic-Auguste Bartholdi and was given to the United States by the people of France as a token of friendship between the two nations. On July 4, 1884, the presentation was made in Paris, and the statue was unveiled on Liberty Island in New York Harbor on October 28, 1886. The statue's official name is "Liberty Enlightening the World" and has become a symbol of the freedom and opportunity enjoyed by people who live in this democracy.

Irving Berlin, the composer who adopted the lyrics for his music, was born in Russia and came to the United States with his parents when he was five years old. Without question, Berlin is the most prolific popular song writer in American history. His music embodies the American spirit and stirs patriotic feelings for the many generations who have listened and responded to it.

"When Johnny Comes Marching Home"

Words and music by Patrick S. Gilmore

The first printing of "When Johnny Comes Marching Home" had the following inscription:

MUSIC INTRODUCED IN THE
SOLDIER'S RETURN MARCH
BY GILMORE'S BAND
Words and Music by Louis Lambert

Many references still list Louis Lambert as the composer of this song, but Louis Lambert was actually the pseudonym of Patrick Gilmore, one of the great bandmasters of the nineteenth century. He was born in Ireland in 1829, and emigrated to America during the Irish potato famine of the 1840s. He served as bandmaster for the Union Army during the Civil War and, in 1863, while on a tour of duty in New Orleans, wrote this song.

The origin of Gilmore's melody is somewhat obscure. Some historians state that it is similar to an Irish folk tune entitled, "Johnny, I Hardly Knew Ye," but Gilmore said he learned the tune from "a traveling Negro singer."

In any event, the song was written during the war between the states (1860–1865), and yet its greatest popularity came during the Spanish-American

War, some 35 years later. Because of its lively tune and optimistic text, ballads of this nature became very popular during this period of American history. The tune has also been incorporated into two other pieces: "American Salute" by Morton Gould and "An American Overture" by Roy Harris some years later.

"WHEN JOHNNY COMES MARCHING HOME"
When Johnny comes marching home again, Hurrah! Hurrah!
We'll give him a hearty welcome then, Hurrah! Hurrah!
The men will cheer, the boys will shout,
The ladies they will all turn out,
And we'll all feel gay when Johnny comes marching home!

Let love and friendship on that day, Hurrah! Hurrah!
Their choicest treasures then display, Hurrah! Hurrah!
And let each one perform some part,
To fill with joy the warrior's heart,
And we'll all feel gay when Johnny comes marching home!

Get ready for the jubilee, Hurrah! Hurrah!
We'll give the heroes three times three, Hurrah! Hurrah!
The laurel wreath is ready now,
To place upon his loyal brow,
And we'll all feel gay when Johnny comes marching home!

Multicultural Music

Multicultural music refers to a great variety of ethnic, racial, and cultural songs and dances. It is the music that mirrors the life and times of all peoples in all levels of society. Some of the music featured here is ethnic; other selections look at other cultures like the American seaman and cowboy. One could also introduce traditional dance music for Irish jigs, Filipino stick dance, or the Jewish hora to help students understand the concept of multiculturalism being more than just a matter of race and/or ethnicity.

"Roll, Jordan, Roll"

Many of those who spoke out against and worked for the abolition of slavery were also the first to recognize and appreciate the significance of the black spirituals. This group consisted of ministers, intellectuals, teachers, and union soldiers who both recorded the music and kept records of the artisans who performed them. "Roll, Jordan, Roll" was a hymn sung by ex-slaves in a Baptist church on St. Helena Island off the coast of Africa in the Atlantic Ocean. It was later recorded by Lucy McKim in 1862. This particular song was heard at a public celebration in 1862, on the first Independence Day celebrated by the newly freed slaves.

African-American music has always been a rich and powerful art form in this country. Many years before it was recognized and legitimized, Black spirituals and hymns were passed on from generation to generation of African-American families.

"ROLL, JORDAN, ROLL"
My brother sittin' on the tree of life,
And he heard when Jordan roll,
Roll, Jordan, roll, roll, Jordan, roll
Chorus: O march, the an-gels march
          O march, the an-gels march,

O my soul a-rise in Heav-en, Lord,
For to hear when Jor-dan roll.

My sister sittin' on the tree of life,
And she heard when Jordan roll,
  Roll, Jordan,
  Roll, Jordan,
  Roll, Jordan, roll!

Chorus

Massa Lincoln sittin' on the tree of life,
And he heard when Jordan roll,
  Roll, Jordan,
  Roll, Jordan,
  Roll, Jordan, roll!

Chorus

Little children, learn to fear the Lord,
And let your days be long,
  Roll, Jordan,
  Roll, Jordan,
  Roll, Jordan, roll!

Chorus

O, let no false or spiteful word,
Be found upon your tongue,
  Roll, Jordan,
  Roll, Jordan,
  Roll, Jordan, roll!

Chorus

The Juba

The word *Juba* likely originated in West Africa and came to America with the slaves. The literal meaning has long since disappeared, but it probably evolved from the word *giblet,* referring to leftovers. Originally it may have come from an African word given to the days and also female given names. Many variations of the dance called the Juba can be found in some islands in the Caribbean. In the United States, the word *Juba* is found in songs and stories reminiscent of the days of slavery. The following rhyme is accompanied by explanations in parentheses (Bessie Jones, 1972). As Jones describes in the final aside, this is a play. The African-American slaves began playing this, clapping and dancing as well, to "get off their brains and minds" for a while their turmoil.

"THE JUBA"

Juba this and Juba that	(That means a little of this and a little of that.)
And Juba killed a yellow cat	(That means mixed-up food might kill the white folks. And they didn't care if it did, I don't suppose.)
And get over double, trouble, Juba	(Someday they meant they would be over double trouble.)
You sift-a the meal, you give me the husk,	(You see, so that's what it would always mean—the mother would
You cook-a the bread, you give me the crust,	always be talking to them about she wished she could give them
You fry the meat, you give me the skin,	some of that good bread or hot whatnot, but she couldn't. She
And that's where my mama's trouble begin,	had to wait and give that old stuff that was left over.)

And then you Juba,
You just Juba.
Juba up, Juba down,
Juba all around the town
Juba for Ma, Juba for Pa, Juba for
    your brother-in-law.

(And then they began to sing and
    play it. . . .) (That mean
    everywhere.) (All around the
    country.)
(See, that meant everybody had
    Juba. And they made a play out
    of it. So that's where this song
    come from, they would get all
    this kind of thing off their brains
    and minds.)

"Cielito Lindo" ("Lovely Little Heaven")

This traditional Mexican folk song is a love song that also illustrates the values
and attitudes of that culture. It glorifies women and compares them to all that
is beautiful and appreciated in nature. This is most typical of Hispanic love
and folk songs.

"LOVELY LITTLE HEAVEN" ("CIELITO LINDO")
Only on Sunday
I see your face
When you go to mass
In the morning.

Ay, ay, ay . . .
Ay! I wish
Every day of the week
Cielito Lindo
Were Sunday.

When you go out into the fields,
Maiden of my love,
At your feet I bow
All the flowers.

Ay, ay, ay . . .
Ay! The beautiful ones bow,
Because you are the queen,
Cielito Lindo,
Of them all.

Those white hands of yours,
So tiny,
When I see them, they seem
Only on Sunday
Like two daisies.

Ay, ay, ay . . .
Ay, so exquisite.
Where are they going to rest,
Cielito Lindo,
The butterflies.

Your red lips contain,
Maiden of my love,
Two precious rows
Of fine pearls.

Ay, ay, ay . . .
Ay, such rare pearls,
That even the Virgin herself,
Cielito Lindo,
Would envy them.

When I talk to you of love,
And you do not listen,
The flowers grow sad,
The birds silent.

Ay, ay, ay . . .
Ay! But when you answer,
The birds and flowers,
Cielito Lindo,
Rejoice with me.

"Los Huapango"

This selection differs from the others in that it illustrates a traditional Mexican dance. Los Huapango, (pronounced wha-pango) is the dance of the platform and couples performed on an elevated floor covered in thatch. It is said that the dance was originally organized by merchants who used the occasion to sell their wares to customers. The occasion was announced to field hands in towns and on ranches by exploding firecrackers and fireworks.

Traditionally, young men would come directly from their place of work while the young women were always accompanied by their mothers or chaperons. To begin the dance, the men would place themselves in front of one of the women, indicating that they would be partners. As the music begins, the women would step forward and the dance would commence. If a man who was not dancing wanted to "cut in," he simply would place his hat on the head of the man he wished to replace.

Sometimes, men would balance such things as bottles on their heads during the dance, or the most skilled dancers would tie knots in sashes during the dance without losing the pace or rhythm of the music. When the band tired, it would play the song "The Bakers," which was a signal for the young men to take their partners for refreshments.

"Wakan'tanka Hears Me"

This is one of the many songs that honors the Great Spirit Wakan'tanka of the Teton Sioux. This song was part of the sun that which took place in midsummer during the full phase of the moon. The medicine men began praying for favorable weather and crops a month in advance of the ceremony. The ceremony itself was meant to show respect to Wakan'tanka in hopes of receiving health and prosperity for the tribe. The dance featured men painted in bright colors of blue for clear sky, red for sunset, and yellow for lightning. Young boys and girls sang to Wakan'tanka, asking for gifts promising to do good deeds in return.

"WAKAN'TANKA HEARS ME"
Wakan'tanka hears me, When I pray to him.
Wakan'tanka loves me, When I'm very good
He is strong and truthful, Blessings he will give,
Wakan'tanka grants me everything that's good.

"Git Along, Little Dogies"

This cowboy anthem illustrates the contrast between romantic myth and dreary truth surrounding a cowboy's existence. Optimism was often absent from this life-style and could be glorified only through music. The mundane task of "cowpunching" paired with hard travel across rugged, often unfriendly country inspired many of these songs. They were sung during the ride to calm the herd, entertain colleagues, and generally pass the time.

"Git Along, Little Dogies" was sung to an Irish lullaby tune and meant to describe the drive from Texas to Wyoming on the Dodge City trail. The various jobs described in this song were reflective of the daily routine for the men on the drive. Each stanza, beginning with the second, describes a particular responsibility of the cowboys on the drive.

"GIT ALONG, LITTLE DOGIES"

As I was a-walking one morning for pleasure,
I spied a cow-puncher all rid-ing a-lone.
His hat was throwed back and his spurs was a-jingling,
and as he approached he was sing-ing this song:

Chorus: Whoop-ee, ti yi yo, git a-long, little dogies!
          Its your mis-for-tune and none of my own.
          Whoo-pee, ti yi yo, git a-long, little dogies,
          For you know Wy-o-ming will be your new home!

Early in the spring, we round up the dogies,
Mark and brand and bob off their tails,
Round up our horses, load up the chuckwagon,
Then throw the dogies up on the trail.

Its whooping and yelling and driving the dogies,
Oh how I wish you would go on!
Its whooping and punching and go on little dogies,
For you know Wyoming will be your new home.

When the night comes on, we herd them on the bedground,
These little dogies that roll on so slow,
Roll up the herd and cut out the strays,
And roll the little dogies that never rolled before.

Your mother, she was raised in Texas,
Where the jimpson weed and sand burrs grow.
Now we'll fill you up on prickly pear and cholla,
Till you are ready for the trail to Idaho.

Oh, you'll be soup for Uncle Sam's Injuns,
Its beef, heap beef, I hear them cry.
Git along, git along, little dogies,
You're going to be beef steers by and by.

"Haul the Bowline"

The origin of "sea shanties" are unknown except that they were traditional work songs of sailors who passed them down for generations. This shanty was a work song used specifically as a hauling song while performing the arduous task of heavy pulling in a coordinated motion by a group of sailors. The accents fell on the beginning of the pulling movement.

In nautical terms, a bowline is a knot tied in a rope to prevent it from slipping from one's grip. Hauling songs are some of the oldest shipboard shanties. A great many shanties originated in England and were later adopted by American seamen as their own. "Kitty," a general female reference, was a common affectation frequently used by all male crews who often gave feminine names to their ships as well as mentioning women in songs and stories.

"HAUL THE BOWLINE"
Haul the bowline—for Kitty she's my darlin',

Chorus: Haul the bowline, th' bowline HAUL!

Haul the bowline—Kitty lives in Liverpool.

Haul the bowline—Liverpool's a fine town.

Haul the bowline—so early in the mornin'.

Haul the bowline—before day wuz dawnin'.

Haul the bowline—the Cape Horn gale's a-howlin'.

Haul the bowline—the cook he is a growlin'.

Haul the bowline—we'll either break or bend it.

Haul the bowline—we're men enough to ter mend it.

Haul the bowline—we'll haul away tergether.

Haul the bowline—an' burst the chafin' leather.

Haul the bowline—we'll hang for fine weather.

Protest and Social Commentary Music

The history of the United States of America has also been dotted with artisans and music that challenged mainstream values and notions. This music has always been part of our history but probably became most popular during the Vietnam and post-Vietnam eras. Be it a warning like Bob Dylan's "The Times They Are a Changin'" or an anti-war song like "Where Have All the Flowers Gone?," protest music has played a key role in depicting the mood of at least a significant part of the population. Indeed, some of the music became anthems and hymns of the protesting segment of the population who ultimately altered our collective history.

"The Times They Are A-Changin'"

Bob Dylan was born in Duluth, Minnesota, on May 24, 1941. He taught himself to play the guitar, piano, and harmonica. He formed a band in 1955 and attracted attention with his "talking blues," a distinctive speech-song style in the late 1950s and early 1960s. Essentially, he synthesized the popular styles of the mid-1950s into the folk song revival style of the 1960s. Most certainly, his lyrics caught the mood of American youth, and several songs became the anthems of the protest and civil rights movement of that turbulent historical era.

"THE TIMES THEY ARE A-CHANGIN'" *
Come gather 'round people
Wherever you roam
And admit that the waters
Around you have grown
And accept it that soon
You'll be drenched to the bone.
If your time to you
Is worth savin'
Then you better start swimmin'
Or you'll sink like a stone
For the times they are a-changin'

Come writers and critics
Who prophesize with your pen
And keep your eyes wide
The chances won't come again
And don't speak too soon
For the wheel's still in spin
And there's no tellin' who
That it's namin'.
For the loser now
Will be later to win
For the times they are a-changin'.

Come senators, congressmen
Please heed the call
Don't stand in the doorway
Don't block up the hall
For he that gets hurt
Will be he who has stalled
There's a battle outside
And it is ragin'.
It'll soon shake your windows
And rattle your walls
For the times they are a-changin'.

Come mothers and fathers
Throughout the land
And don't criticize
What you can't understand
Your sons and your daughters
Are beyond your command
Your old road is
Rapidly agin'.
Please get out of the new one
If you can't lend your hand
For the times they are a-changin'.

The line it is drawn
The curse it is cast
The slow one now
Will later be fast
As the present now
Will later be past
The order is
Rapidly fadin'.
And the first one now
Will later be last
For the times they are a-changin'.

TEACHER-DIRECTED ACTIVITIES FOR STUDENTS
1. Identify a famous composer and research his or her life and times. In your profile, identify some personal things about the person, such as background, family, children, and so on. Look at the circumstances of why this person wrote the music and perhaps why it has become a part of our history.
2. Review American history through music (e.g., the music of the "Great Depression," patriotic songs of World Wars I and II, protest songs of the Vietnam era, etc.). Discuss how music reflects a culture and history of a people.
3. Listen to other national anthems and compare them to ours. Review the histories and identify what *all* national anthems have in common.

4. If we were going to create a new national anthem, what might we include in our song? How would it reflect our life, times, and history?
5. Are there any songs today that might become important in our history? For example, will "Tie a Yellow Ribbon . . . ," become a classical patriotic song? Why? Why not?
6. Research your own family history/heritage and create a folk song that reflects your own personal background.
7. Research the history of your school, community, region, or state and write a folk song.
8. Discuss the reasons why some songs were written and how they reflected and affected history. Also discuss why some music endures while other songs become obsolete.

References

Allen, F., Garrison, L., & Ware, c. (1971). *Slave Songs of the United States.* New York: Books for Libraries Press.

Bierhorst, J., & Servello, J. (1974). *Songs of the Chippewa.* New York: Farrar, Straus and Giroux.

Burke, F. (1985). *Sounds of History.* National Archives and Records Administration.

Carey, G. (1976). *A Sailor's Songbag.* Amherst: University of Massachusetts Press.

Carmer, C. (1942). *Songs of the Rivers of America.* New York: Farrar and Rinehart.

Cohen, M. (1966). *101 Plus 5 Folk Songs for Camp.* New York: Faculty Press.

Cooper, I., et al. (1959). *Music in Our Life.* Morristown, NJ: Silver Burdett.

Cooper, I., et al. (1960). *Music in Our Life.* Morristown, NJ: Silver Burdett.

Curtis, N. (1968). *The Indians' Book: Songs and Legends of the American Indians.* New York: Dover Publications.

Dawley, M., & McLaughlin, R. (1961). *American Indian Songs.* California: Highland Music Company.

Densmore, F. (1972). *Music of the Indians of British Columbia.* New York: Da Capo Press.

Densmore, F. (1972). *Nootka and Quileute Music.* New York: Da Capo Press.

Dwyer, R., & Lingenfelter, R. (1968). *Songs of the American West.* London: Cambridge University Press.

Glass, P. (1974). *Songs and Stories of the North American West.* London: Cambridge University Press.

Goodman, A. (1974). *Abe Lincoln in Song and Story.* Goodman.

Hawes, B., & Jones, B. (1972). *Step It Down: Games, Plays, Songs & Stories from the Afro-American Heritage.* Athens and London: University of Georgia Press.

Hofman, C. (1968). *Frances Densmore and American Indian Music.* New York: Museum of the American Indian Heye Foundation.

Hugill, S. (1969). *Shanties and Sailor Songs.* New York: Frederick A. Praeger, Inc.

Jenkins, J. (1970). *Ethnic Musical Instruments.* London: Hugh Evelyn, Ltd.

Keeling, R. (1989). *Women in North American Music.* Indiana: The Society for Ethnomusicology.

Mitchell, T. (1980). *Music and Civilization.* London: British Museum Publications.

Parsons, J., & Sagel, J. (1990). *Straight from the Heart.* Albuquerque: University of New Mexico Press.

Reeder, B., & Standifer, J. (1972). *Source Book of African and Afro-American Materials for Music Educators.* Contemporary Music Project; Music Educators National Conference.

Schwendener, N., & Tibbels, A. (1975). *Dances of Old Mexico.* New York: A. S. Barnes and Co.

Scott, J. (1966). *The Ballad of America.* New York: Bantam Books.

Serposs, E. H., & Singleton, I. (1962). *Music in Our Heritage.* Morristown, NJ: Silver Burdett.

FOLKLORE AND FOLKTALES: THE MULTICULTURAL LOOKING GLASS

Folklore and folktales, especially in elementary and middle-level classrooms, have frequently provided children with their first encounter in multicultural education. Folk literture and folk music have often served as the impetus for role-playing and simulation activities, sociodramas, and creative writing exercises that encourage children to recognize the similarities while exploring the differences among people. Because folktales and folklore reflect the accumulated wisdom and artistic achievements of everyday people, they provide likely vehicles to study culture and ethnicity, compare environments, review values and attitudes, and allow each child an opportunity to reflect on his or her own culture during the process.

In the broadest sense, folklore includes virtually everything from ethnic foibles to traditional music, dances, and games. It often includes information about legends, myths, and historical figures that are a part of every culture. Folktales, on the other hand, are often stories about the life and times of ordinary people, making them somewhat more popular with younger learners. Perhaps this can be explained by the fact that many of these stories include examples of appropriate morality and social behaviors as well as understandable examples of concepts like bravery, cowardice, humor, grief, avarice, altruism, friendship, hate, and love. Each of these emotions are well understood by young learners who have themselves probably experienced or witnessed them in their young lives. Equally significant to children is the fact that most folktales also reflect cultural characteristics like food, clothing, family and social roles, school, careers, toys, and leisure time—essentially, many of the same components emphasized in multicultural and/or global education curriculums.

Sadly, folk literature is rarely infused with the social studies curriculum. In fact, great pains have often been taken to separate these subjects that fit so well together and greatly enrich one another. Indeed, one might ask, How can a person successfully teach, learn, or understand history without being exposed to literature, art, or music of a people and their culture? Clearly one cannot, but that is essentially what has traditionally been done with the elementary and middle-level curriculums.

It is reasonable to suggest that there are two basic ways to infuse folktales into the school curriculum: (1) teachers read aloud or tell folktales in a group setting and (2) teachers encourage students to select and independently read folktales. Either process or some combination is an acceptable learning strategy, but the former has some exceptional merit. Stories read aloud or narrated by an adult can present a sophisticated vocabulary or contain complex sentences and still maintain a very high level of interest among the young listeners. Conversely, all but the very best readers will lose interest rather quickly when they review a book with multisyllabic words, long sentences, and few illustrations.

Perhaps the inherent lessons here are that even the most sophisticated tales are appropriate for elementary children when presented and discussed by teachers or other adults in a classroom setting.

Folk literature can provide interesting information that will enrich the study of social studies, but, like any powerful learning tool, it requires knowledge and good judgment. Knowledge of what materials are appropriate and how to infuse them into the social studies content are of paramount importance. Teachers must do their homework if folk literature is to be used effectively in a classroom setting.

In developing a curriculum that permeates folklore and literature into the social studies, it is important to think of folklore and folktales as the kinds of stories people share with one another in their everyday lives. The following activities are designed to assist teachers in the development of this curriculum:

TEACHER-DIRECTED ACTIVITIES FOR STUDENTS

1. Recite or write a family story and discuss different types of living groups. These might include stories about vacations, travel, or funny events. *Teachers could also share in the exercise!*
2. Read occupational-career stories and discuss the world of work.
3. Discuss American folktales like Pecos Bill or Paul Bunyan and compare them to the folklore from other cultures.
4. Find examples and discuss the oral history tradition of cultures like those of Native Americans.
5. Think of history as a story told by one person to another. Research an event (e.g., the completion of the transcontinental railroad in 1869) and then discuss the task from a Chinese or Irish laborer's point of view. Another idea might be to look at the American Revolution from a British soldier's or Tory's perspective.
6. Create plays from folktales and folklore (write a script, have props, plan music and costumes, etc.).
7. After reading ethnic folktales, write your own stories applying the information learned about a particular culture to the tale.
8. Prepare some of the foods described in folktales.
9. Using the "Inquiry Island" simulation in this book, create your own folklore.
10. Have a storytelling show where you and your classmates select and present a folktale to one another.

Folklore Activities

As discussed, folklore often constitute the stories, tales, proverbs, foibles, and fables that have been passed down from one generation to the next. The following student activities are designed to illustrate some of these concepts about oral history and its role in holding families, ethnic and cultural groups, and even nations together.

TEACHER-DIRECTED ACTIVITIES FOR STUDENTS

1. Oral History
   a. Collect stories about your family and present them orally to your classmates or at school/parent nights.

    b. Conduct interviews and re-create a historical event that took place in your community.

    c. Invite guest speakers into the classroom and have them share stories about their lives and times.

2. Its a Very Small World

Materials:
Large world map
Pushpins
Yarn
Art supplies
Books

    a. Read one of the following books:
      Anansi the Spider by Gerald McDermott (African)
      Arrow to the Sun by Gerald McDermott (Native American)
      Stone Cutter by Gerald McDermott (Japan)
      African Dream by Eloise Greenfield (Africa)
      I Am Eyes by Leila Ward (African)
      Where Children Live by Thomas Allen (diverse home environments from different cultures)
      How We Live by Anita Harper (diverse life-styles)
      Boy of Nepal by Peter Larson (Nepal)
      A Boat to Nowhere by Maurine Warski (Vietnamese)
      The First Morning by Margery Bernstein (African)
      Growing Up Masai by Tom Shactman (African)
      The Black Snowman by Leonard Bernstein (African American)

    b. On a map, locate where the story takes place with a pushpin and trace, with yarn that location to your hometown. (The result might look something like the illustration here.)

    c. Draw a picture about what you read.

Our Friends Throughout the Year

Name of story, characters, picture, interesting facts

Huge world map

    d. List the characters, setting, human values, similarities, and differences from those of our culture.

    e. Write a letter to the country or city you read about for information. Bring back all the information and then share it during class discussion time.

Bibliography

Some selected materials that may be used in developing folktale/folklore units include the following:

Asbjornsen. (1975). *The Squire's Bride.* New York: Atheneum.

Banks, J. A. (1989). Integrating the curriculum with ethnic content: Approaches and guidelines. In J. A. Banks & C. A. McGee Banks (eds.), *Multicultural Education: Issues and Perspectives* (pp. 189–207). Boston: Allyn and Bacon.

Bettelheim, B. (1976). *The Uses of Enchantment: The Meaning and Importance of Fairy Tales.* New York: Alfred A. Knopf.

Chase, R. (1943). *The Jack Tales.* Cambridge, MA: Riverside Press.

Collier, J. L., & Collier, C. (1974). *My Brother Sam Is Dead.* New York: Four Winds Press.

Courlander, H. (1942). *Uncle Bouqui of Haiti.* New York: Wm. Morrow and Co.

Creel, J. L. (1960). *Folk Tales of Liberia.* Minneapolis: T. S. Denison and Co.

Dorson, R. M. (1959). *American Folklore.* Chicago: University of Chicago Press.

Edmonds, W. D. (1941). *The Matchlock Gun.* New York: Dodd, Mead.

Estes, E. (1944). *The Hundred Dresses.* New York: Harcourt, Brace, Jovanovich.

Forbes, E. (1946). *Johnny Tremain.* New York: Houghton Mifflin.

Harding, D. W. (1978). The author as creator of a social relation. In M. Meek, A. Warlow, & G. Barton (eds.), *The Cool Web* (pp. 201–215). New York: Atheneum.

Heuscher, J. E. (1963). *A Psychiatric Study of Fairy Tales.* Springfield, IL: Charles C Thomas.

Hickman, J. (1974). *The Valley of the Shadow.* New York: Macmillan.

Luthi, M. (1970). *Once Upon a Time: On the Nature of Fairytales.* Translated by L. Chadeayne & P. Gottwald. New YOrk: Frederick Unger.

Mohr, N. (1979). *Felita.* New York: Dial Press.

Nelli, E. (1974). *Encouraging Creative Verbal Processes with Preschool and Elementary School Children.* Lexington: Center for Professional Development, College of Education, University of Kentucky.

Opie, I., & Opie, P. (1974). *The Classic Fairytales.* London: Oxford University Press.

Politi, L. (1976). *Three Stalks of Corn.* New York: Scribner.

Rudman, M. K. (1976). *Children's Literature: An Issues Approach* (2nd ed.). New York: Longman.

Sawyer, R. (1936). *Picture Tales from Spain.* New York: Frederick A. Stokes Co.

Serwadda, W. M. (1974). *Songs and Stories from Uganda.* New York: Thomas Y. Crowell.

Singer, I. B. (1980). *The Power of Light: Eight Stories for Hanukkah.* New York: Farrar, Straus, & Giroux.

Sutherland, Z., & Arbuthnot, M. H. (1977). *Children and Books,* 5th ed. Glenview, IL: Scott, Foresman and Co.

Taylor, M. (1976). *Roll of Thunder, Hear My Cry.* New York: Dial.

Thompson, S. (1951). *The Folktale.* New York: Dryden Press.

Toye, W. (1979). *The Fire Stealer.* Toronto: Oxford University Press.

Uchida, Y. (1971). *Journey to Topaz.* New York: Scribner.

Van Woerkom, D. (1975). *The Queen Who Couldn't Bake Gingerbread.* New York: Alfred A. Knopf.

Welty, E. (1963). And they all lived happily ever after. *The New York Times Book Review,* November, 10, 3.

Westerberg. C. (1977). *The Cap That Mother Made.* Englewood Cliffs, NJ: Prentice Hall.

Wolkstein, D. (1976). *Lazy Stories.* New York: Seabury Press.

Yolen, J. (1975). *The Little Spotted Fish.* New York: Seabury Press.

Zemach, M. (1976). *It Could Always Be Worse.* New York: Farrar, Straus & Giroux.

Zemach, H., & Zemach, M. (1973). *Duffy and the Devil.* New York: Farrar, Straus & Giroux.

SOCIAL STUDIES AND ART: IDEAS AND CLASSROOM PROJECTS

Art and art projects can be easily integrated into the social studies curriculum, enriching both subject areas. The following pages provide some illustrations and teacher-directed activities that clearly show teachers how to infuse these subject areas into meaningful learning experiences for their students.

Geometric Shapes and Social Studies

TEACHER-DIRECTED ACTIVITIES FOR STUDENTS

1. Using several shapes, create a mobile that depicts the significant events or important data about a person or historical event. (See the example illustration.)

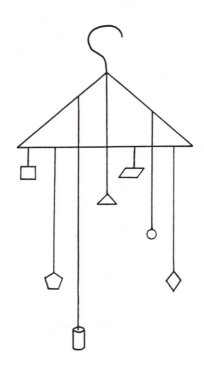

2. Select and research a person, place, thing, or event. After researching, illustrate on each side of a geometrical figure the significant information you discovered about your subject. (See the example illustration.)

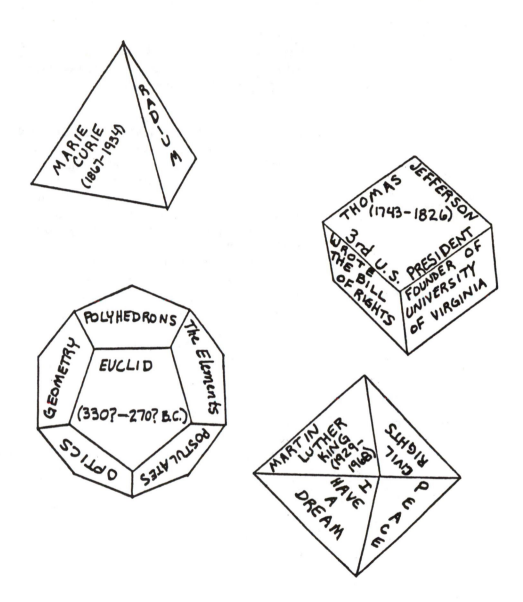

Blue Moose Chronicles (Grade Levels 3–5)

This activity is designed to provide children with an opportunity to use art and literature in a social studies lesson. In essence, it is a problem-solving activity that incorporates several subject areas and allows children to make 3-D maps and sequence events while building their mapping skills. Three-dimensional maps give children a visual as well as tactile experience in the re-creation of story segments.

It is important to note that for this activity to be a successful learning experience for children, the teacher must first (1) teach the concept of community;

(2) generate a list of items that are commonly found on maps (directions, colors, roads, etc.); and (3) give children the opportunity to do some problem solving both individually and collectively.

Materials:
Blue Moose by Manus Pinkwater
Art supplies: Paper scraps, cardboard boxes, assorted junk, paints and large sheets of butcher paper

TEACHER-DIRECTED ACTIVITIES FOR STUDENTS
1. *Blue Moose* by Manus Pinkwater.
2. Make 3-D maps to use when retelling the story. These would include Mr. Bretan's restaurant, Mr. Bretan's woodpile, the woods, Dave's secret place, the owl's home, the nearest town, other towns that people come from, and the place where Mr. Moose goes to visit his uncle.
3. With a small group of your classmates, do the following:
   a. Draw a map using N, S, E, W directions on a small sheet of paper.
   b. Generate a list of materials needed for the project.
   c. Assign roles. (Who does what? When? How?)
   d. Make a map on very large butcher paper. You may glue your map on the butcher paper, paint a map, or whatever.
   e. Your class will end up with five to six very "large" handmade maps using a compass point and a key/ledger.
   f. Write stories about how the moose goes from one place to another.

Cultural Diversity and Change (Grade Levels K–8)

This activity, though not new, is a terrific way to get children to visualize the concept of self and the diversity among all human beings.

Materials:
Overhead projector
Large sheets of butcher paper
Magic markers
Tape

TEACHER-DIRECTED ACTIVITIES FOR STUDENTS
1. At the beginning of the year, ask a partner to trace your outline on butcher paper.
2. "Color" in your outline and identify your likes and dislikes. You may change your list of likes and dislikes at any time during the year; if you do, you must share with your classmates the reasons for the change.
3. Either inside or outside your room post your outline for the rest of the year. (See the example illustration.)
4. In May, repeat the activity and compare and discuss how you have grown and changed from the September picture.

Mr. Ruff's Great Group

Visual Time Lines (Grade Levels K–4)

Materials:
Colored papers
Markers
Tape

TEACHER-DIRECTED ACTIVITIES FOR STUDENTS
1. Keep a visual month-to-month record of the important or significant events for the year. Using pictures, photos, stories, and class handouts, you can chronicle the year you spend in this class. (See the example illustration.)

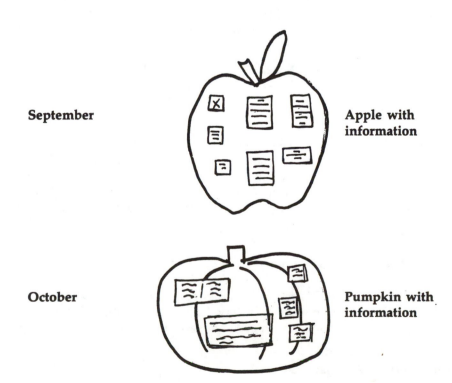

September — Apple with information

October — Pumpkin with information

November      Leaf with information

December      Pine tree with
                                                  information

Global Studies

The author first saw this activity at a *National Geographic* workshop in Bellevue, Washington. Since that time, it has been used successfully in both pre- and in-service classes to introduce global and geographic education. The exercise can be used as a springboard to discuss several issues, such as why most students placed the Western hemisphere in the middle, the relative size of each continent, or to introduce the continental drift theory.

Materials:
Seven sheets of different colored paper
Masking tape

TEACHER-DIRECTED ACTIVITY FOR STUDENTS
1. Utilizing large sheets of construction or butcher paper, (do not cut) the outlines of the seven continents and place them on a bulletin board or wall. You will be surprised at how well you put most things where they should be on a map, without using globes or maps as guides.

Historical Murals (Grade Levels 3–8)

This activity is designed to give students an opportunity to pictorially visualize an event in history. Utilizing art supplies like tempera paint or crayons, students are encouraged to research the event before they begin to reproduce it on paper.

Materials:
Butcher paper
Crayons or paint

TEACHER-DIRECTED ACTIVITY FOR STUDENTS
1. On large sheets of butcher paper, reproduce a scene or significant event in history (e.g., Neil Armstrong's walk on the moon, Christopher Columbus landing in the Caribbean in 1492, Lewis and Clark camping on the Missouri River, the Berlin wall coming down, Mario Polo visiting China, etc.).

LITERACY DEVELOPMENT AND SOCIAL STUDIES

Social studies should be an integral part of the daily curriculum, not an auxiliary to it. Great effort should be made to infuse it into every study unit throughout the academic year. Journal writing exercises, vocabulary development, and reading biographies and/or autobiographies are but a few ways to accomplish this. Here are some suggestions.

Journal Writing

Students could respond to historical concepts or quotes from famous people. They could also keep a current events notebook or a record of significant events that occur during the school year. They could also record information learned on field trips or from guest speakers.

Examples of quotes:
"I'm still learning."—Michelangelo's motto
"The future belongs to those who believe in the beauty of their dreams."—Eleanor Roosevelt
History is only a confused heap of facts."—Earl of Chesterfield
"I hate people who are intolerant."—Laurence Peters

Vocabulary Development

Each unit of study provides opportunities for teachers to introduce new words and build the students' vocabulary. Keeping lists, referring to them frequently, and infusing them into class discussions will greatly enhance the retention and use of new vocabulary.

The Name Game

This fun activity encourages students to create sentences about the word being learned.

Examples:
Can be big or small.
Inner cities need to be renovated.
The biggest city in the world is Mexico City, Mexico.
Your state has both cities and towns.

Third president of the United States.
He and John Adams died on July 4, 1826.
Only red-haired president.
Monticello is the name of his home in Virginia.
Author of the Bill of Rights.
Sent Lewis and Clark to explore the Louisiana Purchase.

John Adams was his political rival.
Elected president in 1800 and 1804.
Founder of the University of Virginia.
First democratic party president.
Entered the presidency as a widower.
Ran against Aaron Burr for presidency in 1800.
Selected to be our ambassador to France.
One of the authors of the Declaration of Independence.
Nationalism was important to Thomas Jefferson.

Other words that may be used in this exercise include the following:

Me	Canadian
Family	African
Home	Asian
School	Rights
American	Responsibility
Mexican	Amish

Abbreviations

Distribute a list of abbreviations to the students.

Examples:

1. ACLU	18. AFL
2. OPEC	19. USA
3. UN	20. JDL
4. NAACP	21. NBA
5. FBI	22. NATO
6. CIA	23. UNICEF
7. FDIC	24. AA
8. NOW	25. FAO
9. EPA	26. FAA
10. ERA	27. USDA
11. GSA	28. NFL
12. CSA	29. FSLICA
13. VFW	30. NASA
14. PLO	31. FDA
15. KKK	32. UNESCO
16. BSA	33. EEC
17. DAR	34. FHA

35. YMCA	47. USFWA
36. MADD	48. IRS
37. HUD	49. NHL
38. AMA	50. NCAS
39. SADD	51. WHO
40. YWCA	52. CDC
41. ADA	53. NIH
42. OAS	54. ANC
43. CIO	55. DEA
44. NEA	56. FTC
45. PTA	57. LULAC
46. UAW	58. FCC

(See the following pages for answers.)

TEACHER-DIRECTED ACTIVITIES FOR STUDENTS
1. Identify each of these abbreviations and discuss how, if any, these organizations have or could affect you in the future.
2. Select one group from the list and trace its history and its political and social influence. Predict its future in U.S. society.
3. Identify those groups that are directly opposed to one another. List the reasons why they oppose one another and discuss the possibility of them ever reconciling their differences.

A Common Thread

Distribute to the students a list of names or items that have something in common.

Example:
John Wilkes Booth
Charles Guiteau
Leon Czolgosz
Gavrilo Princip
Lee Harvey Oswald
James Earl Ray
Sirhan Sirhan

TEACHER-DIRECTED ACTIVITIES FOR STUDENTS
1. Identify these people and discuss how each has changed history.
2. Discuss such terms as *assassination* or *terrorism*. Discuss how political violence affects each of us.

"Isms"

Distribute a list such as the following to the students. Discuss how these terms are both similar and dissimilar.

Example:
Communism
Socialism
Fascism
Nazism
Capitalism

TEACHER-DIRECTED ACTIVITIES FOR STUDENTS
1. Define the concept of government and discuss how it affects the daily lives of ordinary people.
2. Compare and contrast several different types of political philosophies.
3. Identify the nations that have capitalist, socialist, or fascist forms of government.

Contributions by Others

Distribute a list such as the following to the students.

Example:
Dr. Jonas Salk
Copernicus
Dr. Robert Ballard
Marie Curie
Sir Isaac Newton
Dr. Linus Pauling

TEACHER-DIRECTED ACTIVITIES FOR STUDENTS
1. Identify and discuss what these people have in common.
2. Discuss the contributions of these scientists and how they affect our lives today.

Activists

Distribute a list such as the following to the students.

Example:
Mohandas Gandhi
Ho Chi Minh
Vladimir Lenin
Martin Luther King
Ayatollah Khomeini
Thomas Paine

TEACHER-DIRECTED ACTIVITY FOR STUDENTS
1. Discuss how these people influenced not only their own nations but world politics as well.

Abbreviations Answer Sheet

1. ACLU – American Civil Liberties Union
2. OPEC – Organization of Petroleum Exporting Countries
3. UN – United Nations
4. NAACP – National Association for the Advancement of Colored People
5. FBI – Federal Bureau of Investigation
6. CIA – Central Intelligence Agency
7. FDIC – Federal Deposit Insurance Agency
8. NOW – National Organization of Women
9. EPA – Environmental Protection Agency
10. ERA – Equal Rights Amendment
11. GSA – Girl Scouts of America
12. CAS – Confederate States of America
13. VFW – Veterans of Foreign Wars
14. PLO – Palestine Liberation Organization
15. KKK – Ku Klux Klan
16. BSA – Boy Scouts of America
17. DAR – Daughters of the American Revolution
18. AFL – American Federation of Labor
19. USA – United States of America
20. JDL – Jewish Defense League
21. NBA – National Basketball Association
22. NATO – North Atlantic Treaty Organization
23. UNICEF – United Nations International Children's Education Fund
24. AA – Alcoholics Anonymous
25. FAO – Food and Agriculture Organization
26. FAA – Federal Aviation Association
27. USDA – United States Department of Agriculture
28. NFL – National Football League
29. FSLIC – Federal Savings and Loan Insurance Corporation
30. NASA – National Aeronautical and Space Administration
31. FDA – Food and Drug Administration
32. UNESCO – United Nations Educational, Scientific and Cultural Organization
33. EEC – European Economic Community
34. FHA – Fair Housing Administration
35. YMCA – Young Mens Christian Association
36. MADD – Mothers Against Drunk Drivers
37. HUD – Housing and Urban Development
38. AMA – American Medical Association
39. SADD – Students Against Drunk Driving
40. YWCA – Young Women's Christian Association
41. ADA – American Dental Association
42. OAS – Organization of American States
43. CIO – Congress of Industrial Organization
44. NEA – National Education Association
45. PTA – Parent Teacher Association
46. UAW – United Auto Workers
47. USFWA – United States Farm Workers Association
48. IRS – Internal Revenue Service
49. NHL – National Hockey League
50. NCAA – National College Athletic Association
51. WHO – World Health Organization
52. CDC – Center for Disease Control

53. NIH–National Institute of Health
54. ANC–African National Congress
55. DEA–Drug Enforcement Agency
56. FTC–Federal Trade Commission
57. LULAC–Labor Union of Latin American Commission
58. FCC–Federal Communication Commission

INQUIRY ISLAND: A SIMULATION/ROLE-PLAYING EXERCISE

Topographical Map

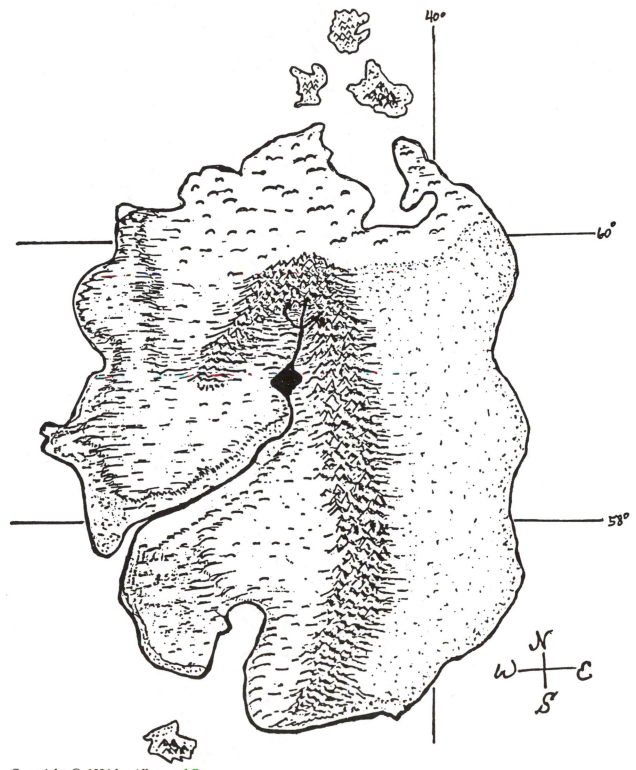

Political Map

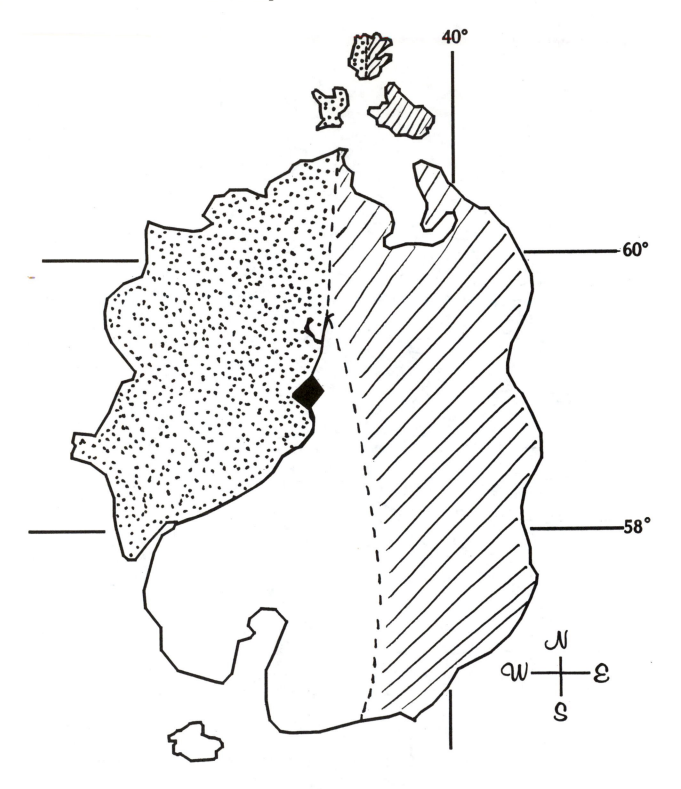

Inquiry Island Activities

Activity 1: Exploration and Colonization

This activity is designed to introduce students to basic map skills as they simulate the exploration and eventual colonization of Inquiry Island. Among other things, students will be able to discern:

1. The size of the island (approximately 420 miles north to south by 240 miles east to west, or about 1,000 square miles)
2. The location of the island (North Atlantic Ocean off the southern tip of Greenland)
3. The topography (mountains, river, lake, arid regions, grass plains, and rolling hills)
4. The climate (much like Iceland)

This basic information is important to have before a site can be selected for the initial settlement.

The teacher, using copies (or a transparency) of the topographical map, directs the class through the simulation activity by creating the scene and asking appropriate questions.

The Scenario:
- The year is 1800 A.D.
- A group of pilgrims (the class) have come upon this island.
- Nearly out of fresh water and travel weary, the group decides to stop and explore the island as a possible site for its colony.
- Sailing around the island, the group explores the island, looking for the very best place to land and establish a settlement.

TEACHER-DIRECTED QUESTIONS FOR STUDENTS
1. What do we need to know about the island before we select a site?
2. What resources and conditions must exist to ensure our survival?*
3. Why did you select this particular site and what makes it a good choice?
4. Do we all agree that this is a good site to establish our colony?

Once a site has been selected, the task is to create a safe and secure environment.

TEACHER-DIRECTED ACTIVITIES FOR STUDENTS
1. Using art supplies, construct a nineteenth-century settlement that will provide adequate housing and other structures to ensure your collective survival.
2. Discuss issues regarding clothing, homes, food, animal life, and so on, all related to the location, topography, and climate of the island.

Materials:
Globes
Atlases
Art Supplies

*Obviously, the original site must be located somewhere along the river or adjacent to the lake but *students* must come to this realization themselves. Consequently, it is essential that students be constantly reminded that the initial settlement must be located where there are natural resources that will ensure survival.

Adventure stories like *Robinson Crusoe* and *Swiss Family Robinson,* which can provide information about survival on an island environment from about the same historical period

Activity 2: Creating and Establishing a Nation

Using the political map, engage students in a role-playing activity that allows them an opportunity to create a nation and establish a national identity.

The Scenario:
- Three generations (about 75 years) have passed and the island has separated into three independent and autonomous nations.

Divide the class into three groups and ask each to create an identity for their nation by responding to the following organizational questions.

TEACHER-DIRECTED QUESTIONS FOR STUDENTS
1. What is the name of your country?
2. Have you created a flag and national symbol?
3. Have you written a national anthem (to be performed in class)?
4. Why did your ancestors come to the new area or why did they stay at the original site?
5. What are the names and locations of the major urban areas?
6. What are your natural resources and where are they located?
7. What kind of people are you (related to geography, etc.)?
8. What difficulties had to be overcome for you to establish and maintain your nation?
9. Which neighbors do you get along the best with?
10. Which do you not get along with and why?
11. What do you predict for the future of your nation?

Materials:
Almanacs
Atlases
Art supplies
Musical instruments

Activity 3: Internationalism and Diplomacy

This activity provides students with an opportunity to engage in dialogue and diplomacy common to international politics. It attempts to illustrate the difficulties nations sometimes face as they attempt to resolve political issues that often directly impact their nation and national security.

The Scenario:
- Each nation must select leaders (including an ambassador) and begin interacting with the other two nations.
- Issues to be reviewed and resolved:
    River usage
    Fishing rights
    Ecological issues
    Environmental issues
    Militarism

Chauvinism
Threat of war
Threat of invasion from an outside force

General Information about the Activities

- Allow plenty of time for each activity.
- Tie each activity to the other.
- Have materials available for student use.
- Use good questioning and discussion strategies.
- Be organized.
- Review each activity and discuss what was learned from the experience.

SPECIAL DAYS AND HOLIDAYS

Recognizing and/or celebrating one of the many holidays that appear on the school calendar does not mean that we must abdicate our teaching responsibilities and simply accept these as "throw-away" days. To the contrary, observing almost any one of the special days can be an excellent opportunity to introduce multicultural and global education to our students. Certainly, it provides teachers with a vehicle to build an integrated curriculum around a holiday theme by infusing social studies with art, music, literature, mathematics, and virtually every other school subject.

The following pages provide a list of special days and holidays that are recognized and celebrated around the world, as well as several teacher-directed activities for classroom use.

Labor Day	Cinco de Mayo
American Indian Day	Rosh Hashanah
United Nations Day	Columbus or Discoverer's Day
Yom Kippur	Halloween
Election Day	Veterans Day
Thanksgiving Day	Hanukkah
Christmas Day	New Year's Day
Martin Luther King Jr.'s Birthday	Ground Hog Day
Chinese New Year	Lincoln's Birthday
Black American Day	Washington's Birthday
Valentine's Day	Easter
St. Patrick's Day	Law Day
Arbor Day	Memorial Day
Mother's Day	Father's Day
Flag Day	Equinox
Solstice	TET

TEACHER-DIRECTED ACTIVITIES FOR STUDENTS

1. Create and maintain a "special day" time line on which you record special days and/or events that occur during the school year.
2. Research why certain colors and/or symbols are associated with specific holidays.
3. Prepare lists of those holidays that are religious, political, and/or associated with nature. Discuss why there are so many different kinds of holidays.
4. Identify those holidays that are universally celebrated by people all over the world.
5. Add to the list of traditional holidays a day you believe should be recognized and/or celebrated (e.g., October 15, Grouch Day; February 11, Inventor's Day; March 8, International Woman's Day; etc.).
6. For American-Indian Day, read *The Story of Jumping Mouse* as retold by John Steptoe. Discuss how Native Americans utilized legends to explain how things were created or why they happened. These stories, usually oral, were recorded on storyskins for future generations to remember. No words were used in the description, only pictures to retell the event. Understanding that, read other Native-American tales and then create your own storyskins about a legend or special event in Native-American history and folklore.

7. Read (or ask the teacher to read) *The Jungle* by Upton Sinclair. Discuss the working conditions as cited in the book. Do you think there are still places in the world where people must work in dangerous and horrid conditions? Why does the United States of America no longer allow the conditions described in the book to still exist? Discuss also the concept of Labor Day and explore if any other nations celebrate the holiday.

APPROPRIATE AND EFFECTIVE USES FOR CLASSROOM BULLETIN BOARDS

Bulletin boards can be used in a variety of ways to enhance and enrich social studies content. Generally, bulletin boards can be categorized into (1) teacher made, (2) student made, (3) student and teacher made, and (4) commercially made. All have their merits and should be incorporated into the classroom during the academic year.

Teacher-made bulletin boards are those that have been conceptualized, assembled, and displayed by the teacher with essentially no outside help. The teacher decides on what, when, and how the display will be used. The teacher also determines how students will obtain and disseminate the information.

Student-made boards should be of a high quality; the aesthetic qualities of the board should complement the academic information. Students should be encouraged to be creative and accurate in their presentations.

Student- and teacher-made bulletin boards should be the best of both worlds. The teacher can organize the effort by assigning tasks and providing an outline and direction. The students would be responsible for assembling, editing, and reporting on the information illustrated on the board.

Commercially made bulletin boards obviously save time and effort in acquiring information for a display. They also clearly focus on a specific theme by providing the pictures, printed materials, and documents that are sometimes difficult for teachers and students to obtain. Unfortunately, it is sometimes difficult to find exactly what one wants or needs for a given subject area. Often commercially made bulletin boards look too "flat."

Depending on the teacher's needs and circumstances, each type of bulletin board can be used during the course of an academic year, but the student- and teacher-made bulletin boards are the most fun and rewarding for both parties involved. It allows students an opportunity to work with the teacher in a less structured environment, giving them a unique view of the teacher, academic cooperation, and success.

Generally, there are some specific guidelines to be observed in creating an informative and operational bulletin board. They should:

1. Clearly convey information and ideas to students.
2. Have balance and order, and be colorful.
3. Not be too cluttered with information.
4. Be interesting, motivational, topical, thoughtful, and fun.
5. Illustrate a variety of subject areas with social studies, such as, for example, the Green Peace movement and global education.
6. Be academic—that is, used to introduce and/or review units of study, instruct and inform, and focus on specific knowledge skills and content.
7. Be appropriate to the grade level(s).
8. Be changed frequently.

Topics that are especially suitable for bulletin board displays are:

Global interdependence
Intercultural communication
Current events
Special days/holidays
Great people and great events
Humankind
Subjects such as war, ecology, aging, local history, etc.

To ensure that bulletin boards are a relevant and meaningful academic experience for students, the teacher must be prepared to discuss and illustrate the significance of the information being displayed. Consequently, the teacher must prepare as well as he or she would for any other academic lesson taught in the class setting. There must be a specific *objective, a series of questions to be asked and resolved,* and *closure.*

CHAPTER 7

Basic Information: Classroom Applications

History does not unfold: it piles up! —ROBERT ADAMS

A YEAR IN THE LIFE OF PLANET EARTH

Much of history is chronological and sequential in nature and this frequently creates problems for students who labor to memorize the data or understand cause and effect. History, because it is history, demands knowledge and understanding before a person can synthesize and evaluate the information to be learned and applied. Indeed, the study of history requires basic comprehension before one can be a successful inquirer. The challenge, then, seems to be: How do teachers make learning the facts both relevant and fun for students?

As previously noted, educators can infuse social studies into other areas like art and music to make learning the facts of history more digestible. Another meaningful and fun exercise is to highlight only the significant events of a given period of time. Essentially, this means reducing pages of content information into a series of highlights that can be readily viewed and easily understood by students. One can start with last year and ask students to recall what they remember about that year. A list could be compiled, the events discussed, and the concepts of history, chronology, and sequence reviewed. Listed here are the highlights from several years in our history. They simply illustrate how clearly and easily one can condense information, allowing teachers and students to proceed with more analytical and evaluative processes.

1800
- U.S. Congress convenes for the first time in Washington, DC.
- John Adams becomes the first U.S. President to live in the White House.
- Thomas Jefferson is elected as the third President of the United States of America.

- William Young of Philadelphia designs shoes for left and right feet.
- China sends first tea exports to Great Britain.
- First alkaline battery is developed.
- A new constitution is enacted in France.
- Napoleon Bonaparte becomes First Council of France.
- Library of Congress is established with books from President Jefferson's library as the nucleus.
- Land Act is enacted.
- Negro minstrel shows begin to appear in public as entertainment.
- *American Musical Magazine* is published in Northhampton, Massachusetts.
- *Life of Washington* by Mason L. Weems becomes a best-seller.
- U.S. population is estimated at 5.3 million.

1810
- Yale medical school is established.
- United States annexes west Florida.
- Hawaii is unified by King Kamehameha.
- Berlin University is founded.
- Composer Frederick Chopin is born.
- Mexico gains independence from Spain.
- Napoleon Bonaparte marries Marie Louise of Austria.
- Sweden declares war on Great Britain.
- Washington Irving, America's first great internationally recognized author, has a best-seller entitled *History of New York*.

1820
- James Monroe is elected as the fifth President of the United States of America.
- Florence Nightingale is born.
- U.S. population is estimated at 10 million.
- Quinine is discovered in France.
- Moses Austin (father of Stephen A. Austin) is granted a Spanish charter to settle 300 families in Texas.
- Missouri Compromise is ratified.
- Portuguese revolution is successful.
- First steamship crosses the Atlantic Ocean in 26 days.
- Kingdom of Columbia (South America) begins its successful revolution from Spain.
- Platinum is discovered in the Ural Mountains.
- *The Sketch Book* by Washington Irving is a best-seller. Contains such stories as "Rip Van Winkle" and "The Legend of Sleepy Hollow."

1830
- Andrew Jackson is serving as President of the United States.
- Indian Removal Act moves many American Indians from their traditional homes to lands west of the Mississippi River.
- Ecuador and Venezuela gain independence from Columbia.
- Simon Bolivar, President of Columbia, dies.
- First wagons cross the Rocky Mountains.
- First British railway is established—Liverpool to Manchester.
- Cholera epidemic in eastern Europe kills thousands.
- Captain Black of Great Britain establishes settlement in Astoria (Oregon).
- British settlers kill all of the native population in Tasmania.

- The play "Pocahontas" by G. W. Palke opens in New York.
- *Book of Mormon* by Joseph Smith is published.
- The waltz becomes a popular dance.

1840

- William Henry Harrison—"Old Tippecanoe"—is elected the ninth U.S. President. He dies after only one month in office (April 4, 1841).
- "Tippecanoe and Tyler too" becomes a popular election song.
- Napoleon Bonaparte is buried in France.
- Russian composer Tchaikovsky is born.
- Great Britain claims New Zealand as a colony.
- Quadruple Alliance is formed by Russia, Austria, Prussia, and Great Britain.
- College of Dental Surgery is established in Baltimore, Maryland.
- The saxophone is invented by Aldophe Sax.
- Opium War between Great Britain and China begins.
- Canadian Samuel Cunard, with a British mail subsidy, establishes a steamboat line servicing Liverpool and Boston, Massachusetts.
- *The Pathfinder* by James Fenimore Cooper and *Two Years Before the Mast* by Richard Henry Dana are best-sellers.

1850

- California becomes the thirty-first state to join the Union.
- Bunson burner is invented.
- Denmark "sells" Ghana to Great Britain.
- First formal expeditions are made into Central Africa.
- Territories of Utah and New Mexico are established.
- Clayton-Bulwer Treaty is ratified.
- Beethoven performs his Fifth Symphony.
- The Chicago-Burlington-Quincy railroad is established.
- Vacuum freeze is invented.
- Compromise of 1850 is ratified.
- Women's Medical College of Pennsylvania, the first school of medicine exclusively for women, is established.
- Best-sellers are *The Scarlet Letter* by Nathaniel Hawthorne and *The Wide Wide World* by Susan Bogert Warner.

1860

- Abraham Lincoln is elected the sixteenth President.
- South Carolina becomes the first state to secede from the Union.
- First Pony Express ride reaches California.
- Gold is discovered in Humboldt and Esmeralda, Nevada.
- Repeating rifle is introduced by Oliver Winchester.
- Golf championships are introduced.
- Florence Nightingale opens the first nurse training schools.
- Oil wells begin to appear in and around Titusville, Pennsylvania.
- Peru increases its national wealth by exporting bird droppings as fertilizer.
- There are 387 daily, 3,173 weekly, 79 semiweekly, and 86 triweekly newspapers in the United States.
- Stephen Foster's "Old Black Joe" is a popular song.
- Poets Walt Whitman ("Calamus") and John Greenleaf Whittier ("Ichabod") have best-sellers.
- Detective-fiction novels are popular.

- Elizabeth Peabody introduces the kindergarten concept to U.S. education.

1870
- Ulysses Grant is serving as President of the United States of America.
- Charles Dickens dies.
- Rome becomes the capital of Italy.
- Manitoba becomes a Canadian province, ending a rebellion.
- John Rockefeller creates the Standard Oil Company.
- Diamonds are discovered in South Africa.
- Adolf Nordenskiold explores the interior of Greenland.
- The Royal Cricket Club of England is formed.
- Congress passes the KKK Acts.
- France declares war on Prussia.
- Texas "boom" begins. The number of farms triple in the decade.
- "Saratoga," a social comedy by Gronson Howard, is popular.
- *Luck of the Roaring Camp* by Bret Harte is a best-seller.

1880
- James Garfield is elected as the twentieth President of the United States of America.
- France annexes Tahiti.
- DeBeers Mining Company is established in South Africa.
- Thomas Edison opens a lightbulb factory.
- Douglas MacArthur is born.
- George Eastman invents the first successful roll of film.
- There are 15 nursing schools in the United States of America.
- Streets in Philadelphia, Cleveland, and New York are being lit by electric lights.
- Best-sellers include *Uncle Remus* by Joel Chandler Harris, *Ben Hur* by General Lew Wallace and *Five Little Peppers and How They Grow* by Harriet Lothrop (Margaret Sydney).
- Spring Symphony by Theo Thomas of Cambridge, Massachusetts, is performed.
- "Pirates of Penzance" is the most popular production of the year.

1890
- Benjamin Harrison is serving as President of the United States of America.
- Dwight David Eisenhower is born.
- Charles de Gaulle is born.
- Emil von Behring isolates diphtheria and tetanus viruses in Germany.
- The "electric chair" is introduced in New York.
- Eveready batteries first marketed.
- Charles B. King invents the pneumatic hammer.
- Sherman Anti-Trust Act is passed.
- Battle of Wounded Knee in South Dakota.
- Vincent van Gogh commits suicide.
- Free elementary education is instituted in Great Britain.
- Idaho (43) and Wyoming (44) join the union.
- Spain grants universal voting rights.
- Botswana and Uganda come under British Control.
- William Clyde Fitch's play "Beau Brummel" opens.

1900
- William McKinley is serving as President of the United States of America.
- World exposition opens in Paris, France.
- Gold Standard U.S.A.—U.S. Currency Act declares paper and other money redeemable in gold.
- Private postal services abolished in Germany.
- Hawaii organized as a territory of the United States.
- Max Planck elaborates quantum theory.
- William Crookes separates uranium.
- Browning revolver is invented.
- First Zeppelin trial flight.
- J. S. Bach Festival established in Bethlehem, Pennsylvania.
- The cake-walk dance is introduced.
- D. F. Davis presents International Challenge Cup for lawn tennis (USA is first winner).
- First advertisement in a national magazine in United States.
- American League (baseball) formed.
- Writer Oscar Wilde dies.
- Metro is opened in Paris, France.
- Best-sellers are *To Have and Hold* by Mary Johnston and *Sister Carrie* by Theodore Dreiser.

1910
- William Taft is serving as President of the United States of America.
- Mark Twain dies.
- Mount Etna erupts.
- The Mexican Revolution begins.
- Japan annexes Korea.
- Leo Tolstoy dies.
- The Manhattan Bridge opens.
- Florence Nightingale dies.
- Royal Canadian Navy is established.
- Thomas Edison experiments with "talking" motion pictures.
- Haleys Comet passes within 13 million miles of the earth.
- Jack Johnson beomes the first black man to become the heavyweight boxing champion of the world.
- Gene Stratton Porter's *Girl of the Limberlost* is popular reading.
- "A Perfect Day" by Carrie Jacob Bonds and "Ah! Sweet Mystery of Life" by Rida Johnson Young and Victor Herbert are the most popular musical pieces.

1918
- Woodrow Wilson is serving as President of the United States of America.
- Denmark grants independence to Iceland.
- World War I; 10 million casualties are reported.
- President Woodrow Wilson proposes his Fourteen Points for world peace.
- Three color traffic lights are installed in New York city.
- Women, 30 years of age or older, get the right to vote in Britain.
- Treaty of Versailles is signed.
- Daylight Savings Time is introduced in the U.S.
- Soviet Union moves the national capital to Moscow.

1927
- Calvin Coolidge is serving as President of the United States of America.

- The first talking movie, "The Jazz Singer," starring Al Jolsen, opens.
- Stalin consolidates his power in the Soviet Union.
- Economic conference is held in Geneva, Switzerland (52 nations attend).
- International "Peace Bridge" between United States & Canada is opened.
- Charles A. Lindbergh flies from New York to Paris in 37 hours.
- Helen Wills wins one of her eight Wimbledon tennis titles.
- Duke Ellington becomes a popular musical personality.
- The foxtrot dance is popular.
- "Black Friday" in Germany.
- Babe Ruth hits 60 homeruns during the season.
- Jack Dempsey versus Gene Tunney in World Heavyweight Championship fight (Tunney won).
- First TV telecast in front of a large audience.
- Top box office star is Greta Garbo.
- Hit songs are "Ol Man River" and "Me and My Shadow."
- Best-sellers are (fiction) *Elmer Gantry* by Sinclair Lewis and (nonfiction) *The Story of Philosophy* by Will Durant.
- Harlem Globetrotters is organized.
- World Series winner is New York Yankees; New York Giants (football) is founded.
- Strong language like *lousy, damn,* and *hell* enters the popular arts and replaces words like *grand* and *swell.*
- First appearances: all-electric jukebox, A & W root beer, car radio, Gerber baby food, Hostess cakes.

1939
- Franklin Delano Roosevelt is serving as President of the United States of America.
- World War II begins in Europe.
- Sigmund Freud dies.
- Paul Miller invents DDT.
- Grandma Moses becomes a popular artist.
- President Franklin Roosevelt asks for $552 million for defense.
- Hitler and Mussolini sign ten-year political and military alliances; the "Pact of Steel."
- Neutrality Act of 1937 is amended.
- Pan-American Airways begins regular commercial flights between United States and Europe.
- First air-conditioned car is produced.
- Baseball Hall of Fame dedicated in Cooperstown, New York.
- Edward R. Murrow broadcasts nightly from London.
- Popular films include "The Wizard of Oz," "The Hunchback of Notre Dame," "Pinocchio," and "Goodbye Mr. Chips."
- Academy Awards: Best Picture, Best Director, and Best Actress—"Gone with the Wind."
- Popular songs are "Ding-Dong! The Witch Is Dead," "Roll Out the Barrel," and "Last Time I Saw Paris."
- Best-sellers are (fiction) *The Grapes of Wrath* by John Steinbeck and (nonfiction) *Days of Our Years* by Pierre van Paassen.
- Karl Landsteiner and Alexander Weiner discover the Rh factor in blood.
- Lou Gehrig retires from baseball.
- World Series: New York Yankees.
- Al Capone is released from prison.
- Clara Adams is first woman to fly around the world.

- College fads are swallowing goldfish, roller skating, knock-knock jokes.
- Popular dances are Chicken Scratch, Chestnut Tree, Boomps-a-Daisy.
- The helicopter becomes operational.

1941

- President Franklin Roosevelt sends Lend-Lease Bill to Congress.
- Japanese bomb Pearl Harbor, Hawaii, and the United States enters World War II.
- Joe DiMaggio hits in 56 straight baseball games.
- Dacron is introduced.
- An aircraft crosses the Atlantic Ocean in 8 hours (a new record).
- The "Manhattan Project" on atomic research begins (led to the development of the atomic bomb).
- Joe Louis retains his heavyweight title.
- Ted Williams hits .406 (the last player to hit over .400).
- U.S. population is 131 million (China, 450 million; India, 389 million, and USSR, 182 million).
- Popular films are "Dumbo," "Dr. Jekyll and Mr. Hyde," and "Citizen Kane."
- Best-Sellers are (fiction) *The Keys of the Kingdom,* and (nonfiction) *Berline Diary.*
- Horse racing: Whirlaway wins the Triple Crown.
- Popular fads are the saying "Kilroy was here," the Congo, Lindy Hop, and Kangaroo Jump.
- First appearances: Cheerios, rationing of silk stockings, municipally owned parking.

1945

- World War II ends (VE Day and VJ Day).
- Charles de Gaulle is elected President of France.
- Potsdam Conference.
- Vitamin A is discovered.
- Franklin Delano Roosevelt dies and Harry S Truman becomes the thirty-third President of the United States of America.
- Vietnam and Cambodia declare independence from France.
- Republic of Indonesia is established.
- Best-sellers are *Forever Amber, Animal Farm, Age of Reason,* and *Brave Men.*
- Popular films are "The Lost Weekend," "The Bells of Saint Mary," and "National Velvet."
- "Bebop" dancing is introduced.
- Popular songs are "Let It Snow," "June Is Bustin' Out All Over," and "Rhapsody in Blue."
- Most popular broadway play is "The Glass Menagerie."
- The United Nations meet for the first time.
- World Series: Detroit Tigers (AL).
- Truman: "The buck stops here" and "If you can't stand the heat, get out of the kitchen."
- First appearances: frozen orange juice, ballpoint pens, Tupperware, trademark "Coke" registered, Swanson & Sons' frozen dinners.

1950

- Harry S Truman is serving as the President of the United States of America.
- Korean War begins

- Speed of light readings are accurately measured for the first time.
- Uruguay wins the World Cup in soccer.
- Picasso produces "The Goat."
- George Orwell dies.
- George Bernard Shaw dies.
- Alger Hiss is found guilty of perjury.
- First series of riots in Johannesburg (South Africa) is provoked by racial policies.
- Development of hydrogen bomb in the United States.
- Population of London is 8.3 million; Chicago is 3.6 million.
- Successful kidney transplant is performed.
- NATO leaders agree on 5-year Integrated Defense Plan.
- Senator Joseph McCarthy charges communist infiltration of State Department—"McCarthyism" begins.
- Top TV shows are "Texaco Star Theater," "The Colgate Comedy Hour," and "Hopalong Cassidy."
- Popular films are "All about Eve," "Father of the Bride," "Samson and Delilah," and "Sunset Blvd."
- Popular songs are "My Heart Cries for You," and "Autumn Leaves."
- Popular musicals are "Guys and Dolls," and "Peter Pan."
- Best-sellers are (fiction) *The Cardinal* and (nonfiction) *Betty Crocker's Picture Cook Book.*
- Ben Hogan wins the U.S. Open (golf).
- World Series: New York Yankees (AL).
- NBA Championship: Minneapolis Lakers.
- Bomb shelters are being built in United States.
- New words and usages: Apartheid, captive audience, ratpack, H-bomb.
- Fads: the mambo, square dancing, and Hopalong Cassidy outfits and toys for kids.
- First appearances: Sugar Pops, Miss Clairol, Smokey the Bear, Minute Rice, "Peanuts" cartoon introduced.

1959

- Dwight David Eisenhower is serving as President of the United States of America.
- Fidel Castro assumes power in Cuba.
- TV quiz show scandals are exposed.
- First drive-in bank established in Liverpool, Great Britain.
- Alaska becomes the forty-ninth state and Hawaii the fiftieth state to join the Union.
- First nationally accepted credit card is introduced.
- President Eisenhower and Nikita Khrushchev of the USSR meet at Camp David.
- Pope John Paul convenes the first Vatican Council.
- American Football League is formed.
- World Series: Los Angeles Dodgers.
- "Mercury Seven" astronauts chosen.
- Eighty-six percent of all Americans own a TV set.
- Rock 'n' roll stars Buddy Holly, Ritchie Valens, and The Big Bopper are killed in a plane crash.
- Top TV shows are "Gunsmoke," "Have Gun, Will Travel," "Father Knows Best," and "The Price Is Right."
- Popular films are "Ben-Hur," "Pillow Talk," "North by Northwest," "Gidget," and "Gigi."

- Popular songs are "Everything's Coming Up Roses," "Put Your Head on My Shoulder," and "Do-Re-Mi."
- Popular play is "The Miracle Worker."
- Best-sellers are (fiction) *Exodus* and (nonfiction) *Twixt-Twelve and Twenty*.
- Fads: go-karting, black leotards, and do-it-yourself activities.
- First appearances: Weather station, nuclear merchantship, European free trade market.

1963
- John F. Kennedy is serving as President of the United States of America.
- Britain is refused entry into Common Market.
- End of New York newspaper strike after 114 days.
- Winston Churchill becomes an honorary citizen of the United States.
- US-USSR agreement on "hotline" from the White House to the Kremlin.
- Riots over school desegregation in Birmingham, Alabama.
- Coup in South Vietnam—President Diem assassinated.
- John F. Kennedy is assassinated in Dallas, Texas. Lyndon Johnson becomes the thirty-sixth President of the United States of America.
- Lee Harvey Oswald is killed by Jack Ruby in Dallas, Texas.
- The Beatles rise to stardom.
- Jackie Robinson is the first black to be voted MVP of the major leagues.
- World Series: New York Yankees.
- Martin Luther King, Jr., gives "I Have a Dream" speech.
- Top TV shows are "Beverly Hillbillies," "Bonanza," and "The Dick Van Dyke Show."
- Popular films are "Tom Jones," "Cleopatra," "How the West Was Won," and "The Birds."
- Popular songs are "Wipeout," "Puff the Magic Dragon," and "Da Doo Run Run."
- Popular plays are "Barefoot in the Park" and "One Flew Over the Cuckoo's Nest."
- Best-seller are (fiction) *The Shoes of the Fisherman* and (nonfiction) *Happiness Is a Warm Puppy*.
- First Human lung transplant is performed.
- Heisman Trophy: Roger Staubach of the Naval Academy.
- New words and usages: Beatlemania, rat fink, fake out.
- First appearances; Weight Watchers, JFK Airport, the "Amazing Spider-man."
- Kenya becomes an independent nation.

1968
- Richard Nixon is serving as the President of the United States of America.
- Nuclear Non-Proliferation Treaty is adopted by the UN.
- Martin Luther King, Jr., is assassinated.
- Civil Rights Bill is passed in Congress.
- Pierre Trudeau becomes Prime Minister of Canada.
- Robert Kennedy is assassinated.
- Color TV sets outsell black and white sets for the first time.
- Top TV shows are "Gomer Pyle," "Bonanza," and "Family Affair."
- Popular films are "Funny Girl," "2001: A Space Odyssey," and "Yellow Submarine."
- Popular songs are "Spinning Wheel," and "Folsom Prison Blues."
- Best-sellers are (fiction) *Airport* and (nonfiction) *Random House Dictionary of the English Language*.

- Amniocentesis is developed.
- First U.S. heart transplant is performed.
- First combined NFL-AFL draft is held.
- Summer Olympic Games held in Mexico City, Mexico.
- Yale College admits women.
- A Florida heiress leaves $450,000 to 150 stray dogs.
- The Vietnam War becomes the longest war in U.S. history.
- First moon orbit is made.

1969
- The first two humans, Neil Armstrong and Buzz Aldrin, walk on the moon.
- Muammar Quaddafi assumes power in Libya.
- Golda meir becomes Prime Minister of Israel.
- Georges Pompidou succeeds Charles de Gaulle in France.
- Ho Chi Minh dies.
- Yasir Arafat becomes the leader of the PLO.
- Automatic banktellers are instituted.
- Steve O'Neal (New York Jets) is the first American football player to punt 98 yards.
- Richard Nixon is the first U.S. President to attend the launching of a manned spaceflight.
- Top TV shows are "Rowan and Martin's Laugh-In," "Gunsmoke," "Family Affair," and "The Doris Day Show."
- Popular films are "Butch Cassidy and the Sundance Kid," "Midnight Cowboy," and "Bob and Carol and Ted and Alice."
- Best-sellers are (fiction) *The Godfather* and (nonfiction) *American Heritage Dictionary of the English Language.*
- First commercial 747 is flown.
- A human egg is fertilized out of the mother's body in England.
- Each major league (baseball) is split into two divisions and pennant playoffs are instituted.
- Super Bowl IV: Kansas City Chiefs.
- Woodstock Concert in Woodstock, New York.
- Fads: underground newspapers, dune buggies.
- New words and usages: downs, uppers, crunch, hair weaving, hung, total, noise pollution.
- First appearance: Frosted Mini Wheats, organized Vietnam protests.

1973
- President Nixon begins his second term.
- President Allende of Chile is overthrown by Chilean armed forces.
- Peace Agreement for Vietnam is signed. U.S. troops begin withdrawing.
- First building in United States is more than 1,400 feet tall—Sears Tower in Chicago.
- University of Miami (Florida) is the first college in United States to offer athletic scholarships to women.
- Top TV shows are "All in the Family," "The Waltons," and "MASH."
- Popular films are "The Sting," "American Graffiti," "The Exorcist," and "The Way We Were."
- Popular songs are "Tie a Yellow Ribbon," "Delta Dawn," "Bad Bad Leroy Brown," and "Rocky Mountain High."
- Yom Kippur War begins in the Middle East.
- The first manned Skylab is launched.

- A computerized brain scanner (CAT) is marketed.
- Congress prohibits TV blackouts for sold-out professional football games.
- Heisman Trophy: John Cappeletti of Pennsylvania State University.
- Screening of airline passengers to prevent hijacking begins.
- Fads: CB radios, martial arts, backgammon.
- New words and usages: Skylab, space shuttle, ego trip, let it all hang out.
- Volcano erupts in Iceland.
- Earthquake hits Mexico.
- Mark Phillips and Princess Anne marry.
- Watergate hearings begin.
- Indian uprising at Wounded Knee.
- Best-seller is *Jonathan Livingston Seagull* by Richard Bach.
- Nobel Peace Prize is awarded to U.S. Secretary of State Henry Kissinger and North Vietnamese negotiator Tho, leading to the end of the U.S. involvement in Vietnam.
- Super Bowl: Miami Dolphins.
- World Series: Oakland Athletics.
- *Pioneer 10* reached its closest approach to Jupiter.
- Academy Award Winning Movie: "The Sting."
- NBA Champs: New York Knickerbockers.
- Former President Lyndon B. Johnson dies.
- Pablo Picasso dies.
- Bahamas becomes independent of Great Britain.
- Egypt resumes diplomatic relations with Jordan.
- Agnew resigns in October of 1973 and Gerald Ford becomes Vice President.

1976
- Jimmy Carter is elected the thirty-ninth President of the United States of America.
- Best-seller is *Curtain* by Agatha Christie.
- Super Bowl: Pittsburgh Steelers.
- Lynn Swann is named MVP of the Super Bowl.
- Leading USA magazine: "T.V. Guide."
- World Series: Cincinnati Reds.
- Earthquake in Guatemala.
- Academy Award Winning Movie: "Rocky."
- Meteorites fall in China.
- NBA Champs: Boston Celtics.
- Winter Olympics are held in Innsbruck, Austria.
- Nixon testifies on wiretapping.
- Patricia Hearst is found guilty of armed robbery.
- Queen Elizabeth I of Great Britain is 50 years old.
- India tightens its birth control policies.
- Earthquake strikes Italy, killing 1,000 people.
- Bicentennial is observed in the United States of America.
- Summer Olympics are held in Montreal, Canada.
- *Viking 2* lands on Mars.
- Agatha Christie dies.
- Teton Dam (Idaho) springs leak and crumbles.
- Nadia Comaneci wins Olympic Gold Medal for gymnastics, scoring perfect 10s.
- Japanese Prime Minister Kakuei Tanaka is convicted for role in Lockheed scandal.

- Hua Kuo-feng becomes China's new Chairman.
- Novelist Saul Bellow wins Nobel Prize.

1981
- Ronald Reagan is inaugurated as the fortieth President of the United States.
- 52 U.S. hostages are freed from Iranian extremists.
- Assassination attempt is made on President Ronald Reagan in Washington, DC.
- Egyptian President Anwar Sadat is assassinated by Muslin extremists.
- Beirut hotel bombing kills 200; wounds 600 U.S. service personnel.
- Islamic republican party headquarters is bombed, killing 150.
- Prince Charles and Lady Diana are wed in London.
- U.S. baseball players strike.
- Fruit fly threatens California produce.
- Writers Guild of America ends strike.
- *Voyager 2* scans Saturn.
- Sandra Day O'Conner becomes first woman Justice of the U.S. Supreme Court.
- Joe Louis dies.
- Natalie Wood dies.
- Super Bowl: Oakland Raiders.
- Jim Plunkett is named MVP of the Super Bowl.
- World Series: Los Angeles Dodgers.
- Academy Award Winning Movie: "Chariots of Fire."
- NBA Champs: Boston Celtics.
- Los Angeles ends mandatory school busing of children in order to achieve racial integration.
- U.S. launches first space shuttle from Cape Canaveral, Florida.
- John Paul II is wounded by a would-be assassin in Vatican City.

1984
- Ronald Reagan wins reelection as President of the United States.
- Geraldine Ferrero is the first woman named as a Vice Presidential candidate on a majority party ticket.
- U.S. Marines withdraw from Lebanon.
- USA wins the largest number of medals at the Summer Olympics held in Los Angeles.
- Soviet Leader Yuri Andropov dies.
- Indira Gandhi is assassinated.
- Prince Harry is born to Prince Charles and Lady Diana of Great Britain.
- Union Carbide gas lead kills 2,500 in Bhopal, India.
- Super Bowl: Los Angeles Raiders.
- Marcus Allen wins MVP Award in the Super Bowl.
- World Series: Detroit Tigers.
- Academy Award Winning Movie: "Amadeus."
- NBA Champs: Boston Celtics.
- Konstantin Chernenko is elected President of the USSR.
- World responds to Ethiopian famine.
- Baby ("Baby Fae") is given a baboon heart.
- Second man receives artificial heart—William Schroeder, age 52.
- Count Basie dies.
- Richard Burton dies.
- Mary Lou Retton wins Gold Medal in gymnastics.

1989
- George Bush is serving as President of the United States of America.
- San Francisco earthquake registers 7.1 on Richter scale.
- *Exxon Valdez* leads 11 million gallons of oil into Prince William Sound off the coast of Alaska.
- Bette Davis, Lucille Ball, and Gilda Radner die.
- Berlin Wall comes down.
- Ayatollah Khomeini dies.
- Political protests are held in Armenia.
- Political unrest and turmoil in Czechoslovakia, Soviet Union, Afghanistan, China, Poland, Bulgaria, South Africa, and Israeli-occupied West Bank.
- World Series: Oakland Athletics.
- Flag amendment fails in U.S. Senate.
- U.S. Senate removes Federal Judge Alcee Hastings of Florida after being convicted of eight articles of impeachment.
- Funding for abortion is vetoed.
- German communists remove Rich Erich Honecker of East Germany from office.
- Hungary is proclaimed a free republic.
- Soviets admit Afghanistan invasion was illegal.
- Spacecraft begins journey to Jupiter.
- Evangelist Jim Baker is sentenced.
- George Bush and Mikhail Gorbachev hold first summit meeting.
- The Pope and Mikhail Gorbachev meet for the first time.
- Emperor Hirohito of Japan dies.
- Best-selling children's book is *The Way Things Work* by David Macaulay.
- Top grossing movie: "Batman."
- Top video rental: "A Fish Called Wanda."
- Best-selling U.S. magazine: *Modern Maturity*.
- Top U.S. newspaper: *Wall Street Journal*.
- Top single: "Look Away" by Chicago.
- Top album: "Don't Be Cruel" (Bobby Brown).
- Top syndicated TV program: "Wheel of Fortune."
- Favorite TV program: "Bill Cosby Show."
- Super Bowl: San Francisco Forty-Niners.
- World Series: Oakland Athletics.
- Best-seller is *All I Really Needed to Know I Learned in Kindergarten*.
- Academy Award Winning Movie: "Driving Miss Daisy."
- NBA Champs: Detroit Pistons.

TEACHER-DIRECTED ACTIVITIES FOR STUDENTS
1. Using almanacs, magazines, and newspaper files, highlight the significant events of the year just passed.
2. Select a particular theme or concept (e.g., air travel or fashion) and trace its development throughout history.
3. Trace the population growth of the United States since 1800 and project future growth and the problems we may face in the twenty-first century.
4. Review the events of the year you were born.
5. Select and read the events of a particular year in history and see if your classmates can guess which year it is.
6. Research the past ten years of your life and see if you can discover the changes in science, politics, art, music, athletics, fashion, or another area.

Time Lines

Time lines are a excellent way to help students visualize history over a given period of time. They can be as simple as charting a person's life to as complex as illustrating the course of events for hundreds of years. The following illustrations are examples of types of time lines that can be used in the classroom.

Personal Time Line

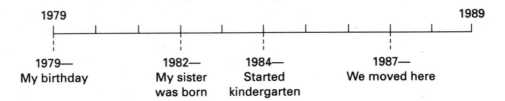

1979   1989

1979—   1982—   1984—   1987—
My birthday   My sister   Started   We moved here
                   was born   kindergarten

Vertical Time Line

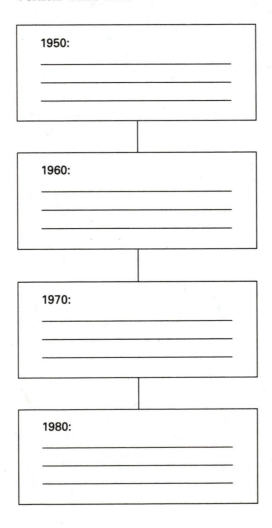

1950:

1960:

1970:

1980:

Historical Time Line

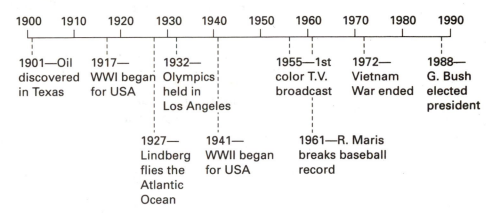

Border Time Line

September	October	November	December	
1. _____	1. _____	1. _____	1. _____	
2. _____	_____	_____	2. _____	etc.
3. _____	2. _____	_____	_____	
4. _____	3. _____	2. _____	3. _____	
5. _____	_____	3. _____	_____	

THE STUDY OF HUMANKIND IS NOT A TRIVIAL MATTER

Although it is true that the study of history often appears to be a pile of unrelated and useless information that defies understanding, let alone relevancy, the notion persists that history can be an interesting and fun school subject. History bridges time and space and gives us an intimate peek at who we were—our successes, failures, and follies. In essence, those things that humanize the study of history make it interesting and relevant.

The question is: How do teachers enliven those textbooks filled with what seems to be mundane, flat information? In part, that will depend on the teacher's attitude toward social studies and how much value he or she places on teaching it to young learners. If the subject is approached with enthusiasm and knowledge, children can find joy in learning history and geography—not to mention having fun in the process.

Content knowledge is important but so is methodology. Even the teacher with limited content information can make social studies a viable and exciting subject for his or her students. The secret is to build on a student's natural curiosity and to share little historical tidbits about the people, places, or things that make up history. Trivia, as we have seen with the popularity of boardgames and TV shows, is an excellent vehicle to stimulate interest and curiosity in the study of history and geography.

The following pages are a compilation of some general information and facts related to the history of humankind. The author encourages the reader to add to this list information found in newspapers, books, journals, almanacs, or even on game shows. Incorporating this kind of information into a classroom is fun and makes studying social studies a bit more palatable.

The following are some tidbits of history and to share with students.

- The most popular colors for flags are red, white, and blue.
- Elizabeth Peabody, the founder of American kindergartens, encouraged teachers to "educate the whole child," which, in 1860, revolutionized American education.
- The largest continents (land size) are north of the equator.
- The largest river complexes in the world are:
  1. Nile (Africa)
  2. Amazon (South America)
  3. Mississippi/Missouri (North America)
  4. Yangtze-Kiang (Asia)
  5. Ob-Irtysh (Asia)
- At least 189 people perished while defending the Alamo against the Mexico army in 1836. Interestingly, at least 31 of these defenders came from countries other than the United States, such as Denmark, England, Ireland, Scotland, and Germany.
- Ancient Greeks created the first popularly used textbooks: Euclid for geometry, Dionysus for grammar, and Diophantus for algebra.
- The following U.S. Presidents play(ed) musical instruments:
  1. Thomas Jefferson (violin)
  2. John Tyler (violin)
  3. Warren Harding (alto horn)
  4. Calvin Coolidge (harmonica)
  5. Harry Truman (piano)
  6. Richard Nixon (piano)
  7. William Clinton (saxophone)
- The caricature of "Uncle Sam" was first depicted by cartoonist Thomas Nast. Dan Rice, a circus clown, was the model.
- Abraham Lincoln and George Washington were circus buffs.
- Christopher Columbus made four voyages to the "New World":
  1. 1492: He explored San Salvador, Northern Cuba, and Hispaniola with three ships.
  2. 1493–1496: With 17 ships, he explored southern Cuba and Puerto Rico.
  3. 1498–1500: He explored the eastern coast of South America.
  4. 1502–1504: He explored the Central American coast and the northern coast of South America.

  Columbus died in 1506 after years of ill health and essentially without recognition from the Spanish Crown. No one knows with absolute certainty where he is buried.
- John Howard Payne, a lonely and destitute wanderer most of his life, wrote the song "Home Sweet Home."
- These U.S. Presidents wrote the most books (of 36 or more pages):
  1. Theodore Roosevelt (39 books)
  2. John Quincy Adams (24 books)
  3. Herbert Hoover (16 books)
  4. Woodrow Wilson (14 books)
  5. Thomas Jefferson (11 books)
  6. Grover Cleveland (10 books)
- The United States of America has had nine capitals:
  1. Philadelphia (1774–1776)
  2. Baltimore/Philadelphia (1776–1777)
  3. Lancaster, Pennsylvania (1777)
  4. York, Pennsylvania (1777–1778)

5. Princeton, New Jersey (1783)*
6. Annapolis, Maryland (1783–1784)
7. Trenton, New Jersey (1784)
8. New York City/Philadelphia (1785–1800)
9. Washington, DC (1800 to present)

- George Washington's favorite activities were:
  1. Shopping
  2. Betting on cockfights
  3. Betting on horses
  4. Fox hunting
  5. Attending the theater
  6. Duck shooting
  7. Dancing
  8. Playing cards

- Food firsts:
  1. Canned food (Napoleon's army)—1808
  2. Peanut butter (Saint Louis doctor)—1890
  3. Canned soup (Campbell's)—1897
  4. Ice cream cone (Saint Louis World Fair)—1904
  5. Frozen foods (Bird's Eye)—1930

- The United States granted women the right to vote in 1920. The first countries to grant women the right to vote were:
  1. New Zealand (1893)
  2. Australia (1902)
  3. Finland (1906)
  4. Norway (1913)
  5. Denmark (1915)
  6. Greenland (1915)
  7. Iceland (1915)
  8. USSR (1917)

- Six nations are smaller than Washington, DC (which is 63 square miles):
  1. Vatican City (.17 square mile)
  2. Monaco (.73 square mile)
  3. Nauru (8 square miles)
  4. Tuvalu (10 square miles)
  5. San Marino (24 square miles)
  6. Liechtenstein (61 square miles)

- Around the world Santa Claus is called:
  1. Befana (a woman) (Italy)
  2. Papa Noel (Brazil)
  3. Grandpa Koleda (Bulgaria)
  4. (Ukko) (Old Man Christmas) (Finland)
  5. Pelznickle (Germany)
  6. Jule Nissen (the Yule gnome) (Denmark)

- Animals that migrate great distances:
  1. Arctic terns (migrate 11,000 miles)
  2. Eels (migrate 5,000 miles)
  3. Whooping cranes (migrate 2,000 miles)
  4. Golden plovers (migrate 2,000 miles)

*No formal meeting place existed from 1779 to 1782 because of the American Revolutionary War.

5. Monarch butterflies (migrate 1,250 miles)
6. Hummingbirds (migrate 500 miles)

- Costa Rica in Central America has more plant species than all the rest of North America combined.
- Thomas Paine coined the name "United States of America."
- Authors most frequently translated into other languages:
  1. Agatha Christie
  2. Leonid Brezhnev
  3. Karl Marx
  4. Vladimir Lenin
  5. Jules Vernes
  6. The Brothers Grimm
  7. Jack London
  8. Hans Christian Andersen

- Leonardo da Vinci is credited with inventing scissors.
- How long have they been around?
  1. Needle (prehistoric times)
  2. Button (300 B.C.)
  3. Pin (1817)
  4. Trouser fly (mid-1800s)
  5. Hatpin (1832)
  6. Safety pin (1849)
  7. Snap-fastener (1855)
  8. Zipper (1890)

- Eight state capitals have less population than the New York City police force (about 35,000 officers):
  1. Montpelier, Vermont (pop. 8,120)
  2. Piere, South Carolina (12,000)
  3. Augusta, Maine (20,640)
  4. Dover, Delaware (22,660)
  5. Helena, Montana (24,670)
  6. Juneau, Alaska (25,920)
  7. Frankfort, Kentucky (26,920)
  8. Concord, New Hampshire (32,770)

- The person behind the city:
  1. Orlando, Florida (Orlando Reeves, Indian runner)
  2. Cleveland, Ohio (Moses Cleveland, a Connecticut surveyor)
  3. Dallas, Texas (George Dallas, U.S. Vice President)
  4. Denver, Colorado (James Denver, Governor of Kansas Territory)
  5. Gary, Indiana (Judge Elbert Gary)
  6. Reno, Nevada (General J. L. Reno, Civil War)
  7. Seattle, Washington (Sealth, Indian Chief)

- Peter Cooper invented "Jell-O", ran for U.S. President, made hats, brewed beer, designed the first commercial American steam locomotive (the "Tom Thumb"), helped lay the first Atlantic cable, and founded "Cooper Union" (a free school in the Arts and Sciences).
- Rugby, North Dakota, is the geographical center of North America.
- U.S. casualties in major conflicts:
  1. Revolutionary War, 1775–1783 (4,435 deaths)
  2. War of 1812, 1812–1815 (2,260 deaths)
  3. Mexican War, 1846–1848 (1,733 deaths)
  4. Civil War, 1861–1865 (498,332 deaths, 677,392 casualties
  5. Spanish-American War, 1898 (385 deaths, 4,108 casualties)

    6. World War I, 1971–1918 (53,402 deaths, 320,518 casualties)
    7. World War II, 1941–1945 (291,557 deaths, 1,076,245 casualties)
    8. Korean War, 1950–1953 (33,629 deaths, 157,530 casualties)
    9. War in Southeast Asia, 1964–1975 (47,382 deaths, 211, 438 casualties)

- About 80,000 Americans are injured yearly in gun-related incidents.
- Wilhelm Roentgen won the first Nobel Prize for physics with his invention of the X-ray.
- The following games were invented in these countries:
  1. Bridge—Turkey (1850)
  2. Polo—India (1800s)
  3. Mah-jong—China (1850)
  4. Solitaire—France (1700s)
  5. Lotteries—Italy (1600s)

- The original names for these famous products were:
  1. Cellucotton (Kleenix)
  2. Health Kups (Dixie cups)
  3. Bouncing Table (Trampoline)
  4. C-Curity Fastener (Zipper)
  5. I-Scream Bar (Eskimo Pie)

- Andrew Jackson is credited with being the first president to kiss a baby during an election campaign.
- The most valuable matchbook cover is the Charles Lindberg transatlantic flight commemorative of 1927—only two are known to exist.
- From Neanderthal times, human teeth have been getting smaller.
- Elizabeth Blackwell in 1849 became the first woman in the United States to earn a medical degree.
- Colombia, South America, exports the most fresh-cut flowers to the United States. The Netherlands ranks second.
- Reportedly, the first person to set foot on Plymouth Rock in 1620 was a woman.
- Sir Arthur Conan Doyle, who created Sherlock Holmes, named his character after American judge Oliver Wendell Holmes, whom he greatly admired.
- Virginia Dare was the first child born to English parents in the "New World" at the Roanoke Island Colony in 1587. The colony and all of the settlers mysteriously disappeared without any trace.
- The first surviving colonial child born in the "New World" was named Peregrine White. He was born aboard the *Mayflower* as the ship lay at anchor. The name *Peregrine* is latin for *pilgrim* or a person in a foreign land. Peregrine White lived to be 83 years old.
- The United States in the 1980s:
  1. 5% eat at McDonald's daily.
  2. 10% of truck drivers are women.
  3. 38% dislike rock music.
  4. 61% read a daily newspaper.
  5. 70% own running shoes but don't run.
  6. 84% believe there is a heaven.
  7. 94% of men would like to change their looks.
  8. 99% of women would like to change their looks.
- Approximate sizes of eight mideast countries:
  1. Iraq is more than twice the size of Idaho.
  2. Kuwait is smaller than New Jersey.
  3. Iran is larger than Alaska.

4. Saudi Arabia is less than one-fourth the size of the United States.
5. Ethiopia is less than twice the size of Texas.
6. Syria is larger than North Dakota.
7. Jordan is smaller than Indiana.
8. Egypt is more than three times the size of New Mexico.
- The Democratic party, founded by Thomas Jefferson, is the oldest continuing political party in the world.
- How big are the Great Lakes?
  1. Lake Ontario is the size of Hawaii and Rhode Island.
  2. Lake Erie is the size of Vermont.
  3. Lake Michigan is the size of Delaware, Vermont, Rhode Island, and New Hampshire.
  4. Lake Huron is the size of Missouri, New Jersey, and Connecticut.
  5. Lake Superior is the size of South Carolina and Rhode Island.
- The Pilgrims rarely drank water before they came to the "New World" because of the poor quality of the water where they had previously lived.
- The seven sins, according to Mahatma Gandhi were:
  1. Wealth without work
  2. Pleasure without conscience
  3. Knowledge without character
  4. Commerce without morality
  5. Science without humanity
  6. Worship without sacrifice
  7. Politics without principle
- How long does litter last?
  1. Paper, 2 to 4 months
  2. Orange peels, 6 months
  3. Milk cartons, 5 years
  4. Filter cigarettes, 10 to 12 years
  5. Leather shoes, 25 to 40 years
  6. Aluminum, 80 to 100 years
  7. Disposable diapers, 500 years
  8. Plastic foam, infinitely
- It is said that storytelling is the oldest form of art. Supposedly, no human society with a language did not tell stories.
- It is believed that the most stressful jobs in the United States are:
  1. Inner-city high school teacher
  2. Police officer
  3. Miner
  4. Air-traffic controller
  5. Medical intern
  6. Stockbroker
  7. Journalist
  8. Customer service employee
  9. Waitress
  10. Secretary
- Jimmy Dewar invented Twinkies.
- Charles Lubin of Chicago was the first baker to have supermarkets sell his baked goods. He was also the father of Sarah Lee, whose bakery products are popular today.
- Ages when musicians began to play instruments:
  1. Wolfgang Mozart (Harpsichord), age 3
  2. Ludwig van Beethoven (piano), age 3

   3. Johann Sebastian Bach (violin), age 4
   4. Peter Tchaikovsky (piano), age 4
   5. Johannes Brahms (viola and violin), age 5
   6. Frederic Chopin (piano), age 5 (played original melodies without any lessons)
- Juliette Low, the founder of the Girl Scouts of America, was deaf.
- The name native people call their own country:
   1. Iceland (Lydveldid Island)
   2. Iran (Keshvare Shahanshahiueiran)
   3. China (Chung-hua Jen-min Kung-ho Kuo)
   4. Taiwan (Chung-hua Mink-Kuo)
   5. Ceylon (Sri Lanka)
   6. South Korea (Daehan-Minkuk)
   7. Tibet (Po)
- The first U.S. Thanksgiving took place in mid-October of 1621. Ninety-one Indians and 56 pilgrims dined on venison (brought by the Indians), eel pie, duck, geese, lobster, clams, bass, cornbread, and fresh fruit.
- President Lincoln established the fourth Thursday of November as the official Thanksgiving holiday. In 1931 it became a national holiday.
- Canadian Thanksgiving is celebrated on the second Monday of October.
- Christmas has been an "official" holiday only since about 1891.
- The largest animal in the history of the world is currently alive—the Blue Whale.
- Iceland boasts it has the highest literacy rate in the world. Australia and New Zealand also lay claim to this title.
- By his twentieth birthday, Mozart had composed 30 symphonies, 12 masses, 8 operas, 12 sonatas, and 13 string quartets. He also wrote several serenades, dances, marches, vocal works, and concertos.
- "Twinkle, Twinkle, Little Star" was written by Mozart before he was 5 years old.
- In Benjamin Franklin's day, people powdered their wigs, wiped their teeth, and scraped their tongues. "Toilet" kits of well-to-do colonials often included silver tongue scrapers.
- L. Frank Baum, who wrote *The Wonderful Wizard of Oz*, also wrote *The Art of Decorating Dry Goods Windows and Interiors*.
- There are 30 countries in the world with no coastline.
- The first telephone operators in Connecticut in 1878 answered with "Ahoy" instead of "Hello." Today other countries answer this way:
   1. Greece—"Come in"
   2. Russia—"I am listening"
   3. Spain—"Tell me"
   4. Mexico—"Well?"
   5. India—"Greetings"
   6. Iran—"Yes"
   7. Germany—"Hello, who is speaking?"
   8. Italy—"Ready, with whom am I speaking?"
   9. Japan—Excuse, excuse"
- Abraham Lincoln was the first full-bearded U.S. President and Benjamin Harrison was the last.
- "Bite the dust" isn't from an old cowboy movie. It comes from the *Iliad* by Homer.
- Benjamin Harrison, twenty-third President of the United States, had the most states admitted to the Union during his term of office: North Dakota,

South Dakota, Montana, Idaho, Wyoming, and Washington.

- Geologically speaking, Iceland is the youngest country in the world.
- Youngest presidents at death:
  1. John F. Kennedy (46 years, 177 days)
  2. James Garfield (49 years, 304 days)
  3. James Polk (53 years, 225 days)
  4. Abraham Lincoln (56 years, 62 days)
  5. Chester Arthur (57 years, 44 days)
  6. Warren Harding (57 years, 273 days)
  7. William McKinley (58 years, 228 days)
  8. Theodore Roosevelt (60 years, 71 days)

- Presidential facts:
  1. The youngest to become President was Theodore Roosevelt (43 years old).
  2. The youngest to be elected to the presidency was John F. Kennedy (43 years old).
  3. The oldest to be elected to the presidency was Ronald Reagan (69 years old).
  4. The tallest Presidents were Abraham Lincoln and Lyndon Johnson 6'4").
  5. The shortest President was James Madison (5'3").
  6. The most obese President was William Taft (300+ pounds).
  7. The longest tenured President was Franklin Delano Roosevelt (13 years).
  8. The shortest tenured President was William Harrison (1 month).

- States with less population than Washington, DC (620,000) are:
  1. Wyoming (471,000)
  2. Alaska (513,000)
  3. Vermont (556,000)

- The only elected U.S. Presidents to succeed the President they served were:
  1. John Adams (succeeded George Washington, 1787)
  2. Thomas Jefferson (succeeded John Adams, 1801)
  3. Martin Van Buren (succeeded Andrew Jackson, 1837)
  4. George Bush (succeeded Ronald Reagan, 1989)

- What's in a name?
  1. Michigan (great water)
  2. Connecticut (long river place)
  3. Oklahoma (red man)
  4. Wisconsin (grassy place)
  5. Minnesota (cloudy water)

- The three faces originally scheduled to be carved on Mount Rushmore were:
  1. Kit Carson
  2. Jim Bridger
  3. John Colter

- In Great Britain, Valentine's Day is celebrated by:
  1. Sending cards signed with dots
  2. Receiving gifts of fruit and money
  3. Singing special Valentine songs
  4. Baking buns with seeds or raisins
  5. Women waiting by a window for a man to pass (the old custom said that the first man by the window would become your husband)

- Some of the all-time best-selling books of fiction are:
  1. *The Godfather* (1969)
  2. *The Exorcist* (1971)
  3. *To Kill a Mockingbird* (1960)
  4. *Peyton Place* (1956)
  5. *Love Story* (1970)
  6. *Valley of the Dolls* (1966)
  7. *Jaws* (1974)
  8. *Jonathan Livingston Seagull* (1970)
  9. *Gone with the Wind* (1936)
  10. *God's Little Acre* (1933)

- The most common surnames in the United States are:
  1. Smith
  2. Johnson
  3. Williams
  4. Brown
  5. Jones
  6. Miller
  7. Davis
  8. Martin
  9. Anderson
  10. Wilson

- "Blues" music started in Memphis, Tennessee.
- The most recognizable U.S. brand names worldwide are:
  1. Coca-Cola
  2. Campbell's Soup
  3. Pepsi
  4. AT&T
  5. McDonald's
  6. American Express
  7. Kellogg's
  8. IBM
  9. Levi's
  10. Sears

- Weather extremes in the continental United States:
  1. Warmest is Key West, Florida (avg. 77.7 degrees).
  2. Coldest is International Falls, Minnesota (avg. 36.4 degrees).
  3. Driest is Yuma, Arizona (avg. 2.65 inches rain).
  4. Wettest is Quillayute, Washington (avg. 104.5 inches rain).
  5. Sunniest is Yuma, Arizona (avg. 17 days rain).

- *World Bok Encyclopedia* editors recorded that the most frequently looked up topics by students in school libraries were:
  1. Dog
  2. Snake
  3. Cat
  4. Fish
  5. Bird
  6. Presidents of the United States
  7. Horse
  8. Flag
  9. Dinosaur
  10. Baseball
  11. Whale

12. Animal
13. Abraham Lincoln
14. George Washington
15. Football
16. Airplane
17. Earth
18. Elephant
19. Florida
20. United States

- William Howard Taft was the first U.S. President to play golf.
- In 1789, at first session of Congress, a lack of quorum forced the Congress to adjourn:
  1. Senators—8 of 22 attended
  2. Representatives—13 of 59 attended

- It was Abraham Lincoln who first said "Government of the people, by the people and for the people."
- Humans can swim up to 5 miles per hour. How does that compare to the following?
  1. Sailfish, 65 miles per hour
  2. Bluefish tuna, 40 mph
  3. Swordfish, 35 mph
  4. Barracuda, 30 mph
  5. Dolphin, 25 mph
  6. Sea turtle, 20 mph
  7. Whale, 20 mph
  8. Trout, 5 mph

- For the birds:
  1. The fastest flyer is the Peregrine Falcon (180 mph)
  2. The fastest on land is the Ostrich (40 mph)
  3. The smallest bird is the Bee Hummingbird (2 inches)
  4. The largest bird is the Ostrich (8 feet)
  5. The highest flyer is the Bareheaded Goose (25,000 feet)
  6. The longest traveler is the Arctic Tern (11,000 miles, migration from Arctic to Antarctic)
  7. The deepest diver is the Loon (160 feet)

- The South has been called "Dixie" since about 1850. Credit the Citizens Bank of Louisiana, New Orleans, for that. Before the Civil War, it produced reliable $10 bills accepted nationwide. Printed partly in English and partly in French, the bill showed "Dix," meaning "Ten" on it. The word *Dixie* came to stand for "good currency," and then as a nickname for the South.
- Winning foot racers in ancient Greece received a celery stalk rather than a Gold Medal!
- Sonan is the oldest surviving family name in the United States; descendants go back to 1565 in St. Augustine, Florida.
- What is in a name and how was it named?
  1. Parker House Rolls (Parker House Hotel, Boston)
  2. Dr. Pepper (owner of drugstore where it was developed)
  3. Noxzema (from the words "knocks eczema")
  4. Worcestershire sauce (from Worcester, England)
  5. Murine (chemical formula muriate of berberine)
  6. Avon products (founder loved the works of William Shakespeare)

- The story of *Robinson Crusoe* was based on the life of an old pirate named Alexander Selkirk who, for nine years (1703–1712) was marooned on a Pacific Island.
- The five largest metropolitan areas in the world in the 1990s are:
  1. Tokyo-Yokohama, Japan
  2. Mexico City, Mexico
  3. Sao Paulo, Brazil
  4. Seoul, Korea
  5. New York, USA

- General George Armstrong Custer was a hero at the Battle of Gettysburg.
- China raises more horses than the United States; California more than Texas.
- Thomas Nast, the political cartoonist, had a word coined for his work: "nasty."
- President Rutherford B. Hayes's favorite sport was croquet.
- Woodrow Wilson was so sick with migraine headaches as a child that he did not learn to read until he was 11 years old. He later became a university president and then President of the United States.
- Kissing has been around for a very long time. Poets from ancient India, Greece, and Persia all wrote about kissing some 4,000 years ago.
- Subaru in Japanese is what we call that star cluster known as Pleiades, or the Seven Sisters. Check out the Subaru car emblem!
- The oldest letter of any alphabet is *O*.
- There are no native trees on Antarctica.
- Objects that discriminate against left-handers are:
  1. Band instruments
  2. Microscopes
  3. Auto dashboards
  4. Pencil sharpeners
  5. Watch winding stems
  6. Cameras
  7. Fishing reels
  8. Most instruction booklets (written for right-handers)

- "Lemonade" Lucy Rutherford was so named because she would not allow alcoholic beverages served in the White House during her husband's term of office.
- Thomas Jefferson invented the folding chair.
- In Benjamin Franklin's day, if you had a rug in your house, you were considered rich.
- In 1956 the polio vaccine developed by Dr. Jonas Salk was given to children for the first time. Dr. Salk worked for nearly 20 years developing the vaccine.
- In World War I Germany was the first nation to equip its pilots with parachutes.
- The poorest nation in the world is probably Bhutan; people earn less than $100 a year.
- Youngest first ladies:*
  1. Frances Cleveland (21 years, 226 days)
  2. Julia Tyler (24 years, 53 days)
  3. Jacqueline Kennedy (31 years, 176 days)

---

*Hillary Rodman Clinton was 45 years and 112 days old when her husband was inaugurated in 1993.

4. Edith Roosevelt (40 years, 39 days)
5. Edith Wilson (40 years, 140 days)
6. Dolly Madison (40 years, 288 days)
7. Sarah Polk (41 years, 181 days)
8. Mary Lincoln (42 years, 81 days)

- Canada is a really big country! Vancouver, British Columbia, is closer to Tokyo, Japan, than it is to Nova Scotia's Halifax in its own nation!
- Checkers originated as a game of war strategy in Egypt.
- Before Christopher Columbus came to the "New World," a squirrel, if so inclined, could go by tree top from the Atlantic Ocean to the Mississippi River. Where have all the trees gone?
- Hawaii is the state with the least amount of fresh lake water.
- At least 13 U.S. Presidents have Scottish ancestry: Monroe, Jackson, Polk, Buchanan, Andrew Johnson, Harrison, McKinley, T. Roosevelt, and Wilson.
- Population growth in the world's five largest countries, predicted for the next 30 years (1990 to 2020):
  1. China (34,400 persons per day)
  2. India (47,600 persons per day)
  3. CIS (5,900 persons per day)
  4. USA (3,900 persons per day)
  5. Indonesia (8,900 persons per day)
- The population under age 15 in the world's most populous countries:
  1. Nigeria (45 percent under age 15)
  2. Pakistan (45 percent)
  3. Bangladesh (44 percent)
  4. Indonesia (40 percent)
  5. India (38 percent)
  6. Brazil (36 percent)
  7. China (28 percent)
  8. CIS (26 percent)
  9. Japan (22 percent)
  10. USA (22 percent)
- Illiteracy rate in the world's 10 largest countries (persons age 15 or older):
  1. Bangladesh (74 percent)
  2. Pakistan (74 percent)
  3. Nigeria (66 percent)
  4. India (64 percent)
  5. Indonesia (33 percent)
  6. Brazil (24 percent)
  7. China (23 percent)
  8. Japan (less than 1 percent)
  9. Australia (less than 1 percent)
  10. New Zealand (less than 1 percent)
  11. CIS (less than 1 percent)
- Female life expectancy is lower than male life expectancy in the following countries:*
  1. Afghanistan
  2. Bangladesh
  3. India

*Female life expectancy in the United States is 78. Male life expectancy in the United States is 71.

    4. Iran

    5. Nepal

    6. Pakistan

- Los Angeles County is the largest county in the United States, with about a million people living there.
- The last American Civil War veteran died in 1959.
- The "Star Spangled Banner" became our official national anthem in 1931.
- Thomas Edison failed 24,999 times before inventing a successful storage battery.
- There are about half a million words in the American-English alphabet. The average person has a vocabulary of about 10,000 words.
- The shortest transcontinental railroad (Atlantic to Pacific) is located at the Panama Canal.
- The seven wonders of the modern world as selected by the American Society of Civil Engineers in the 1970s are:

    1. Chicago Sewage Disposal System

    2. Colorado River Aqueduct

    3. Grand Coulee Dam

    4. Hoover Dam

    5. Panama Canal

    6. San Francisco-Oakland Bay Bridge

    7. Empire State Building

What structures could be added to this list in the 1990s?

- The Incas were the first and most prolific road builders in the "New World." One of their roads was 2,500 miles long—going from Colombia to Chile.
- The Cassowary of Australia and New Guinea is the most dangerous bird in the world.
- Buddhist monks in India developed karate about 2,500 years ago.
- Phoenix (Arizona) and Indianapolis (India) are the two largest (by population) capital cities. Montpelier (Vermont) and Pierre (South Dakota) are the two smallest.
- Americans love to munch and snack all day long:

    1. Chicago, per capita, consumes the most Twinkies.

    2. Dallas loves Fritos

    3. New York City devours Hersheys Kisses.

    4. Pikeville (Kentucky) has the biggest per capita consumption of Pepsi Cola.

    5. Miami is tops in Perrier and prune juice consumption.

    6. Portland (Oregon) loves Grape-Nuts.

    7. Salt Lake City has the biggest per capita consumption of Cracker Jacks.

    8. Hartford and New Haven (Connecticut) and Springfield (Massachusetts) are the pasta centers of the United States.

    9. Seattle has the most Hershey bar eaters.

    10. Chicago's O'Hare International Airport sells more hot dogs than any other concession in the country.

    11. Midwesterners are the biggest per capita consumers of lunchmeat.

- One out of every six people currently living in Canada was born somewhere else.
- By act of Congress, only three people have been honored as honorary U.S. citizens:

    1. Sir Winston Churchill

  2. The Marquis de LaFayette
  3. Raoul Wallenberg

- William Wirtz was the only military person executed for "war crimes" at the conclusion of the Civil War. He was the commandant of the infamous Andersonville prison where thousands died.
- The popular and familiar American vision of "Santa Claus" was created by a Coca-Cola magazine ad in the early 1930s.
- In 1874 the elephant, as a Republican party symbol, first appeared in a cartoon by Thomas Nast in *Harper's Weekly*. He used the elephant several times as the symbol and it soon caught on for the Republican Party.
- The donkey was used as a political symbol by Andrew Jackson after his opponents called him a "jackass" during the 1828 election campaign. Later, Thomas Nast, as he had with the elephant for the Republican party, used the donkey to represent the Democratic party in his political cartoons, and it too became the official symbol for the 1880s.
- The first Peace Corps volunteer went to Ghana, Africa, in 1961.
- Names on maps do change:
  1. Uganda was once Buganda.
  2. Bermuda was Somers Island.
  3. Ecuador was Quito.
  4. Ghana was Gold Coast.
  5. Cameroon was German Kamerun.
  6. Mexico was New Spain.
  7. Indonesia was Netherlands East Indies.
  8. Crete was Candia.
  9. Saudi Arabioa was Arabia.
  10. Myanmar was Burma.
  11. Commonwealth of Independent States was Union of Soviet Socialist Republic.

- "I only regret that I have but one life to give for my country." Who said that? Evidently, not Nathan Hale. Recently discovered eye-witness accounts indicate that his last words were: "It's the duty of every good officer to obey any orders given him by his commander-in-chief."
- Even explorers do not always know what they have found or how to get there:
  1. Columbus thought Cuba was China.
  2. Ponce de Leon thought Florida was an island.
  3. John Cabot thought Newfoundland was China.

- William McKinley is the only U.S. President who has no personal residence still standing.
- *Time, People, Sports Illustrated, TV Guide,* and *Newsweek* were the magazines with the highest advertising revenue for 1990.
- The ice cream soda was said to have been invented in Denver, Colorado, in 1871.
- Charles Curtis, Vice President under President Herbert Hoover, was the first native American to serve in that office. His mother was a member of the Kaw tribe.
- Two years before Christopher Columbus sailed to the "New World," a German mapmaker named Martin Behaim made the first geographical globe and called it "Earth Apple." Columbus never saw it, but he, like many educated Europeans, knew the world was round.
- President Theodore Roosevelt held the first press conference.
- Damascus, Syria, is the oldest city in the world.

- The oldest one-family farm in the United States of America is the Tuttle vegetable farm in Dover, New Hampshire, dating back to 1632.
- The first pay phone was installed in Hartford, Connecticut, in 1889.
- Shoelaces were invented in England four years before the United States of America came into being.
- Steelville, Missouri, is said to be the geographical center of the United States of America.
- The Sioux call themselves "Lacotas."
- Anne Bradstreet is considered by some to be the first significant U.S. poet.
- The *Fiji Times* claims that it is "the first newspaper published in the world today." The International Dateline is very near Fiji.
- In 1937, Chester Carbon invented the process used in today's office copy machines.
- Kit Carson's American frontiersman and explorer, dying words reportedly were: "I'm gone, goodbye, doctor. Adios, compadre."
- Iowa raises the most pigs, California the most eggs, Georgia the most peanuts, and Arkansas the most rice.
- The typewriter revolutionized U.S. business when it came on the market in 1888.
- Salmon P. Chase, Abraham Lincoln's Secretary of the Treasury, decided our money should be green.
- Sandra Berenson Abbot of Smith College is considered by many to have been the first person to write the rules for women's basketball.
- The most common names:
  Japan: Suzuki
  France: Martin (pronounced mar-teen)
  CIS: Kuznetsky
  Poland: Kowalski
  China: Wang
  Czechoslovakia: Kovak
  Spain: Gomez
- Christmas and May Day always fall on the same day of the week.
- Benjamin Franklin invented the spelling bee.
- The apricot is considered to be the oldest fruit known to humankind.
- Queen Elizabeth I is given credit for inventing the "gingerbread man" (the Royal Chef probably invented it).
- No American president ever won a majority vote. Lyndon Johnson came the closest, with 38 percent in 1964.
- The first jigsaw puzzle was a map of Europe that was divided into national boundaries as they were in 1766.
- Nellie Ross Taylor was the first woman to be elected governor in the United States (1925, Wyoming).
- Some believe that Lionel Steinbuger invented the cheeseburger at his father's cafe in 1924.
- The only walled metropolis in North America is Quebec City, Canada.
- Juneau, Alaska, is the only state capital not accessible by land.
- President Taft, in 1910, reported that cocaine posed the greatest threat to the United States of America.
- The Great Barrier Reef off the coast of Australia is considered the world's largest living thing.
- Oklahoma has more tornadoes per square mile than any other state.
- Giovani Caboto is explorer John Cabot's real name.
- California was the first state to elect two women to serve concurrently in the Senate (1992).

- Of the Earth's total surface, 75 percent is water; 99.5 percent of that is undrinkable!
- Only five U.S. cities have "The" as the official first word in the city's name:
  1. The Dalles, Oregon
  2. The Village, Oklahoma
  3. The Village of Indian Hills, Ohio
  4. The Plains, Ohio
  5. The Meadows, Illinois

- M&M candy stands for the initials of the inventors, Forrest Mars and Bruce Murrie.
- President Thomas Jefferson predicted it would take 40 generations to conquer the American wilderness. It took only about 4 generations.
- State capitals with "City" in their names:
  1. Salt Lake City, Utah
  2. Jefferson City, Missouri
  3. Carson City, Nevada
  4. Oklahoma City, Oklahoma

- Arthur de Lulli was originally listed as the composer of "Chopsticks" in 1877. In truth, it was a 16-year-old girl named Euphemia Allen who used the name of de Lulli.
- Some famous people born on the Fourth of July were:
  1. Calvin Coolidge
  2. Stephen Foster
  3. Nathaniel Hawthorne
  4. Louis Armstrong
  5. Neil Simon
  6. Ann Landers/Abigail VanBuren (twins)

- Meaning of capital city names:
  1. Jerusalem, Israel: "city of peace"
  2. Beirut, Lebanon: "well"
  3. Bangkok, Thailand: "forest village"
  4. Madrid, Spain: "timber"
  5. Warsaw, Poland: "castle"
  6. Seoul, South Korea: "capital"
  7. Beijing, China: "northern capital"
  8. Ottawa, Canada: "to trade"

- In comparison:
  1. Romania is slightly smaller than Oregon.
  2. Hungary is slightly smaller than Indiana.
  3. Luxembourg is slightly smaller than Rhode Island.
  4. Czechoslovakia is slight larger than New York.
  5. Yugoslavia is slightly larger than Wyoming.
  6. Poland is slightly smaller than New Mexico

- The following magazines have published continuously without missing an issue:
  1. *Scientific American* (146 years)
  2. *Town and Country* (145 years)
  3. *The Atlantic* (134 years)
  4. *Popular Science* (119 years)
  5. *McCall's* (115 years)
  6. *Ladies Home Journal* (108 years)
  7. *Good Housekeeping* (106 years)

8. *The Sporting News* (105 years)
9. *Sports Afield* (104 years)

- A black man from Haiti named Jean Baptiste Pointe du Sable found a settlement in 1772 and called it Eschikagou. Today we call it Chicago.
- About 4 million slaves were officially freed after the American Civil War ended in 1865.
- Rebecca Felton was the first U.S. Senator (appointed in October of 1922).
- Hattie Carroway was the first woman elected to the U.S. Senate (1932).
- Benjamin Franklin invented suspenders in 1736.
- The three most popular natural attractions in the United States are:
  1. The Grand Canyon (Arizona)
  2. Yellowstone National Park (Wyoming)
  3. Niagara Falls (New York)
- Dogs were probably first domesticated in present-day Iran some 2,000 years ago.
- George Washington's favorite soup was made from peanuts.
- The Labor Day holiday was probably created by either Peter McGuire or Matthew Maguire. The argument has never really been resolved.
- The "wildest" river in North America is probably the Yukon in northern British Columbia, Canada.
- Robert Frost, in 1961 at the inauguration of John Kennedy, was the first poet to read a poem during the inauguration ceremony.
- Point Barrow, Alaska, is the northern-most point of the United States.
- The U.S./Canadian border is 3,987 miles long; the U.S./Mexican border is 1,933 miles long.
- The first U.S. zoo was the Philadelphia Zoological Gardens, which opened in 1874. It still exists on the same grounds.
- Elizabeth Hisington was the first female general in the United States Army (appointed in 1970).
- Benjamin O. Davis in 1940 became the first black general in the U.S. Army.
- Ben Nighthorse Campbell of Colorado was the first Native American to be elected to the U.S. Senate (1992).
- Francis Perkins was the first woman to become a cabinet member. She served as Secretary of Labor in the Roosevelt administration from 1933 to 1945.
- Martha Washington was the first woman commemorated on a postage stamp (1918).
- There are 132 Hawaiian Islands. The Hawaiian Islands are only one of the many archipelagos in the world.
- The Humber Suspension Bridge near Hull, England, is the longest bridge in the world. It is 4,626 feet long and was completed in 1981.
- There are eight time zones in North America.
- Oreos are the world's best-selling cookies.
- Herbert Hoover was the first U.S. President born west of the Mississippi River (August 10, 1874) in Iowa.
- Trygve Lie of Norway was the first Secretary-General of the United Nations (1946 to 1952).
- Carol Moseley Braun of Illinois was the first African-American woman to be elected to the U.S. Senate (1992).
- Park is the most common street name in the United States of America.
- Madrid, Spain, at 2,150 feet above sea level, is the highest capital city in Europe.
- Since 1899, it has been illegal for any factory to dump any waste into any body of U.S. water.

TEACHING HISTORY IS A DAILY EVENT

The Calendar

The ordinary everyday daily calendar just might be the most complete, inexpensive, and accessible teaching resource in social studies education. Teachers do highlight a special day here and there but rarely do they use the calendar as a teaching tool to help enrich social studies content.

In the hands of a skillful teacher, the calendar can become a wonderfully exciting instructional tool. Besides serving as a means to mark significant dates in history or as a reminder of someone's birthday, the calendar can also be used to initiate creative writing sessions, art projects, musical productions, or simulation and role-playing activities. In short, the calendar can supplement the more traditional social studies materials and help breathe life into the daily curriculum. It can be used as a tool helping students learn basic research skills. It can also serve as the starting point in inquiry-oriented lessons, providing some answers while children resolve the "why" of history content. Finally, the calendar is a bridge from the past to the present and future.

The following pages are intended to outline some significant dates as well as offer some fun learning/teaching activities. Teachers are encouraged to refer daily to a calendar and to assist children in developing a concept of time and history. Classroom calendars (recording daily school/community events) or class time lines are fun and informational by-products enjoyed by students in this process.

GENERAL INFORMATION ABOUT CALENDARS:

1. *Calend* was the name ancient Romans gave the first day of each new month. The term was adopted and changed to *calendar* by the new Christian nations in Europe after the fall of Rome.
2. The concept of a calendar (the measuring of days) has been around since ancient times. Many ancient cultures, such as the Babylonians, Mayans, Egyptians, and Romans, developed a "calendar" to measure time. Some were lunar (based on the moon) while others were solar (based on the sun). But all were vital in everyday life for the people in these societies.
3. The Jewish calendar, which also has 12 months, celebrates "New Year" in the fall of each solar year. The months are called Tishri, Heshvan, Kislev, Tebet, Shebat, Adar, Nisan, Iyar, Sivan, Tammuz, Ab, and Elul. The Jewish calendar year is calculated by adding 3760 to the date of the Christian calendar. For example, in 2000 the Jewish calendar would be 5760. The number 3760 represents the years the Jewish culture existed before the birth of Jesus Christ, hence the difference in years.
4. the Islamic calendar marks its beginning with Muhammad's flight from Mecca to Medina in A.D. 632 (Christian calendar). Consequently, in the year 2000, the Islamic calendar would 1368. They, too, have a 12-month calendar and those months are Muharran, Safar, Rabi I, Rabi II, Jumada I, Jumada II, Rajab, Shabau, Ramadan, Shawwal, Zulkadah, and Zulhijjah. There are 354 days in the Islamic calendar.
5. The Chinese calendar began in 2367 B.C., which makes it 4367 in the Christian calendar. The calendar is based on cycles of 60. For example, in the year 2000, it will be the seventeenth year in the seventy-eighth cycle. Chinese New Year comes no earlier than January 20th and no later than February 20th.

6. The current Christian calendar (Gregorian calendar) was adopted by Pope Gregory XIII in 1583. This calendar has a cycle of 12 months with 10 or 11 of those months having at least 30 or 31 days. The exception is February, which has 28 days except on a Leap Year when it has 29 days. 1966 is a Leap Year. The calendar is based on the life of Jesus Christ, the Christian savior. A.D. refers to the years following the birth; B.C. refers to the years prior to the birth. Non-Christians sometimes use BCE to refer to "Before Christian Era" and CE as "Christian Era."

7. Days of each week are probably derived and named from ancient calendars. They are:
   Sunday—for Helios (Greek god of the Sun)
   Monday—for Selene (Greek goddess of the Moon)
   Tuesday—for Tyr (Norse god of War)
   Wednesday—for Woden (Norse Ruler of the gods)
   Thursday—for Thor (Norse god of Thunder)
   Friday—for Frigga (Norse goddess of Marriage)
   Saturday—for Saturn (Roman god of Time)

General Activities for the Calendar

Activity 1: Time

Each student in the class finds one quote that pertains to *time* and brings that quote to class. The teacher prepares a large clock and the quotes can be arranged in such a manner that the face of the clock is made up of quotes. (Examples of quotes: "Time waits for no man"; "For those who love, time is eternity"; "Till the end of time"; "It's always the right time to do right"; etc.).

Activity 2: Basic Research Skills

1. Students scan research on Galileo Galilei with particular reference to his "pendulum" discovery. A pendulum can then be constructed in class and Galileo's theory demonstrated.
2. Students can research the life and times of Louis XVI of France with particular reference to his interest in fixing clocks. Parts of a clock can be reassembled in class.

Activity 3: Art Activity

Given the derivation of the days of the week, students can choose one god or goddess and draw their interpretation of that deity.

Activity 4: Music and Time

Find a selection of songs that contain the words "time," "days of the week," or "months of the year." Edit snippets of the songs onto a tape. Students listen to each song and write down all the references to *time, days,* or *months*. (Examples of songs: "Calendar Girl," "Come September," "Time and the River," "Eight Days a Week," "Never on a Sunday," "Autumn in New York," etc.)

Activity 5: Now and Then

On any special day or holiday, students can role-play a "now and then" situation. For example, on Lincoln's birthday, one student can role-play Lincoln from the 1860s and another student can role-play the same scenario from a present-day perspective.

Activity 6: Tracking Time

After a lesson on sundials, take small groups of students outside where they can construct their own sundial. Groups can move around, clockwise or counterclockwise, and attempt to tell the time from each other's sundials.

January

The month of January was named for Janus, a Roman mythological god who has two faces looking in opposite directions. One face looks to the future and one face looks to the past.

> **Some Interesting Facts about January**
> 1. January is the first month of the year according to the Gregorian calendar.
> 2. Anglo-Saxons called January "Wolfmonth" because wolves came into the village in the winter (January) in search of food.
> 3. The Snowdrop is the special flower of the month because it often blooms in the snow.
> 4. The Garnet is the gem for January.

Activity 1

Date: January 10

Event: Sherlock Holmes's Birthday

Level: Grades 3–5

Lesson Plan: Students will have a better understanding of mystery, detection literature, and the nuts and bolts of writing mystery fiction stories.

Activity: Students will read a variety of mystery or detective stories and write one mystery of their own about some aspect of our school. These mysteries will then be drawn at random for the two fifth-grade classes to solve together over the period of three days.

Questions:
1. Who was Sherlock Holmes?
2. What kind of an impression did the character of Sherlock Holmes make on you?
3. What techniques did you recognize that the author, Sir Arthur Conan Doyle, used to create suspense in his books?
4. What techniques did you use to create your own mystery and why did you choose to use this method or technique?

Skills Taught: Knowledge of literature, writing skills, and cognitive thinking skills involved with writing and solving mysteries.

Resources: Plenty of Sherlock Holmes books and any other quality mysteries.

Activity 2

Date: January 15

Event: Martin Luther King, Jr.'s Birthday

JANUARY

1
New Year's Day
- 1st Federal income tax went into effect in the U.S. (1862)
- President Lincoln issued Emancipation Proclamation freeing all slaves in areas still in rebellion (1863)

2
- First commemorative stamp was issued in 1893 depicting Columbus's voyage
- Georgia Admission Day, 4th state, 1788

3
- Lucretia Mott born 1793
- Alaska Admission Day, 49th state, 1959

4
- Utah Admission Day, 45th state, 1896
- Louis Braille's birthday, 1809, developed a touch/writing system

5
- Nellie Taylor Ross of Wyoming became the 1st women Governor, 1925
- Jeannette Ridlon Piccard's birthday, 1st woman to qualify as free balloon pilot in 1934

6
- New Mexico Admission Day, 47th state, 1912
- Armenian Christmas

7
- Millard Fillmore 13th President, born 1800
- First Presidential election held 1789
- First balloon flight across English Channel
- Eastern Orthodox Christmas

8
- Elvis Presley's birthday
- President Woodrow Wilson lays out a 14 pt. peace plan to Congress
- Battle of New Orleans, 1815

9
- Connecticut Admission Day, 5th state, 1788
- Richard Nixon, 37th president, born in 1913

10
- Oil discovered in Texas 1901
- Ethan Allen's birthday, Revolutionary war hero
- Sherlock Holmes's birthday

11
- Nepal National Unity Day
- Alexander Hamilton's birthday, 1755, an American statesman
- Alice Paul's birthday, women's right leader
- Winterfest begins

12
- Jack London, born in 1876
- Ira Hayes's birthday, soldier who raised flag at Iwo Jima, 1945
- Tanzania, Zanzibar Revolution Day

13
- Horatio Alger's birthday
- Stephen Foster, composer 38 dies, 1864

14
- Henry Ford inaugurated his assembly line in 1914
- Benedict Arnold's birthday
- Ratification Day of the U.S. Constitution
- Eastern Orthodox New Year

15
- Humanitarian Day (Chicago region), day of respect towards unsung leaders of Civil Rights Movement
- Martin Luther King, Jr.'s Birthday

16
- Human Relations Day
- Ethel Merman's birthday
- National Nothing Day
- Religious Freedom Day
- Debbie Allen's birthday, 1950
- A.J. Foyt's birthday, 1935

17
- U.S. Air bombed Iraq, War started, 1991

18
- Daniel Webster, born in 1782
- "Pooh Day," birth of Alan Milne, author
- Representatives from 32 allied nations gather in Versailles to discuss Peace Treaty, 1919

19
- James Watt, inventor of the steam engine was born in 1736
- Carrot Festival in Holtville, CA
- Chocolate Festival, Knoxville, TN

20
- Basketball players first dribbled down the court in 1892
- first time U.S. officially observed Martin Luther King Day, 1986

21
- John Fitch's birthday, 1743, American inventor
- Thomas (Stonewall) Jackson's birthday, 1824

22
- National Popcorn Day!!
- F.W. Woolworth opened first 5 and 10 store in N.Y., 1879

23
- John Hancock born 1737
- Joseph Heves birthday, signer of Declaration of Independence
- National Pie Day in Boulder, CO
- National Handwriting Day

24
- Eskimo Pie was patented by Christian Nelson, 1922
- Gold discovered in California, 1848
- Clash Day!, wear brightest mismatched clothes to work

25
- Robert Burn's birthday, Scottish poet, born 1759
- Frederick Wells finds the Cullinan diamond, 1905
- Alexander Graham Bell with Thomas A. Watson made another historic phone call between N.Y. and San Francisco

26
- Michigan Admission Day, 26th state, 1837
- Australia Day since 1788
- Republic Day in India

27
- Mozart born in 1756
- Thomas Edison was granted his patent for the incandescent light in 1880

28
- Great Seal of the U.S. Anniversary, 1782
- First ski tour in 1934 at Woodstock, Vermont
- 1st comm. telephone exchange opened, New Haven, CN, 1878

29
- Kansas Admission Day, 34th state, 1861
- William McKinley's birthday, 25th president, 1843
- Thomas Paine, born in 1737

30
- F.D. Roosevelt, 32nd President, born 1882
- Adolf Hitler 44, leader of Nazi party appointed Chancellor, 1933
- Mohandas Gandhi of India assassinated, 1948

31
- In 1974, New Jersey Division of Civil Rights ruled that Little League baseball teams must let girls play
- Explorer 1 launched by army, 1958, first U.S. earth satellite

Level: Grades 4–8

Lesson Plan: Students will have a better understanding of the feelings for the dreams of Martin Luther King, Jr. They will also have a better understanding of their own future insights and dreams.

Activity: Read or listen to King's speech. Discuss as a class Martin Luther King Jr.'s dreams. Have students write about a dream of their own.

Questions:
1. Why was Martin Luther King such a historical figure in our country?
2. What does the King speech mean to you?
3. If you were alive in King's time, what would you have contributed to the cause of equality for all people?
4. What is a problem in our society today and what can/will you do to improve or solve that problem?

Skills Taught: Appreciation of the problems of our country's past, ability to look for solutions regarding our country's future, and awareness of the African-American culture and history of our country.

Resources: Resources include a video or written copy of the famous speech, "I Have a Dream" given by Martin Luther King, Jr. on August 28, 1963, at the Lincoln Memorial in Washington, DC.

Activity 3

Date: January 27, 1756

Event: Mozart's Birthday

Level: Grades K–4

Lesson Plan: At the conclusion of this lesson, the students will have a better understanding of the power of classical music.

Activity: Students will listen to Mozart's music as they are doing art activities and during any other appropriate times.

Questions:
1. How does Mozart's music make you feel?
2. Do you draw or paint according to the message that the music is sending you?
3. What is your favorite part about listening to this music?
4. What would you change about this music?

Skills Taught: How to create art through identification with music and the message it sends.

Resources: Resources include Mozart's musical pieces.

February

The month of February comes from the Latin word *februarie*, which means to purify.

Some Interesting Facts about February
1. February is the shortest month of the year (28 days, 29 days in Leap Year).
2. According to tradition, the Roman Emperor Augustus took one day from February and added it to August, which is the month named after him, to make February the month with 28 days.

FEBRUARY

1	2	3	4	5	6	7
-American Heart Month since 1964 -American History Month -Black History Month -National Snack Food Month -Boy Scout Month	-William Rose Benet, American poet born in 1886 -Groundhog Day	-Norman Rockwell born in 1894 -First paper money was issued in America, 1690 -Space Shuttle Challenger was launched on its 4th trip	-Charles Lindbergh born in 1902 -USO birthday since 1941 -George Washington chosen President, 1789	-Hank Aaron, born 1934 -Weatherman's Day, birth of one of America's 1st weathermen, John Jefferson, 1744	-Massachusetts, Admission Day, 6th state, 1788 -Babe Ruth's birthday in 1895 -Mid-winters Day Celebration, Ann Arbor, MI	-Author Charles Dicken's birthday, 1812 -Ballet introduced to the U.S. -Granada: Independence Day -No Talk Day, write to communicate without talking

8	9	10	11	12	13	14
-The Confederate States of America formed, 1861 -Boy Scouts of America founded 1910 -Arbor Day, Arizona	-William H. Harrison, 9th President, born in 1733 -Carrot Day -Zoo Affair, NC	-In 1933 the Postal Telegraph Co. introduced the singing telegraph -Queen Victoria marries her cousin Prince Albert, 1840	-Inventor Thomas Edison born, 1847 -Iceland: Bun Day -White Shirt Day in Flint, MI -Burt Reynold's birthday	-Henry Lindfield became the 1st automobile fatality, 1898 -Abraham Lincoln, 16th President, 1809 -Charles Darwin, author and naturalist born, 1809	-Grant Wood, American artist, born 1892 -First public school in America was established in Boston in 1635	-Arizona Admission Day, 48th state, 1912 -Oregon Admission Day 33rd state, 1859 -St. Valentine's Day

15	16	17	18	19	20	21
-Susan B. Anthony's birthday, 1820 -Chinese New Year!	-Dinosaurs and more exhibit in Pocatello, ID -Lithuania, Independence Day! -Teddy Bear Tea in Barstow, CA	-Geronimo died on this day, 1909 -National Youth Workout Day	-The planet Pluto first seen, 1930 -Cyprus: Green Monday -Gambia: Independence Day -Presidents Day - U.S. Holiday	-Nicolaus Copernicus, astronomer, born 1473 -Washington's birthday -Germany: Demotechnia, International Trade Fair	-First American in space John Glenn, Jr., 1962 circled earth 3 times in the Mercury capsule -National Art Gallery paid 6 million for a portrait by Da Vinci, 1967	-Edwin Holmes invented the burglar alarm in 1858 -Richard Trevithick invents first steam locomotive, 1804 -New Yorker Magazine's birthday

22	23	24	25	26	27	28
-George Washington, 1st President, born in 1732 -St. Lucia Independence Day -French Fry Friday, Tri-Cities, WA	-W.E.B. Dubois, Black American educator born in 1868 -Santa Anne attacked the Americans in the Alamo, March 23, ended attack, 1836	-A 31 year old German soldier (Adolf Hitler) addressed 2,000 members of the National Socialist German workers, 1920	-Samuel Colt patented the first U.S. six gun in 1836 -Kuwait: National Holiday -Suriname: Revolution Day	-Grand Canyon became a National Park, 1919 -Dominican Republic: Independence Day -Robert Watson-Watt, demonstrates use of apparatus for the detection of air craft by radio methods, 1935	-Eclipse, a very famous race horse dies, 1789 -St. Gabriel Possenti Feast Day -Gulf War cease fire, 1991	-Republican party formed in Ripen, WI, 1854 -Charro Day in Texas

203

3. The Primrose is the flower for February.
4. The Amethyst is the gem for February.

Activity 1

Date: February 21, 1858

Event: Edwin Holmes invented the burglar alarm

Level: Grades 5–8

Lesson Plan: Students will have a better understanding of why and how the burglar alarm was invented.

Activity: Each student will have the opportunity to do some research from tradebooks and encyclopedias on how burglar alarms were invented. After learning about the burglar alarm, students will create their own alarm, using paper to draw it or a variety of mediums to build it.

Questions:
1. Who was Edwin Holmes?
2. Why did he see a need to create a burglar alarm?
3. If you were to build an alarm, what would you be protecting and how would you build this special alarm to protect it?
4. If you were a burglar, what would you do if you found out that there was an alarm created to catch you?

Skills Taught: The reasoning behind a technological invention, how to create one for themselves, and how it feels to look through a burglar's eyes at an alarm.

Resources: Tradebooks and encyclopedias about Edwin Holmes and burglar alarms.

Activity 2

Date: February 22

Event: George Washington's Birthday

Level: Grades 3–7

Lesson Plan: Students will have a better understanding of the history of George Washington and some of his character traits that made him the first President of America.

Activity: Cut out a picture of the American flag. For each star or stripe, students will write facts about George Washington, the era in which he lived, or reasons why he is so respected and honored today.

Questions:
1. Who was George Washington?
2. What do you think it was like growing up during the time of George Washington and his presidency?
3. If you could be any president in the history of our country, which one would you be and why?
4. Using what you know about our nation's history, what do you suppose were some of the major problems facing our country during Washington's presidency?

Skills Taught: To apply their knowledge about one of our nation's leaders toward problem solving and using a creative vehicle to present that information.

Resources: Resources include books on George Washington and the history of that era, as well as books researching the changes in the American flag throughout the history of our country.

Activity 3

Date: February 17

Event: National Youth Workout Day

Level: Grades K–4

Lesson Plan: Students will have a better understanding of health and fitness and its importance throughout our lives.

Activity: Students will participate in many health activities throughout this week, including fitness checks. We will also use movement in the classroom to help use our muscles while using our brains. For instance, in math class we will add people to people and boys to boys and girls to girls. We can use movement and literature together to have students show their comprehension by acting out the story.

Questions:
1. Why is fitness important to our health?
2. What is your favorite form of exercise?
3. How can you improve the overall fitness of your family?
4. If you were to teach a subject of learning, how would you include movement into the lesson?

Skills Taught: Understanding that classroom exercise is not only beneficial but enjoyable.

Resources: Information from P.E. instructor.

March

The month of March is named to honor Mars, the Roman god of War.

Some Interesting Facts about March
1. March is the month that ends winter and begins spring.
2. March comes in like a lion and goes out like a lamb.
3. The Violet is the official flower for March.
4. The Bloodstone and Aquamarine are the gems for March.

Activity 1

Date: March 3, 1814

Event: National Anthem Day

Level: Grades 3–6

Lesson Plan: Students will have a better understanding of why and how we acquired "The Star-Spangled Banner" as our national anthem.

Activity: Students will create their own words to the musical background of "The Star-Spangled Banner" dealing with current events around the world. This can be achieved as a class or in small groups. Ideas can be collected and these can be sung at the next assembly or open house.

Questions:
1. Who wrote "The Star-Spangled Banner" and when?

MARCH

1	2	3	4	5	6	7
-Congress passed Civil Rights Act, 1875 -Nebraska Admission Day, 37th state, 1867 -Ohio Admission Day, 17th state, 1803 -President John F. Kennedy set up Peace Corps, 1961	-Dr. Seuss's birthday, 1904 -Hog calling contest in Weatherford, OK -Sam Houston's birthday, American soldier and politician -Texas Independence Day	-Florida Admission Day 27th state, 1845 -National Anthem Day, on this day, 1931, we adopted the Star Spangled Banner	-Vermont Admission Day, 14th state, 1791 -Thomas Jefferson became first president to be inaugurated at new capital, Washington DC, 1801	-Australia's Labor Day -Crispus Attucks Day -Montana and Nevada introduce first state pension for the elderly in the U.S., 1923	-Michelangelo's birthday 1475 -Elizabeth Barrett Browning, poet, 1806 -Dred Scott decision by U.S. Supreme Court, 1857	-Luther Burbank born, 1849 -Alexander Graham Bell was granted the patent for the telephone, 1876
8	**9**	**10**	**11**	**12**	**13**	**14**
-International Women's Day -First train crossed the newly completed Niagara Falls suspension bridge, 1855	-Yuri Gagarin's birthday, 1934 -First patent for false teeth was given to Charles Graham, 1822 -Mexican Revolutionary Francisco "Pancho" villa goes on shooting spree, 1916	-Anniversary of the Salvation Army in the U.S. since 1880 -Fun Mail week to share letter enthusiasm and encourage letter writing	-Johnny Appleseed Day -Canada: Commonwealth Day -Human Services Day	-U.S. Post Office was established, 1789 -American Girl Scouts founded, 1913 -Fireside Chat Day started by President Franklin Roosevelt	-First earmuffs patented in 1877 -Good Samaritan Involvement Day, NY -Grenada: National Holiday	-Albert Einstein's birthday, 1879 -Dade County Youth Fair, Miami, FL
15	**16**	**17**	**18**	**19**	**20**	**21**
-Maine Admission Day 23rd state, 1820 -Andrew Jackson, 7th President, 1767 -The buzzards return to Hinckley, Ohio	-James Madison, 4th President, 1751 -First downhill ski races, 1866	-St. Patrick's Day -Camp Fire boys and girls birthday -Children and Hospitals Week, Bethesda, MD	-Rudolph Diesel, 1858 -Grover Cleveland, 22nd President, 1837 -Soviet Cosmonaut Alexei Leonov floats in space, 1965	-The swallows return to San Juan Capistrano, CA -Australia: Canberra Day	-Earth Day! -Beginning of Spring -"Snowman Burnout", reading of poetry to bring in Spring and put winter away, Sault Ste. Maine	-Benito Juarez's birthday, 1806 -Persia changes name to Iran, 1935 -Vernal Equinox
22	**23**	**24**	**25**	**26**	**27**	**28**
-National Goof Off Day -Marcel Marceau born 1923 -Johann Wolfgang Von Goethe dies, 1832	-"Give Me Liberty or Give Me Death" speech, Patrick Henry, 1775 -Elisha Graves Otis installed the first passenger elevator, 1857	-First American gasoline car was sold in 1898 -Art week	-Bela Bartok, composer born in 1881 -Greek Independence Day -Global understanding Day, Grand Blanc, MI -Maryland Day, MD, commerates first settlers	-Robert Frost, poet, birthday, 1874 -Bangladesh Independence Day -Ludwig Van Beethoven 56, dies of pneumonia, 1827	-First color T.V. broadcast 1955 -Dr. Abraham Gesner discovered process to refine oil into what he called Kerosene, 1856	-Teacher's Day in Czechoslovakia -Three Mile Island Nuclear accident
29	**30**	**31**				
-John Tyler, 10th President, 1790 -Coca-Cola was invented in 1886 -Good Friday -Stamp Expo in Van Nuys, CA	-Treaty of Paris ended the Crimean War, 1856 -First dance marathon, 1923, Alma Cummings danced continuously 24 hrs -Alaska sold to USA, 1867 -Kansas split between proslavery & antislavery factions, elections 1855	-Eiffel Tower officially opened in Paris 1889 -The Treaty of Kanagawa opened Japan to the West 1854				

206

2. What were the circumstances surrounding the creation of this song?
3. Why do you think this song was chosen as our national anthem?
4. What affect will your song have on the history of our class, school, state, or country?

Skills Taught: Learned the importance and the circumstances that led to the creation of our national anthem; musical and writing skills will also be learned through writing a song of their own.

Resources: "The Star-Spangled Banner" by Francis Scott Key.

Activity 2

Date: March 28, 1979

Event: Three Mile Island Nuclear Accident

Level: Grades 4–12

Lesson Plan: At the conclusion of this lesson, students will have a better understanding of not only the need for nuclear power but the hazards of creating, using, and disposing of its waste.

Activity: Students will become the leaders of a small town in Pennsylvania trying to decide how the issue of nuclear power (its creation and disposal of wastes) will be handled in their town. They will study and research the reports written before and after the accident at Three Mile Island and will make a decision of how they will individually deal with nuclear power.

Questions:

1. What happened on March 28, 1979, at the Three Mile Island reactor in Middletown, Pennsylvania?
2. What could have been done to prevent an accident such as this one?
3. How would you have handled this situation?
4. Using your knowledge of the Three Mile Island incident and nuclear power, how will you deal with this situation in your small town in Pennsylvania?

Skills Taught: Learned facts about the positives and negatives of nuclear power; learned the process for making group decisions and dealing with real problematic situations.

Resources: Resources include reports, articles, and any information about nuclear power and the Three Mile Island reactor in Middletown, Pennsylvania.

Activity 3

Date: March 29, 1806

Event: Invention of Coca Cola

Level: Grades K–4

Lesson Plan: Students will have a better understanding of the invention of cola and the production of cola drinks today.

Activity: Students will take a tour of the Coca Cola processing plant and write a letter to the president of Coca Cola, presenting an invention for a new drink, its ingredients, and a reason why people will buy it.

Questions:

1. Why do you think Coca Cola is so popular today?
2. What did you learn at the Coca Cola factory?

3. What were your reasons for creating the drink that you did?

4. How will you get people to try your newly invented drink?

Skills Taught: Learned how Coca Cola is produced, why it is so popular with people today, and how to create a drink of their own that might be tested by the Coca Cola Company.

Resources: Students will tour a Coca Cola processing plant.

April

The name *April* comes from possibly two sources. One source may be the Latin word *Aprilis,* meaning "to open," because in the temperate zones of the Northern hemisphere growth starts in flowers and trees and the hibernating animals are coming out of their dens. The other source may be the word for the Greek goddess of Love, *Aphrodite.*

Some Interesting Facts about April

1. It is the fourth month of the Gregorian Calendar.
2. April has 30 days.
3. It is considered the first month of spring in the Northern hemisphere and the first month of fall in the Southern hemisphere.
4. Many religious holidays are celebrated all over the world in April, such as Christian Easter (usually in April), the Jewish Passover, the Chinese Pure and Bright Festival, and the Canadian and British St. George's Day (patron saint of England).
5. The Daisy is the official flower for April.
6. The Diamond is the gem for April.

Activity 1

Date: April 2

Event: Birthday of Hans Christian Andersen

Level: Grades 4–7

Lesson Plan: Students will be able to discuss how social climate or activities can affect the writing of an author.

Activity: This is an integrated social studies/literature experience activity using the literature of Hans Christian Anderson. Provide a selection of his works in the classroom for students to read. Display a map of Denmark. Choose the fairy tale, *Thumbelina,* for reading to the class and discussion of the story. Have students research the life of Andersen for a few life history facts and write a short journal article about one of them and how it might have affected his writing.

Questions:

1. Locate the birthplace of Andersen on a map of Denmark.
2. Discuss and have students web some of the major events of his life.
3. Why do you think Anderson wrote stories with the themes that he chose?
4. What do you notice about the climate of many of his stories (the climate is often wintery)?
5. How could this theme of a cold climate relate to one's feelings?

APRIL

1	2	3	4	5	6	7
-April Fool's Day -Cancer Control Month	-Hans Christen Anderson born 1805 -Ponce de Leon discovers Florida, 1513 -International Childrens Book Day, Switzerland	-American author, Washington Irving born in 1783 -Pony Express opened 1860	-Civil Rights leader Martin Luther King, Jr. was shot in Memphis 1968 -Flag Act of 1818, Congress approved the first U.S. Flag	-Booker T. Washington's birthday, 1856 -Buddha Day in Japan -Student Government Day -Arthur Hailey's birthday author/poet	-First modern Olympic Games, 1896 -First theater in colonies opened in Williamsburg, VA, 1716 -The U.S. declared war on the Central Powers, 1917 (WWI)	-World Health Day -Days of Remembrance for those who died in holocaust (WWII)
8	9	10	11	12	13	14
-Hank Aaron hit his 715th home run in 1974	-American Civil War ended 1865	-1898 Walter Hunt patented the safety pin -1866 American Society for the prevention of cruelty to animals	-Jackie Robinson is the first black to play major league professional baseball in 1947	-Russian Yuri Gagarin became the first human in space, 1961 -Harry S. Truman became President, 1945 -The American Civil War began, 1861	-Thomas Jefferson, 3rd President, born in 1743 -First elephant arrived in U.S., 1796	-Titanic strikes iceberg, sinks, 1912 -Thomas A. Edison kinescope, motion picture, invented, 1894 -President Abe Lincoln shot, 1865
15	16	17	18	19	20	21
-1900 First organized automobile race in U.S. -Boston Marathon -Income Tax Day	-Wilbur Wright aviation pioneer born in 1867 -Slavery abolished in District of Columbia Anniversary, 1862	-Sirimavo Bandaranaike world's first woman prime minister, the Republic of Sri Lanka -Verrazano Day, discovery of New York Harbor, 1524	-Paul Revere made his midnight ride, 1775 -San Francisco earthquake and fire in 1906	-Lord Byron, 36 years old, dies in Missolonghi, Greece while helping free the country from Turkish rule, 1824	-Apollo 16 astronauts explore the surface of the moon, 1972 -Patriots Day, Maine and Massachusetts	-German educator Friedrich Froebel born, 1782, founded first kindergarten in 1837 -First railroad train crossed Mississippi, 1855
22	23	24	25	26	27	28
-Earth Day was celebrated for the first time in 1970	-James Buchanon, 15th President, 1791 -Book Day in Spain, 1714 -William Shakespeare's birthday, 1564 -Moving Pictures introduced to U.S., 1896	-First soda in 1874 by Robert Green -Professional Secretaries Day	-Automobile license plates required in 1901 -Iceland: First day of summer -Confederate Memorial Day, Florida and Georgia	-James Audubon born in 1785 -World YWCA Day	-Ulysses Grant, 18th President, 1822 -Ferdinand Magelan died in 1521 -Edward Gibbon, historian and author born in 1737 -Fast Day in New Hampshire	-Maryland Admission Day, 7th state, 1788 -James Monroe, 5th President, 1758 -Great Poetry Reading Day
29	30					
-Confederate Army Memorial Day	-Louisiana Admission Day, 18th state, 1812 -Hamburgers were first introduced in 1904 at the St. Louis World's Fair -Vietnam War ends, 1975					

Skills Taught: Reading, writing, map skills, and analysis of a story for theme and relationship to personal experience.

Resources: Resources include a map of Denmark, a biography about Andersen, and several copies of his work, such as *Thumbelina, The Ugly Duckling, The Steadfast Tin Soldier,* and others.

Activity 2

Date: April 18

Event: Paul Revere's Ride (with William Dawes) in 1775.

Level: Grades 4–7

Lesson Plan: Students will be able to trace Revere's ride on a map, explain its affect on the American Revolution, and recite a portion of Longfellow's poem.

Activity: Read Longfellow's poem, *Paul Revere's Ride.* Also read excerpts from *Johnny Tremain* by Esther Forbes. Display a map of the Boston-Concord-Lexington (Massachusetts) area.

Questions:
  1. Why did Revere and Dawes ride that night?
  2. What impact did their ride have on the American Revolution?
  3. Trace the route on a blank map of the area.
  4. Calculate the distance they rode.
  5. Write a newspaper article as if the event was actually happening.

Skills Taught: Reading, listening, map skills, mathematics, and the analysis of an event in regard to other events and writing.

Resources: *Johnny Tremain* by E. Forbes (Houghton Mifflin, 1946); *Paul Revere's Ride* by H. W. Longfellow (Greenwillow, 1985); and *The World Almanac and Book of Facts* (World Almanac, 1990).

Activity 3

Date: April 22

Event: Earth Day

Level: Grades K–8

Lesson Plan: Students will be able to name local environmental pollutants and describe what can be done to eliminate them.

Activity: Obtain posters and other information about Earth Day and other environmental information. Discuss and display the posters around the room. Read the poem "Sarah Cynthia Sylvia Stout Would Not Take the Garbage Out."

Questions:
  1. What would a home be like if no one took out the garbage?
  2. What would happen to our world if no one ever cleaned up the garbage and trash?
  3. Name some things we have on our playground that are environmental pollutants (paper scraps, plastic, etc.).
  4. (For older students) List some of the more serious environmental pollutants (nuclear waste, acid rain, etc.). Do some art work or get pictures from magazines to make a bulletin board that depicts some of the pollutants found in the local area.

5. (For younger students) Draw a picture of something you could do to clean up your home, school, or community. Color the picture and hang it up in the room.

Skills Taught: Listening, observing, writing, and art and analysis.

Resources: Various posters and handouts about Earth Day; and *Where the Sidewalk Ends* by S. Silverstein (Harper and Row, 1974).

May

The month of May is probably named for Maia, the Roman goddess of Spring and growth. The name seems to be related to the Latin word for growth and warmth.

Some Interesting Facts about May
1. It is the fifth month of the year.
2. May has 31 days.
3. May Day (May 1) has been celebrated since ancient Roman times with parades, flowers, dancing, and other festivities.
4. The famous horse race, the Kentucky Derby, has been run in May since 1875.
5. The Lily of the Valley is the official flower for May.
6. The Emerald is the gem for May.

Activity 1

Date: May 5

Event: Cinco de Mayo

Level: Grades 4–8

Lesson Plan: Students will be able to describe the significance of Cinco de Mayo and be able to compare the Mexican holiday with the Fourth of July celebration in the United States.

Activity: Display a map of Mexico and locate Puebla, the site of the decisive battle. Students will research the event and write a short journal article explaining the events leading to the battle. With school policy in mind, perhaps some Mexican-style foods may be used in classroom for a festive mood or a piñata may be made.

Questions:
1. Why did the Mexicans fight the war?
2. How do people in Mexico celebrate this holiday?
3. What does "El Cinco de Mayo" mean?
4. What U.S. holiday is Cinco de Mayo like?
5. Who was Mexico's "George Washington"?

Skills Taught: Reading, writing, analyzing information, and research.

Resources: A map of Mexico, encyclopedias, and tradebooks such as *Fiesta Days of Mexico* by G. E. Fay (University of Northern Colorado, 1970).

Activity 2

Date: Last Monday in May

Event: Memorial Day

MAY

1	2	3	4	5	6	7
-Lei day in Hawaii -First U.S. postcard issued, 1873 -Construction began on the first skyscraper in Chicago, 1884 -May Day	-Robert's Rules Day, birth of Henry Robert, 1837 -French Revolution began 1814	-Sun Day celebrated since 1977 to promote solar energy -International Tuba Day	-Invisible Ink was first used in France, 1776 -Nikolai Lenin born, 1870 -China: Youth Day	-Cinco de Mayo -Children's Day in Japan -The first train robbery occurred at North Bend, OR, 1865	-First postage stamp with glue 1840 -Roger Banister broke the 4 minute mile at Oxford University, 1954	-Johannes Brahms's birthday, 1833 -Peter Tchaikovsky's birthday, 1840 -First presidential inaugural ball anniversary, 1789
8 -Harry Truman, 33rd President, born 1884 -World Red Cross Day	**9** -U.S.S.R. Victory Day -Native American Day -Billy Joel's birthday, singer, 1949 -Candice Bergen's birthday actress, 1946	**10** -Transcontinental railroad completed 1869 -Hot air balloon stampede in Walla Walla, WA	**11** -Minnesota Admission Day, 32nd state, 1858 -Station WGY in New York began the first scheduled TV programming three times a week, 1928	**12** -Florence Nightingale's birthday -Limerick Day - write a limerick	**13** -Astronomy Day -Mother's Day -The U.S. declared war on Mexico, 1846	**14** -Jamestown settled in 1607 -Gabriel Fahrenheit born in 1686 -"Stars & Stripes Forever Day", first public performance of John Philip Sousa
15 -Police Memorial Day -First baseball stadium opened in Brooklyn, NY 1862 -U.S. returns Okinawa to Japan, 1972	**16** -First nickel was authorized in 1866 -Henry Fonda's birthday, actor, 1905 -Biographers Day	**17** -Racial segregation in Public Schools found unconstitutional by Supreme Court, 1954 -National Defense Transportation Day	**18** -International Museum Day -Mt. St. Helen's erupted 1980 -Armed Forces Day!	**19** -Ringley Brothers opened their circus complete with an animal act and band in 1884	**20** -Homestead Act was approved granting farmers right to settle 1862	**21** -Charles Lindbergh, 25, landed in Paris on first solo flight, 1927 -Amelia Earhardt first women to fly solo across the Atlantic Ocean, 1932
22 -1st public showing of a motion picture, 1891 -American artist, Mary Cassat's birthday, 1844 -The last soldiers killed in the Civil War, 1865 -"The Savannah", a wooden ship, fist steam ship to cross the Atlantic, 1819	**23** -S. Carolina Admission Day, 8th state, 1788 -Start of Mexican War, 1846 -Memory Days!, Grayson, KY	**24** -First SST Supersonic plane landed in the U.S. in 1977 -First message over first telegraph line sent by Samuel R. B. Morse, 1844 -Brooklyn Bridge opened, 1883	**25** -African Freedom Day -Constitutional Convention Anniversary 1787	**26** -Sally Kristin Ride, first American woman in space, born 1951	**27** -Amelia J. Bloomer's birthday, 1818 -Rachel Carson born in 1907 -Golden Gate Bridge opened in San Francisco in 1937	**28** -James Francis Thorpe, athlete, born 1888 -Moon Phase: Full moon
29 -Rhode Island Admission Day, 13th state, 1790 -Wisconsin Admission Day, 30th state, 1848 -J. F. Kennedy, 35th President, born 1917	**30** -First auto accident, New York City, 1896 -Traditional Memorial Day	**31** -American poet Walt Whitman's birthday 1819 -The Union of South Africa was proclaimed 1910				

212

Level: Grades 3–8

Lesson Plan: Students will be able to explain why Memorial Day is celebrated and how it has changed slightly from the original idea of honoring the soldiers of our country to remembering all loved ones.

Activity: Ask a member of the local VFW organization to speak to the class about the history of the holiday. Each student will make a small 6″ × 8″ flag using white fabric and fabric paint to make the blue field and the red stripes to display in the room. Students will bring names of people they know who have died in U.S. wars and conflicts, write the names on cards, and post the cards near the flags.

Questions:
1. Why do we celebrate Memorial Day?
2. How is it different from Veteran's Day?
3. How has the holiday changed in regard to who is remembered?
4. Why is it the last Monday of May?
5. When was Memorial Day first celebrated?

Skills Taught: Listening, art, and researching names for cards as well as history of Memorial Day.

Resources: A speaker from VFW, a world almanac, and encyclopedias.

Activity 3

Date: May 8

Event: World Red Cross Day

Level: Grades 2–8

Lesson Plan: Students will be able to list the many ways the Red Cross helps people all over the world.

Activity: Have a speaker from the local Red Cross address the class about the founding of the Red Cross and some of the work it has done over the years both here in the United States and in other countries.

Questions:
1. What does the Red Cross do?
2. Name some different emergencies that the Red Cross helps with.
3. Who can work for the Red Cross?
4. Draw a picture of one thing the Red Cross does.
5. Write a newspaper article that tells about a recent instance of the Red Cross helping people.

Skills Taught: Listening, writing, and art work.

Resources: A speaker from the Red Cross and Red Cross promotional material.

June

The name *June* probably comes from *Juno,* the Roman goddess of marriage. Some records show that it could also have been a family name, *Junius,* which was a powerful family in early Roman history.

Some Interesting Facts about June
1. It is the sixth month of the Gregorian Calendar.
2. June has 30 days.

JUNE

1	2	3	4	5	6	7
-Kentucky Admission Day, 15th state, 1792 -Tennessee Admission Day, 16th state, 1796	-First baseball game played under electric lights, 1883	-Jefferson Davis's birthday 1808 -American Lung Association Trans-America Bicycle Trek, Seattle, WA	-Gemini IV astronaut White "space walks" for 20 minutes, 1965 -Ice Cream capers, free ice cream from 12:00 to 1:00, Columbus, OH	-World Environment Day -Stories in a cove, Olive Hill, KY	-Flag Day in Sweden -D-Day, 1944 -Korea: Memorial Day -Superman celebration in Metropolis, IL	-Boone Day in Kentucky to honor Daniel Boone, great frontiersman -Donut Day in Chicago IL -Red Earth celebration Oklahoma City, OK
8 -Frank Loyd Wright's birthday 1867 -Patent granted for the sweeping machine or vacuum cleaner, 1869 -Fieldens' Factory Act passed; reduced women and children's work days to 10% hours, 1847	**9** -In 1790 the Philadelphia Spelling Book was the first copyrighted book in the U.S.	**10** -First log cabin was built in 1800 -Alcoholics Anonymous founded, 1935, Akron, OH	**11** -Jacques Cousteau's birthday, 1910 -Joe Montana's birthday, football player, 1956	**12** -First human-powered flight across the English Channel, 1979	**13** -The New York Times ran the first installment of the Pentagon Papers, 1971 -Pecan Festival, Okmulgee, OK	**14** -Harriet B. Stowe's birthday, 1811 -Flag Day -Children's Day
15 -Arkansas Admission Day, 25th state, 1836 -Magna Carta Day -first ice cream factory opened 1854 -Benjamin Franklin flying kite in thunderstorm, invented lightening rod, 1752	**16** -U.S.S.R.'s Valentina Teresh-Kova became the first woman in space, 1963	**17** -Watergate Day, 1972 -Father's Day -Bunker Hill Day, Suffolk, MA, 1775, Battle on this day	**18** -Battle of Waterloo anniversary, 1815 -Amelia Earhart became first woman passenger to fly across Atlantic, 1928 -Congress declared war on England, 1812	**19** -Maximilian emperor of Mexico was executed, 1867 -Garfield the Cat's birthday, 1978	**20** -West Virginia Admission Day, 35th state, 1863 -U.S. Government adopted the Great Seal 1782 -Anne Murray birthday, singer	**21** -New Hampshire Admission Day, 9th state, 1788 -Summer begins -Solstice Day, celebrate first day of Summer
22 -In 1870 the U.S. Dept. of Justice was created -Aebleskiver Day in Tyler Maine celebrate Danish Heritage	**23** -At 12:00 am Jacob Pirait declared Liberia the first independent African Republic, 1847 -A workers Revolution, called the June days, broke out in Paris, 1848	**24** -First reported sighting of UFO's in 1947 -Mermaid Festival, North Webster, IN, carnival, festival, parade and ball -Samuel R. B. Morse, 1844	**25** -Virginia Admission Day 10th state, 1788 -George Orwell's birthday 1903 -Battle of Little Big Horn or "Custer's Last Stand" 1876	**26** -Chicken clucking contest in Baltimore, MD -Lunar Eclipse, 11:43 pm EST, 1991	**27** -Helen Keller's birthday 1880 -Watermelon thump champion seed spitting contest, Luling, TX -Captain Kangaroo, Bob Keeshan's, birthday, 1927	**28** -World War I ends with the signing of the Treaty of Versailles in 1918 -Henry VIII born -Queen Victoria was crowned at West Minster Abbey, 1838
29 -Trek Fest in Riverside, IA in celebration of TV show Star Trek -Elizabeth Hanford Dole birthday, Secretary of Labor, 1936	**30** -Zaire Independence Day -Charles Blondin walked over Niagara Falls on a tightrope, 1859 -Novel by Margaret Mitchell published, "Gone With the Wind", 1936					

3. It is often called the Month of Roses.
4. It has also been called the wedding month since Ancient Roman times.
5. The Rose is the official flower for June.
6. The Pearl is the gem for June.

Activity 1

Date: June 6

Event: D-Day (Allied Forces invaded Normandy during World War II)

Level: Grades 5–12

Lesson Plan: Students will be able to explain the purpose and describe the complexity of the Allied invasion to retake Europe during World War II.

Activity: Display a large map of Europe. Pinpoint the beaches of Normandy with flags printed with names assigned to the beaches. With an overhead and various colored transparencies, show with colored acetate arrows the different Allied forces involved in the assault. Use a tradebook or textbook as a resource and explain the logistics and objectives of the military exercise.

Questions:
1. What are some of the difficulties involved in planning an effort such as this?
2. Name the principal Allied countries involved.
3. Why was it necessary to have an amphibious landing in order to retake Europe?
4. On a blank map locate Normandy, England, the beaches used for the landings and the various occupied countries.
5. Write a short essay on why the success of the invasion was a turning point in the war.

Skills Taught: Observation, analysis, map skills, and writing

Resources: Various history books and maps, encyclopedias, and almanacs.

Activity 2

Date: June 14

Event: Flag Day

Level: Grades 4–8

Lesson Plan: Students will be able to state the history and origin of the United States flag and describe the Code of Etiquette for its use.

Activity: Students will select various historical U.S. flags to make paper and paint replicas and display them on the bulletin board. They will read the *Code of Etiquette* and the history of the flag from *The World Almanac*.

Questions:
1. What are the different ways that different people salute the flag (i.e., soldiers, nonmilitary men and women)?
2. What uses of the flag are prohibited?
3. Why do we have stars and stripes on the flag?
4. Was there really a Betsy Ross and did she design and make the first flag?
5. Make labels for the flags you have made that gives the year they were first flown.

   Skills Taught: Reading, art, writing, and research.

   Resources: *The World Almanac* (current year).

Activity 3

Date: June 10

Event: Maurice Sendak's Birthday

Level: Grades K–4

Lesson Plan: Students will be able to explain who Maurice Sendak is, what he does, and how his work often tells about how people feel and get along.

Activity: For this integrated social studies/language arts activity, display tradebook posters of the author and a selection of his work. Read several of the books to the class. Also read a biography of the author so he becomes a real person to the students. (There is a video about him.)

Questions:
1. Who is Maurice Sendak?
2. What does he do?
3. Name some books he has written.
4. How do his books show how people feel and get along?
5. Draw a picture of your favorite story and tell why it is your favorite.

Skills Taught: Reading, writing, listening, and analysis.

Resources: Various works of Maurice Sendak, posters, and a video.

July

July's name comes from *Quintilis,* which means "fifth." It was changed to July when the calendar was changed and July became the seventh month.

Some Interesting Facts about July
1. July has 31 days.
2. July 2 marks the half-way point of the year—182½ days have passed and 182½ days remain.
3. July is known as the hottest month of the year.
4. The Liberty Bell rang for the first time on July 8.
5. The Lily is the official flower for July.
6. The Ruby is the gem for July.

Activity 1

Date: July 13

Event: All-American Teddy Bear Picnic

Level: Grades K–3

Lesson Plan: Students will be able to identify where Lahasla, Pennsylvania, is and the importance of teddy bears.

Activity: As a class, read a *Teddy Bear's Picnic* and listen to the tape. All students will bring their teddy bears from home and have an all-class sharing of teddy bears and picnic.

Questions:
1. Where did the teddy bear originate?
2. Why does Lahasla, Pennsylvania celebrate All-American Teddy Bear Picnic?
3. What is the importance of teddy bears?

JULY

1	2	3	4	5	6	7
-Dominion Day in Canada -First adhesive postage stamps on sale, 1847, (Franklin 5 cents, Washington 10 cents)	-James A. Garfield shot in Washington DC, 1881 -Halfway point of year, 182½ days passed and 182½ days to go in the year	-Idaho Admission Day, 43rd state, 1890 -Air conditioner appreciation days in Northern Hemisphere -First Bank opens in U.S. in NY, 1819	-Declaration of Independence drafted, 1776 -John C. Coolidge, 30th president birthday, 1872 -Fourth of July -First U.S. passenger railroad was begun, 1828	-Author Washington Irving appointed American ambassador to Spain, 1842 -Kids Art Festival in Tacoma, WA, Pt. Defiance Park	-John Paul Jones, Naval Officer, born, 1747 -International Cherry Pit Spitting contest in Michigan	-Japan Star Festival (Tanabata) -Be nice to New Jersey week
8	**9**	**10**	**11**	**12**	**13**	**14**
-Video Games Day -Declaration of Independence first public reading 115th anniversary, 1776, Liberty Bell rang out to indicate America's freedom, 1776	-Elias Howe, inventor, born in 1819 -14th amendment to U.S. Constitution ratified, 1868 -Tom Hank's birthday, 1956	-Wyoming Admission Day, 44th state, 1890 -Bahamas Independence Day -Chesapeake turtle derby 10 races to determine champ	-John Q. Adams, 6th President, 1767 -National Cheer up the Lonely Day -Fur Trade Days, Chadron, Neb., to celebrate heritage of early settlers -Solar Eclipse 1991, begins 12:23pm EST-ends 3:48pm	-Henry David Thoreau's birthday, 1817 -Golden Days in Fairbanks, AK, celebrate the finding of gold in Alaska	-Abraham Lincoln birthplace founders day weekend, Hodgenville, KY -All American Teddy Bear picnic, Lahaska, PA -Old Fashion Ice Cream Festival, Rockwood Museum, Willimington, DE	-Gerald Ford, 38th President, born 1913 -Edward Whymper scaled the Matterhorn, 1865 -Children's Festival in Jacksonville, OR -Space week July 14 to 20
15	**16**	**17**	**18**	**19**	**20**	**21**
-Clement C. Moore, author, born, 1823 -National Ice Cream Day -The first successful steamboat trip (U.S.)	-Flower Day -Atomic Bomb Day, first atomic bomb explosion 5:30 am, 1945, NM -District of Columbia established, 1790	-Civil war broke out in Spain, 1930 -Hog calling contest, Baltimore, MD -Crab and clam bake in Smers Cove Marine, MD -Nelson Mandela's birthday, Black Civil Rights activist, 1918	-Hot Dog night in Luverne, MN, more than 12,000 hot dogs served free of charge -Logger Days in Libby, Montana	-First women's rights convention, 1843 -Bloomer Day, first introduced for women to wear, 1848	-Moon Day, first man on the moon, Neil Armstrong and Edwin Aldrin 1969 -Anti-Cruelty Society Dogwash in Chicago, IL	-Guam Liberation Day -Ernest Hemingway's birthday, American short story writer
22	**23**	**24**	**25**	**26**	**27**	**28**
-"Spooner's Day" William Spooner born in 1844 -Poland: National Holiday	-Ice cream cones invented 1904 -First U.S. swimming school opening, 1827, Boston, MA	-Amelia Earhart's birthday, 1937 -Detroit's birthday, 1701 -Pioneer Day in Utah	-Walter Payton's birthday, 1954, football player -Test-tube Baby player	-New York Admission Day, 11th state, 1788 -New York Ratification Day	-The House Judiciary Committee voted to impeach President Nixon, 1974 -Beanhole Bean Fest Oxford, ME -Take your house plant for a walk day	-President Hoover ordered army to drive out WWI vets camped in Washington, 1932 -Comedy Celebration Day San Francisco, CA Golden Gate Park -Singing telegram birthday, 1933
29	**30**	**31**				
-Benito Musselini's birthday, Italian Fascist Leader, 1833 -Norway: Olsoker celebrate Viking King St. Olav	-Henry Ford born, 1863 -World footbag championships in Golden, CO	-Samuel Hopkins received the first U.S. government patent, 1790				

4. Who has teddy bears?
5. How old is the teddy bear?

Skills Taught: Research, listening, reading, and mapping skills.

Resources: Teddy bears and *Teddy Bear's Picnic* by W. du Boir.

Activity 2

Date: July 23

Event: Ice cream cones invented

Level: Grades 3–8

Lesson Plan: Students will be able to identify where the ice cream cone was invented and be able to make ice cream.

Activity: After discussion of the history of the ice cream cone, students will create their own serving of ice cream in a paper cup. Discuss the scientific changes that take place when ice cream is made (the state of matter).

Questions:
1. Where was the ice cream cone invented?
2. How long has the ice cream cone been around?
3. What would we do without ice cream?
4. Where is ice cream most popular?
5. What is ice cream made of?

Skills Taught: Research, social, and application skills.

Resources: Recipe and ingredients for the production of ice cream.

Activity 3

Date: July 11

Event: Cheer Up the Lonely Day

Level: Grades 7–12

Lesson Plan: Students will understand and have compassion for those who are lonely. Further, students will have a understanding of how to help those feel less lonely.

Activity: Discuss the issue of being lonely and how it feels. Divide the class into groups and have each group adopt an elderly person from a nursing home to be their friend. Throughout the year, students will be responsible for doing things for their adopted friend (e.g., write letters, visit, make gifts). Tell students to treat their new friend as they would like to be treated.

Questions:
1. What makes you feel good?
2. How does it feel to be lonely?
3. What can we do to make others less lonely?
4. Why are people lonely?
5. Who gets lonely?

Skills Taught: Research, social, and analysis skills.

Resources: Pen pals from a nursing home.

August

The name for August comes from the word *Sextilis,* which means "sixth." The Romans used this term and renamed the month August to honor the emperor Augustus.

Some Interesting Facts about August
1. August is the month during which the first picture of the moon was taken from space.
2. There are 31 days in August.
3. August takes one day away from February, leaving February with 28 days.
4. The first Lincoln penny was issued in August.
5. The Poppy and Gladiolus are the official flowers for August.
6. The Sardonyx and Peridal are the gens for August.

Activity 1

Date: August 2

Event: Friendship Day

Level: Grades 1–5

Lesson Plan: Students will be able to recognize the importance of their friends and how important it is to be a good friend.

Activity: Discuss as a class the importance of friends and how we see friends treat one another. Read the book *Do You Want to Be My Friend?* and discuss the feelings the little boy had when no one would be his friend. Using magazines, create collages that express what friends do for one another and how they treat one another.

Questions:
1. What is a friend?
2. How can a person be a friend?
3. What do you like about friends?
4. What do we do when we have friends?
5. How do you treat your friends?
6. How do your friends treat you?

Skills Taught: Research, reading, social, and creative skills.

Resources: *Do You Want to Be My Friend?* by E. Carle.

Activity 2

Date: August 28, 1963

Event: Dream Day

Level: Grades 4–8

Lesson Plan: Students will be able to recognize the "I Have a Dream" speech and be able to identify their own personal dreams.

Activity: After reading and discussing the "I Have a Dream" speech by Martin Luther King, Jr., students will relate what he said to what is going on today in the country. Students will be asked to identify their own dreams relevant to their lives and the nation's happenings. Once dreams have been identified and discussed, students will create a speech and share it among a small group of students.

AUGUST

1 -Colorado Admission Day 38th state, 1876 -Francis Scott Key's birthday, 1799 -First Emancipation Day declared in the British Empire, 1834	**2** -Friendship Day -Bratwurst Days, Sheboygan, WI	**3** -Columbus Sailing Day Anniversary, 1492 -Colorado Day	**4** -Save the Whale commemorative postage stamps were issued -American Family Day Arizona/Michigan	**5** -National Mustard Day -First English Colony in N.A. founding anniversary -Australia Picnic Day	**6** -American Family Day -Hiroshima Day, 1945 -Bolivia least major area in South America to be freed from Spanish rule, 1825 -First man executed in electric chair, NY, 1890	**7** -First picture of earth from space, 1959 -Iran invades Kuwait, 1990
8 -Jesse Owens won his fourth Olympic Gold Medal -Baby Parade in Ocean City, NJ	**9** -National Hobo Convention in Britt, IA -Omak, WA Stampede and suicide race	**10** -Missouri Admission Day 24th state, 1821 -Herbert Hoover, 31st President, born 1874 -Blueberry Festival, Ketchican, AK	**11** -Daughter's Day -Herbert Hoover Day in Iowa -Presidential Joke Day -Hulk Hogan's birthday, 1953	**12** -U.S.S.R. National Sports Day -First continuous-stitch sewing machine made for domestic use by Isaac M. Singer, 1851 -First transatlantic telegraph cable was completed, 1858	**13** -National Alcoholism Awareness Day -Central Africa Republic Independence Day -Fidel Castro's birthday, President of Cuba, 1927	**14** -Victory Day -The last shot fired in World War II, 1945 -Liberty Tree Day in Messachusetts
15 -Panama Canal officially opened, 1914 -Transcontinental railroad completed in 1870 -Napoleon Bonaparte's birthday 1769	**16** -Bennington Battle Day Vermont, 1777 -Stamp Expo "91", CA -Timothy Hutton's birthday Actor	**17** -David Crockett, born 1786 -Geology and Astronomy weekend, West Virginia -Nelson Piquet's birthday autoracer, 1952	**18** -Marshall Field's birthday 1835	**19** -Orville Wright's birthday 1871 -Gail Borden patented condensed milk in the U.S., 1856	**20** -Benjamin Harrison, 23rd President, 1833 -Little League baseball world series, Aug 20-24 Williamsport, PA	**21** -Hawaii Admission Day, 50th state, 1959 -American Bar Association Anniversary -The Mona Lisa stolen from the Louvre Museum in Paris, 1911
22 -Archibald M. Willard's birthday, 1836, painted the Actor Rudolph Valentino, Spirit of "76"	**23** -Romania Liberation Day silent film star, died 1926	**24** -India, Onam -India Amarnath Yarta -Italy Vesurlieus Day	**25** -Bret Harte born 1836 -Be Kind to HumanKind week, Aug 25-31	**26** -Lee de Forest, inventor born 1873 -Susan B. Anthony Day in Messachusetts -American women receive the right to vote by the 19th amendment, 1920	**27** -First jet plane taxied down runway in Germany, 1939 -L. B. Johnson, 36th President, 1908 -J.A.C. Charles, French Physiatrist, tested first hydrogen balloon -15 nations signed Kellogg Briand Pact to settle all differences without war-1928	**28** -"Dream Day" in commeration of Dr. M. L. King's speech, 1964 -first undersea telegraph cable completed between Dover, England and Calais, France, across English Channel, 1850
29 -Oliver Wendell Holmes's birthday, 1809 -The Beatle's last performance, 1966	**30** -Oatmeal Festival, TX -Huey P. Long Day, Louisiana	**31** -Capital Day -Debbie Gibson's birthday, singer, 1970				

Questions:
1. Who was Martin Luther King, Jr.?
2. Why is his speech so famous?
3. Why did people listen to Martin Luther King, Jr.'s dreams?
4. Did King's dreams come true?
5. How did he make his dream speech so effective?
6. Where was the "I Have a Dream" speech given?

Skills Taught: Research, social, analysis, and creative skills.

Resources: *"I Have a Dream" speech by Martin Luther King, Jr., August, 28, 1963.*

Activity 3

Date: August 6, 1945

Event: Hiroshima Day

Level: Grades 6–12

Lesson Plan: Students will be able to explain the effects of dropping an atomic bomb.

Activity: Students will read *Hiroshima* and discuss the novel while reading it as a class. They will brainstorm and try to think of other solutions rather than using an atomic bomb to resolve conflict. Students will also research the events that took place previous to dropping the bomb.

Questions:
1. Why was the bomb dropped?
2. How did the bomb affect the United States?
3. How did the bomb affect the rest of the world?
4. Who gave permission to drop the bomb?
5. Are the effects of the bomb permanent?

Skills Taught: Research, reading, and interpretive skills.

Resources: *Hiroshima* (a novel by John Hersey) and maps of Asia.

September

September's name comes from the Latin *Septem,* meaning "seven." It used to be the seventh month of the year until Julius Caesar changed the calendar to make January 1 the beginning of the year instead of March.

Some Interesting Facts about September
1. September 21 is the equinox—both night and day are of the same length.
2. September is cable TV month.
3. September is library card sign-up month.
4. September has 30 days.
5. The Morning Glory is the official flower for September.
6. The Sapphire is the gem for September.

Activity 1

Date: September 26, 1774

Event: Johnny Appleseed's birthday

Level: Grades 1–4

SEPTEMBER

1 -An earthquake leveled Tokyo, 1923 -Cable T.V. Month -Library Card Sign Up Month -National Courtesy Month	**2** -Buhl Day, to honor the laboring man -Columbia River Cross Channel Swim, Hood River, OR -V-J Day, Japanese surrender to Allies, 1945	**3** -Prudence Grandall's birthday, school teacher who dared to educate young black girls in 1830's -WWII Declaration, 1939 -Treaty of Paris signing anniversary, 1783	**4** -Marcus Whitman born 1802 -New York Sun broke the credit mobilizer scandal, 1872 -Happy Birthday Los Angeles, 1781 -Labor Day	**5** -Terrorism at the 1972 Olympics in Munich, Germany -Be Late for Something Day -Popcorn Festival, Marion, OH	**6** -Boston Bicycle Club began first 100 mile bike trip in 1882	**7** -Last holdup by Jesse James, 1881 -First bathing beauty contest for the Miss America title, 1921
8 -Baby Safety Week -National Grandparent Day -National Pet Memorial Day	**9** -California Admission Day, 31st state, 1850 -Last public performance by Beethoven, 1825 -National Boss-Employee Exchange Day	**10** -Elias Howe patented the sewing machine, 1846 -Swap Ideas Day to help others with sharing of ideas	**11** -First policeman with full powers to arrest was appointed in Los Angeles 1910 -Pumpkin Festival, Morton, IL	**12** -Jesse Owen's birthday, American athlete won 4 gold medals in 1936 Olympics, born 1913 -Ethiopia National Revolution Day -Guinea Bissau National Holiday	**13** -First pro football game was played in 1895 -Knickerbocker Club founded, first to codify baseball rules, 1845	**14** -Gregorian calendar was adopted by Great Britain and the American Colonies, 1752
15 -William H. Taft, 27th President, 1857 -James Fenimore Cooper's birthday 1789 -Agatha Christie, author, born 1890	**16** -Mayflower departed from Plymouth, England, 1620 -Stay Away From Seattle Day	**17** -Citizenship Day, anniversary of the signing of the U.S. Constitution, 1787	**18** -Herman Melvile published "Moby Dick" 1851 -Anniversary of first sky writing at night in New York City -First edition of New York Times printed, 1851	**19** -George Washington's farewell address, 1796 -First beauty contest held in Belgium, 1888 -International Banana Festival, Fulton, KY -Twiggy's birthday, actress, model, 1949	**20** -Rosh Heshanah -Aloha week Festival celebrate Hawaiian tradition -National Laundry Day, importance of laundry service employees -Sophie Loren's birthday, actress, 1934	**21** -Sandra Day O'Conner as Associate Justice of the U.S. Supreme Court, 1981, first women appointed -Autumnal Equinox
22 -American Business Women's Day -American Heart Association Food Festival, Dallas, TX	**23** -Lewis & Clark expedition ended -Harvest Moon, full moon closest to harvest -Ray Charles's birthday, singer, composer, musician, 1930	**24** -National Hunting and Fishing Day -1,000 army paratroopers help enroll 9 black students safely, 1957	**25** -First transatlantic telephone went into operation, 1956 -Food Service Employees Day -Major leagues baseball first double header, 1882	**26** -Johnny Appleseed born in 1774 -Good Neighbor Day	**27** -Thomas Nast American political cartoonist born in 1840 -First locomotive to pull a passenger train	**28** -A woman arrested in New York City for smoking in public, 1904
29 -Munich Pact, 1958 -Gold Star Mother's Day, Presidential Proclamation -Goose Day, religious holiday feast, Lewistown, PA	**30** -First annual fair in America, 350th Anniversary, 1641 -Happy Fiscal New Year Festival					

Lesson Plan: Students will be able to explain who Johnny Appleseed is and the significance of his character.

Activity: Read the story *Johnny Appleseed* by Stephen Kellogg. Discuss the significant things Johnny Appleseed did and the illustrations that Stephen Kellogg uses to portray those events. Discuss where and how Johnny Appleseed traveled. Students will create a huge apple tree in the classroom, with each apple representing something Johnny Appleseed did.

Questions:
1. Who was Johnny Appleseed?
2. What is Johnny Appleseed known for doing?
3. Where is Johnny Appleseed from?
4. How have we heard about Johnny Appleseed?
5. Was Johnny Appleseed a significant figure in our history?

Skills Taught: Research, reading, and creative skills.

Resources: *Johnny Appleseed* by S. Kellogg, encyclopedias, and maps.

Activity 2

Date: September 20

Event: Rosh Hashanah

Level: Grades 5–7

Lesson Plan: Students will be able to explain what Rosh Hashanah is and what some of its traditions are.

Activity: Read the story "Start with Something Sweet" by Sidney Taylor from the book *Holiday Storybook*. Once the story is read and discussion has taken place, the students will predict what might be their fate for the upcoming year.

Questions:
1. Who celebrates Rosh Hashanah?
2. What is a synagogue?
3. What is Shofar? What kind of noise do you think Shofar would make?
4. What are some of the traditional things done on the eve of Rosh Hashanah?
5. How is it decided what day Rosh Hashanah will fall on?
6. What day is (was) it on this year?

Skills Taught: Research, reading, and discussion skills.

Resources: *Holiday Storybook* by S. Taylor.

Activity 3

Date: September 3, 1939

Event: World War II declared

Level: Grades 8–12

Lesson Plan: Students will be able to discuss the significance of World War II and how it affected our country.

Activity: Have a variety of literature that reflects World War II. Students need to discuss the differences among the books and imagine what it would have been like for them to be living at that time. Students will write down their ideas and then interview a grandparent or someone else to find out what it was really like to live during and be a part of World War II. Compare the similarities and differences between the students' ideas and the results from their interviews.

Questions:
1. Why did World War II take place?
2. Where did World War II take place?
3. Which countries were involved in World War II?
4. How did World War II affect the American people?
5. What other countries were extremely affected by World War II?
6. How was World War II resolved?

Skills Taught: Research, reading, interviewing, and analytical skills.

Resources: Encyclopedias, maps, and source books on World War II.

October

The name for October comes from the Latin word *octo*, which means "eight." October was the eighth month in the early Roman calendar. It later became the tenth month when the ancient Romans moved the beginning of the year from March 1 to January 1.

Some Interesting Facts about October
1. In the Northern Temperate Zone, the first frost usually occurs in October.
2. Leaves change to brilliant crimson, russet, and gold.
3. The frost kills many insects, and most birds have left for the south, but sparrows are fond of October and stay later.
4. The Calendula is the official flower for October.
5. The Opal is the gem for October.

Activity 1

Date: Entire month

Event: Welcoming October

Level: Grades 2–6

Lesson Plans: This activity is designed for primary and intermediate students. Its purpose is to bring an awareness to characteristics of individual months. Students will be aware of the changes that take place during the fall season.

Activity: Work with the students to create a bulletin board of a tree with no leaves (i.e., a maple tree). Have each student make two leaves, one green and the other either gold, orange, brown, or crimson. Glue the two leaves together so the opposite sides are different colors. Place all the leaves on the tree (green side out). As each day passes, turn several of the leaves over to expose the other colors. Near the end of the month, start putting the leaves at the bottom of the tree.

Questions:
1. Why do trees lose their leaves in the winter?
2. What trees do not lose their leaves or needles?
3. What happens to the leaves once they are on the ground?
4. When do the new leaves grow back?

Skills Taught: Understanding and comparing geographical regions.

Resources: Bulletin boards and October posters.

OCTOBER

1	2	3	4	5	6	7
-Jimmy Carter, 39th President, born 1924 -James Meredith became first black student at University Mississippi, 1962 -Computer Learning Month	-Nat Turner, born 1800 -Child Health Day -Mohandas Gandhi's birthday 1869 -Thurgood Marshall sworn in as first black U.S. Supreme Court Justice, 1967	-Andy Griffith show first broadcast, 1960 -Chubby Checker's birthday 1941 -Mrs. W. H. Felton becomes first U.S. women senator, 1922	-Rutherford Hayes, 19th President, born 1822 -U.S.S.R. fired the opening gun of the space race with the launching of Sputnik, 1957 -Ten-Four Day, recognition of ham radio operators	-Chester Arthur, 21st President, born 1830 -Issaquah Salmon Days Festival, Issaquah, WA -ZooFest "91", Asheboro, NC, a celebration of animals, autumn, and the arts	-American Library Association's birthday -Ballpoint pen patented 1921 -First talking motion picture show in New York, 1927 -Lafayette Day	-Child Health Day -London Bridge Day, Lake Havasu City, AZ -National Customer Service Week

8	9	10	11	12	13	14
-Chicago fire anniversary, 1871 -Canadian Thanksgiving	-Viking Leif Erickson in America 1000 -First successful underground oil pipeline laid along oil creek in Pithole, PA, 1865 -California admitted to the union, 1850	-Japan Health Sports Day -Salem Apple Butter festival -Martina Navratilova's birthday, 1956, tennis player	-Weems Parson, traveling bookseller, born 1759 -The Boar War broke out in South Africa, 1899 -General Pulaski Memorial Day	-Discoverer's Day -Christopher Columbus and crew sighted land in the Bahamas, 1492, Columbus Day -International Moment of Frustration and Scream Day	-Alaska Day celebration -American Indian Time of Thanksgiving -Credit Union Week -National School Lunch Week	-Dwight D. Eisenhower, 34th President, born 1890 -Winnie the Pooh's birthday, 1925 -Queen Marie Antoinette found guilty of conspiracy, 1793

15	16	17	18	19	20	21
-National Poetry Day -Gourmet Coffee Week -Lee Iacocca's birthday 1924 -National Grouch Day	-William Douglas, born 1898 -Sweetest Day -Marie Antoinette, 38, guillotined, 1793 -An anesthetic used in major surgery, 1846	-Black Poetry Day -Pope John Paul I's birthday, 1912, 263rd pope of the Roman Catholic Church -U.S. Constitution adopted, 1787	-Alaska Day since 1867 -Chuck Berry's birthday, 1926, singer, song writer -George C. Scott's birthday, 1927, actor	-Autumn Historic Folklife Festival, Hannibal, OH -Oktober Fest Grand Prairie, TX -Sweetest Day	-Barnum & Bailey Circus opened the big top, 1919 -National Cleaner Air Week -National Forest Products Week	-Edison invents the incandescent lamp, 1879 -Somalia National Day -Jamaica National Hero's Day

22	23	24	25	26	27	28
-First parachute jump from a balloon, 1797 -Cuban missile crisis anniversary, 1962 -National Save Your Back Week, to educate public on proper back care, Camp Hill, PA	-Beirut terrorist attack anniversary, 1983 -National Mole Day -T.V. Talk Show Host Day	-United Nations Day -Pony Express service ended due to first transcontinental telegraph line being completed, 1860 -Black Thursday on Wall Street, stock nosedived, 1929	-Pablo Picasso, born 1881 -First postcard mailed in U.S. 1870 -Grenada Invasion, 1983 -National Magic Week	-Erie Canal opened, 1825 -The Shah of Iran born 1919 -Championship Cat Show Indianapolis, IN	-Teddy Roosevelt, 26th President, born 1858 -Dylan Thomas, poet, born 1914 -First rapid transit subway running beneath Manhattan open to public, 1904	-Harvard University founded, 1636 -Statue of Liberty dedicated, 1886 -James Cook birthday, 1728, English Sea Captain & explorer

29	30	31				
-In 1929, Stock Market collapsed -NBA Day in Basketball, Springfield Civic Center, MA	-John Adams, 2nd President, born 1735 -Orson Wells radio dramatization of War of Worlds caused Nationwide scare, 1938 -Some 50,000 members of Fascist party marched on Rome, 1922	-Nevada Admission Day, 36th state, 1864 -Halloween -National Unicef Day -Louisiana Purchase				

Activity 2

Date: October 13

Event: National School Lunch Week

Level: Grades 3–8

Lesson Plan: This activity is designed for primary students and/or can be modified for intermediate and middle schools. Its purpose is to recognize those who we take for granted. Students will appreciate the hard work involved in scheduling, preparing, and serving daily school meals.

Activity: The students will design a "Certificate of Honor" for all of those who work for their school lunch program. Banners and posters will be made to be displayed in the lunchroom in honor of those people.

Questions:
1. Who is responsible for the scheduling, preparation, and serving of your lunch?
2. What does it take to make a healthy meal?
3. What would happen if our bodies did not receive the proper nourishment?
4. How can we improve our own daily meals?

Skills Taught: Appreciation, creativity, application, and social skills.

Resources: Student-made or ready-made certificates, banners, health books, and food nutrition pamphlets.

Activity 3

Date: October 28

Event: Statue of Liberty Day

Level: Grades 1–6

Lesson Plan: This activity can be used effectively with all elementary-grade students (with some modification). Its purpose is to educate students about the origin and meaning of the Statue of Liberty. Students will be able to give information about the history of the Statue of Liberty.

Activity: Locate on the map where the Statue of Liberty is. Discuss with the students why it would be located where it is. Create a scale model of the statue out of paper maché and paint it.

Questions:
1. How did the Statue of Liberty come about?
2. What does it symbolize?
3. What other things do we use to symbolize freedom?
4. If you were going to create something as a gift for freedom, what would it be? Why?

Skills Taught: Map skills, creative thinking, and research skills.

Resources: Pictures of the Statue of Liberty and history books.

November

The name for November comes from the Latin word *novem*, which means "nine." November was the ninth month in the early Roman calendar when March 1 was the beginning of the year.

NOVEMBER

1 -National Author's Day -Wizard of Oz, 1901, by Frank Baum -Aviation History Month -Child Safety and Protection Month	**2** -N. Dakota Admission Day, 39th state, 1889 -S. Dakota Admission Day, 40th state, 1889 -Daniel Boone born, 1734 -James Polk, 11th President, 1795	**3** -John Montague born, 1718 invented the sandwich -American Revolutionary War ended	**4** -Nellie T. Ross became nation's first woman governor, 1924 -First boat from Buffalo using the Erie Canal reached New York City 1825 -Ronald Reagan, 40th President, elected 1980	**5** -Europeans got their first taste of chocolate, 1519 -Florence Nightingale arrived Barrack Hospital, Turkey, during Crimean War, 1854 -Franklin Roosevelt only President in U.S. elected for 3rd term, 1940	**6** -John Philip Sousa born 1854 -James Naismith, 1891, invented basketball using peach baskets and a soccer ball -Abraham Lincoln, age 51, elected President, 1860	**7** -Marie Curie's birthday 1867, winner Nobel Peace prize for discovery of radium -National Notary Public Day
8 -Montana Admission Day 41st State, 1889 -Edmund Haley, astronomer and mathematician born 1656 -Edward Brooke elected as first black U.S. Senator in 85 years, 1966	**9** -Smokey the Bear died, 1976 at the age of 26 -Workers in Berlin walk out on jobs in a revolt 1918	**10** -Edmund Fitzgerald sank in 1975 -Over 30 million Americans and Canadians without power in great power outage "The Night the Lights Went Out," 1965	**11** -Washington Admission Day, 42nd state, 1889 -Veteran's Day -Kate Smith introduced Irving Berlin's song "God Bless America," 1939	**12** -Elizabeth Cady Stanton born, 1815 -Nadia Comaneci born 1961, Olympic gymnast from Romania	**13** -A doctor in St. Louis invented peanut butter, 1890 -National Young Readers Day, Pittsburgh, PA	**14** -Robert Fulton's birthday 1815, inventor of the steamboat
15 -American Enterprise Day -John Coleman's birthday 1935, T.V. meteorologist	**16** -Oklahoma Admission Day 46th state, 1907 -W. C. Handy's birthday 1873, "Father of the blues" -National Eating Disorders Week -National Mom & Dad's Day	**17** -Great American smokeout -Homemade Bread Day -Suez Canal opened for traffic, 1869 -American Education week	**18** -Mickey Mouse's birthday 1928 -Haiti Army Day	**19** -James A. Garfield, 20th President, born 1831 -Abe Lincoln read the Gettysburg Address 1863	**20** -First tank dominated battle took place in Cambrai, France, 1917 -Dick Smother's birthday 1938, comedian	**21** -North Carolina Admission Day, 12th state, 1789 -World "Hello" Day, greet friends
22 -"China Clipper" anniversary, since 1935 -J. F. Kennedy was assassinated, 1963 -National Farm-City Week	**23** -Billy the Kid born, 1859 -Thanksgiving Day -First play by play football game broadcast 1919	**24** -Zachary Taylor, 12th President, born 1784 -Dale Carnegie born 1888	**25** -Automobile speed reduction, 1973, from 70 miles per hour to 55 miles per hour	**26** -Shopping Reminder Day (only 24 days until Christmas) -Charles Monroe Shulz birthday, 1922, cartoonist	**27** -Ginger Bread House competition, Lahaska, PA -Buffalo Bob's birthday 1917, T.V. personality	**28** -William Blake, poet and artist, born 1757 -Macy's Thanksgiving Day Parade -Michigan Thanksgiving Day Parade
29 -Louisa May Alcott's birthday, 1832 -Cowboy Christmas, Wickenburg, AZ, gathering of cowboys who are poets and singers	**30** -Mark Twain born, 1835 -Softball first played 1887 in Chicago, it was invented by George Hancock -Turkey declared war against Russia, 1853					

Some Interesting Facts about November
1. November comes between autumn and winter.
2. In the Northern Temperate Zone, the trees are bare in November.
3. The fallen leaves from October have lost their brilliant colors.
4. The soft grays and browns of northern landscapes are sometimes covered with a light snow.
5. The Chrysanthemum is the official flower for November.
6. The Topaz is the gem for November.

Activity 1

Date: Entire month

Event: Aviation History Month

Level: Grades 2–8

Lesson Plan: This activity is designed for all elementary and middle school grades in recognition of aviation. Its purpose is to stress the significant roles that aviation plays in our lives. Students will understand the importance of aviation in our world.

Activity: The students will research early transportation methods and read about the early attempts at aviation. Construct with them a time line of aviation.

Questions:
1. How does aviation affect our lives?
2. Who were the pioneers of aviation?
3. What were some types of early flying machines?
4. What are some differences and likenesses between early aviation and modern aviation?

Skills Taught: Research, reading, and comparing and contrasting.

Resources: Aviation literature and old and new photographs.

Activity 2

Date: Entire month

Event: Child Safety and Protection Month

Level: Grades K–12

Lesson Plan: This activity is designed to make all students aware of their rights, as well as the things they can do to help themselves. Students will be aware of child safety and protection.

Activity: Visit a public or school library and check out books centering around the topics of child safety. Make these books available to the students and discuss with them all of the major topics.

Questions:
1. Why do children need to be protected?
2. What are some reasons that children may seek help?
3. Where can children seek help?
4. What can be done to improve child safety?

Skills Taught: Research, reading, discussion, and application of knowledge.

Resources: Literature on child safety, counselors.

Activity 3

Date: November 17

Event: Great American Smoke Out

Level: Grades K–12

Lesson Plan: This activity is designed to look at the effects and dangers of smoking. It can be modified for all grade and age levels. Students will be aware of the dangers and risks associated with smoking.

Activity: Make books, pamphlets, and other research material centered around the dangers of smoking available. Students will construct posters, bulletin boards, and signs (older students can create statistical charts) describing the dangers of smoking. If they know someone who smokes, ask those students to give their full support to help the smoker quit.

Questions:
1. What are some of the dangers of cigarette smoking?
2. Why is it so hard for people to quit smoking?
3. Is it possible to reverse some of the effects once the smoker has quit?
4. What can you do to help someone quit smoking?

Skills Taught: Research and social skills.

Resources: Medical pamphlets, brochures, articles, and health books.

December

The name for December comes from the Latin word *decem,* which means "ten." December was the tenth month in the early Roman calendar when March 1 was the beginning of the year.

Some Interesting Facts about November
1. Winter begins during December in the northern half of the world.
2. December 21 or 22 is the shortest day of the year in the Northern hemisphere due to the Winter Solstice, or when the sun appears to have traveled the farthest south.
3. The Poinsettia is the official flower for December.
4. The Turquoise is the gem for December.

Activity 1

Date: December 15

Event: Bill of Rights Day

Level: Grades 5–12

Lesson Plan: This activity is designed for intermediate through high school students. Its purpose is to stress the importance of the Bill of Rights. Students will be able to give the importance of the first ten amendments and list several civil rights given to us in the Constitution of the United States.

Activity: Arrange students in cooperative learning groups and give each group a fictitious nation. Explain to them that they must decide on a government structure, its rules, and a symbol for their nation. Have each group present their "Constitution" to the class. Later, have them improve or make "amendments" to their constitution to make it more effective.

DECEMBER

1
- Rosa Parks Day, 1955
- First drive-in gasoline station opened in Pittsburgh, 1913

2
- Monroe Doctrine opposing European intervention in the Americas, 1823
- Napoleon I and Josephine crowned emperor and empress of France, 1804

3
- First heart transplant done in South Africa, 1967 by Dr. Barnard
- Illinois Admission Day, 21st state, 1818
- First neon sign blinked at the Paris Motor Show in 1910

4
- Manilla paper patented 1843
- National Grange Founding, set into motion first organized agriculture movement

5
- Martin Van Buren, 8th President, born 1782
- Death of Wolfgang Amadeus Mozart (35), 1791
- AFL-CIO founded, 1955

6
- Thomas Edison made first sound recording in 1877
- St. Nicholas's Day

7
- Delaware Admission Day, 1st state, 1787
- Pearl Harbor attacked 1941
- Eli Whitney, born 1765, invented the Cotton Gin and chicken wire

8
- Civil Right Week
- Flip Wilson's birthday, 1933, comedian

9
- Giant Christmas Tree lighting at Rockfeller Center, N.Y.

10
- Mississippi Admission Day, 20th state, 1817
- First domestic jet airliner service in U.S. opened by National Airlines, 1958

11
- Indiana Admission Day 19th state, 1816
- Pinckey Pinchback elected Governor of Louisiana, 1872, the first black man to have that office

12
- Pennsylvania Admission Day, 2nd state, 1787
- W. L. Garrison, born 1805
- Mexico Guadalupe Day
- Hanukkah
- First motor hotel or motel opened in Calif. 1925

13
- St. Lucia's Day
- Mary Todd Lincoln's birthday, 1818, wife of 16th President Abraham Lincoln

14
- Alabama Admission Day, 22nd state, 1819
- George Washington died, Mt. Vernon, 1799
- Norwegian explorer and 4 others reach the South Pole, 1911

15
- Bill of Rights Day, 1791
- Raggedy Ann's birthday
- Bill of Rights 200th anniversary, 1791-1991

16
- Beethoven born, 1770
- Boston Tea Party, 1773
- Battle of the Bulge began, 1944

17
- Aztec Stone Calendar discovery anniversary
- Wright Brother's first plane, 1903
- Pan American Aviation Day

18
- New Jersey Admission Day, 3rd state, 1787
- First Atomic Power Plant in Idaho produced electricity, over 100,000 watts, 1951

19
- U.S. invasion of Panama 1989
- U.S. earth satellite atlas, score sent a Season Greetings back to earth in 1958
- Basketball Hall of Fame gala, Civic Center Spring Field, MA

20
- South Carolina, 1st state to secede from Union, 1860
- Louisiana Purchase Day
- Mudd Day, remembrance of Dr. Samuel A. Mudd who gave medicine to John Wilkes Booth fleeing assassin of Abraham Lincoln

21
- Forefather's Day, commemorates day pilgrims landed at Plymouth Rock, 1620
- First crossword puzzle in U.S. appeared in New York World, 1913

22
- Winter begins in Northern Hemisphere
- Diane K. Sawyer's birthday, 1946, journalist

23
- Engelbert Humperdinck's opera Hansel & Gretel first performed, 1893
- First Non-stop flight around the world without refueling, 1987

24
- Kit Carson's birthday 1809
- First radio program broadcast from Brant Rock, Mass., 1906
- Christmas Eve

25
- Christmas Day
- Hirohito became the 124th emperor of Japan 1926

26
- First feature length film produced in Australia, 1906, "The Story of the Kelly Gang"
- Boxing Day, day those who rendered services were given gifts in honor (postman, lamplighter, dustman) in England

27
- Louis Pasteur inventor of the pasteurization process, born 1822

28
- Iowa Admission Day 29th state, 1846
- Woodrow Wilson, 28th President, born 1856
- Australia proclamation Day

29
- Texas Admission Day, 28th state, 1845
- Andrew Johnson, 17th President, born 1808
- Anniversary of Wounded Knee Massacre, 1870

30
- John Altgeld, born 1847
- Simon Guggenheim born 1867, American capitalist and Philanthropist

31
- Last day of the year
- Annual World Peace Mediation, Focus on Peace
- Make up your mind day
- New Year's Eve

Questions:
1. Who decides what rights we as citizens have?
2. What control over the government do we have?
3. What were the first ten amendments and who is affected by them?
4. What can we as citizens do to improve our nation?

Skills Taught: Cooperative learning, decision making, creative thinking, and application of knowledge.

Resources: Encyclopedias, books on government, and history books.

Activity 2

Date: December 21 or 22

Event: Winter Solstice Observation

Level: Grades 4–12

Lesson Plan: This activity is designed to enhance students' awareness of the earth-sun relationship. It can be modified to accommodate any grade level. Students will be able to understand and demonstrate the position of the earth during the winter and summer solstices.

Activity: Take a picture of a western horizon and make copies of it, one for each student. Draw the same pictures on a bulletin board. The students will record sunsets by drawing an arrow at the point where the sun set. Enter the time and date next to the arrow. This should be done about a week before the December 21 and carried through about a week after. The students should notice the pattern. Use a globe and light to demonstrate to the students what is taking place.

Questions:
1. Why do the days get shorter?
2. Why do the days get longer?
3. When would the hours of daylight be equal to darkness?
4. During which solstice is it the warmest? Why?

Skills Taught: Application skills and analysis.

Resources: Globes, light sources, sunset charts, and pictures of earth-sun relationship.

Activity 3

Date: Before December 31

Event: Reflecting on the Past Year

Level: Grades 4–12

Lesson Plan: This activity is designed for most grade levels. Its purpose is to reflect on all the changes and advances the students have witnessed or participated in. The importance of this lesson is to ensure that all the information is relevant and meaningful. Students will understand that time past is history.

Activity: Students will collect old newspapers, magazines, photographs, and assignments. Pull out the main topics (i.e., politics, national events, local events, etc.) and make a chart. Discuss with them all the events and reflect on all the information.

Questions:
1. What is history?
2. What is the importance of studying history?
3. How can we keep track of historical events?

Skills Taught: Research, discussion, analysis, and evaluation.

Resources: Old newspapers, magazines, and photographs.